Jean Dunbabin is Fellow and Tutor in
Modern History at St Anne's College, Oxford.

A HOUND OF GOD

A HOUND OF GOD

*Pierre de la Palud
and the
Fourteenth-Century Church*

JEAN DUNBABIN

CLARENDON PRESS · OXFORD
1991

Oxford University Press, Walton Street, Oxford OX2 6DP
Oxford New York Toronto
Delhi Bombay Calcutta Madras Karachi
Petaling Jaya Singapore Hong Kong Tokyo
Nairobi Dar es Salaam Cape Town
Melbourne Auckland
and associated companies in
Berlin Ibadan

Oxford is a trade mark of Oxford University Press

Published in the United States
by Oxford University Press, New York

British Library Cataloguing in Publication Data
Dunbabin, Jean
A hound of God.
1. Christian church. La Palud, Pierre de
I. Title
270.5092
ISBN 0-19-822291-2

Library of Congress Cataloging in Publication Data
Dunbabin, Jean.
A hound of God / Jean Dunbabin.
Includes bibliographical references and index.
1. Petrus, de Palude, Patriarch of Jerusalem, d. 1342.
2. Catholic Church—Bishops—Biography.   3. Church history—Middle
Ages, 600-1500.   I. Title.
BX4705.P44125D85   1991
282'.092—dc20
[B]   90-38706
ISBN 0-19-822291-2

Typeset by Downdell Limited, Oxford
Printed and bound in
Great Britain by Bookcraft Ltd
Midsomer Norton, Bath

To John

Preface

Apart from popes and kings, few medieval men have left enough evidence of their activities to attract a biographer. Pierre de la Palud is therefore worthy of note on this count alone. But I did not write this book purely because it was possible. Rather, since the strands that gave colour to his life also ran through early fourteenth-century ecclesiastical pre-occupations, I thought Pierre's story had illustrative value. And as witness to the events in which he participated, Pierre has solid virtues: the broad range of his concerns, his synthetical approach, his vitality, and his concrete mind imparted to his literary output a multi-faceted complexity which, though sometimes baffling, enlarges our insight into the confusing and tension-ridden world he inhabited. Lawyer, advocate, preacher, reformer, theologian, politician, encyclopaedist, crusader, Pierre was all of these; and the voice of each can be heard in his writings. So too can many other voices; for it was characteristic of him that he could not hear a new point of view without recording it somewhere. This trait, the enemy of incisiveness, has injured his reputation as a thinker. But for the historian it is precious, in that it provides evidence of the welter of overlapping, intertwining, and yet diverging opinions prevailing among those who strove to create norms for the early fourteenth-century church to follow.

Worn down by the struggle for clarity, Pierre turned increasingly from pure to applied science. His decision to concentrate on the friar's pastoral functions should make us hesitate before judging the way of life he espoused as already in terminal decline. Clericality had not yet sapped dry the original inspiration of St Dominic. But if Pierre could mould his learning to the needs of preaching and hearing confessions, his upbringing proved less malleable. As a consequence he exercised his mission primarily among those who enjoyed his own privileges of breeding and education. At the height of his career, as Patriarch of Jerusalem, he cut a fine figure in French society. Behind his noble mien lay the aristocratic virtues of courage, breadth of vision, and initiative, backed—in his non-academic works—by a certain colourfulness of language that can still endear him to the twentieth-century reader. These character-istics make him an interesting figure in his own right, reinforcing his significance as a mouthpiece for his times.

I am very conscious that Pierre's theological writings get little coverage in this book. More should have been said about his position in the ranks of second-generation Thomists and about the significance of his Biblical commentaries. I can only plead my incompetence in these matters. But it is my impres-sion that recent commentators, particularly Stella, Vereecke, Duval, and Marcuzzi, have tended to focus especially on Pierre's ethical and political teaching, which is also part of my theme.

Personal names have provided an irritating problem. In the end I decided to use the French form for 'Frenchmen' (not for-getting the ambiguities in such a label at this period) and the English form for others. But where consistency would have led to pedantry, as with the names of kings, popes, and a few other well-known figures, I have broken the rule.

I am very grateful to the Institute for Advanced Study in Princeton for electing me to membership in the second semester of 1988–9, thereby providing an excellent opportunity for peaceful reflection. Betty Rutson gave me much useful advice on literary matters; Robert Lerner, David d'Avray, Malcolm Barber, and Malcolm Vale answered my questions. My chief academic debt is to Bill Courtenay, who saved me from many errors and made some most constructive suggestions. The staff of the Institut de recherche et d'histoire des textes were admirably prompt in providing me with a microfiche of Pierre's sermons; and I have met with kind assistance in a number of libraries. My respect for the Dominican Order was aroused many years ago by my then supervisor, Father Daniel Callus. The dedication expresses my gratitude for help of other kinds.

J.D.

1990

Contents

Abbreviations

AFH	*Archivum Franciscanum Historicum*
AFP	*Archivum Fratrum Praedicatorum*
AHDLMA	*Archives d'histoire doctrinale et littéraire du moyen âge*
Baluze–Mansi, *Miscellanea*	S. Baluze, *Miscellanea novo ordine digesta*, ed. J. Mansi (Lucca, 1756–62)
Baluze–Mollat, *VPA*	S. Baluze, *Vitae Paparum Avinionensium*, ed. G. Mollat (4 vols.; Paris, 1914–28)
BEC	*Bibliothèque de l'École des chartes*
BEFAR	Bibliothèque de l'École français d'Athenes et de Rome
BEHE	Bibliothèque de l'École des hautes études
BIHR	*Bulletin of the Institute of Historical Research*
CUP	*Chartularium Universitatis Parisiensis*, ed. H. Denifle and E. Chatelain, ii (Paris, 1891)
DA	*Deutsches Archiv für Erforschung des Mittelalters*
DPP	Pierre de la Palud, *Tractatus de potestate Papae*, ed. P. T. Stella (Zurich, 1966)
EHR	*English Historical Review*
Fournier, *HLF*	P. Fournier, 'Pierre de la Palu, théologien et canoniste', *Histoire littéraire de la France*, xxxvii (Paris, 1938), pp. 39–84
HLF	*Histoire littéraire de la France*
Lettres communes, ed. Vidal	*Benôit XII: Lettres communes*, ed. J. M. Vidal (Paris, 1903–11)
Lettres communes, ed. Mollat	*Jean XXII: Lettres communes*, ed. G. Mollat (16 vols.; Paris, 1904–47)
Lettres secrètes, ed. Coulon	*Jean XXII: Lettres secrètes et curiales relatives à la France,*

	ed. A. Coulon and S. Clemencet (Paris, 1906–72)
MGH SS	*Monumenta Germaniae Historica: Scriptores*
Mortier	D. A. Mortier, *Histoire des mâitres généraux de l'ordre des Frères Prêcheurs* (8 vols.; Paris, 1903–20)
Ordonnances des roys de France	*Ordonnances des roys de France de la troisième race*, ed. E.-J. de Laurière *et al.* (Paris, 1723–1857)
QFIAB	*Quellen und Forschungen aus Italienischen Archiven und Bibliotheke*
QSL	Petrus de Palude, *Quartus Sententiarum liber*, ed. Vincent Haerlem (Paris, 1514)
Rashdall	H. Rashdall, *The Universities of Europe in the Middle Ages*, ed. F. M. Powicke and A. B. Emden, 3rd edn. (3 vols.; Oxford, 1936)
Raynaldus, *Annales ecclesiastici*	O. Raynaldus, *Annales ecclesiastici ab anno 1198*, ed. J. D. Mansi (Lucca, 1747–56)
RTAM	*Recherches de théologie ancienne et médiévale*
Reichert, ed., *Acta*	B. M. Reichert, ed., *Acta capitulorum generalium Ordinis Praedicatorum* (Monumenta Ordinis Fratrum Praedicatorum Historica, 3 and 4), i (Rome, 1889) and ii (1899)

1. Youth

(a) Childhood

Some time between 1275 and 1280, in a castle high above the river Ain in the old kingdom of Burgundy, Pierre de la Palud was born to Marguerite, wife of Gerard de la Palud, knight. Gerard was lord of Varembon, a significant bundle of lands stretching from St Martin du Mont above Pont d'Ain in the north to Maximieux in the south, largely contained within Dombes, the southern half of the county of Bresse.[1] His family name derived from the marshy landscape of the area, with its infinity of small lakes and man-made ponds, many of which have survived to this day. The rivers Saône and Ain both defined the region's borders and linked it with the outside world; but within, stretches of water which the flinty soil could not absorb hampered communications at every turn. As a consequence the inhabitants of Dombes had learned to live on their own resources, both physical and emotional. In the middle of the thirteenth century the Dominican inquisitor Étienne de Bourbon had found, to his deep disgust, peasants on the banks of the river Chalaronne venerating a holy greyhound said to heal sick babies and children.[2] The isolation which encouraged unsanctioned forms of devotion (and protected this cult long after Étienne had condemned it) also put brakes on the pace of social change. A Northern Frenchman, travelling there at about the time of Pierre de la Palud's birth, would have found it very old-fashioned.

To the eye of the historian, the time lag is most evident in the political situation. Like the French royal demesne in the eleventh century, Dombes in the late thirteenth was dotted with castles owned by feuding lords, who had successfully resisted, and until the early fifteenth century were to continue

---

[1] E. L. Cox, 'Political and Social Institutions in Bresse (1250–1320)', Ph.D. dissertation (Johns Hopkins University, Baltimore, 1958), p. 239. I have drawn on this work for what is said about the political situation in Dombes.

[2] Étienne de Bourbon: Anecdotes historiques, légendes et apologues, ed. A. Lecoy de la Marche (Paris, 1877), pp. 325–8. For a recent study see J.-C. Schmitt, The Holy Greyhound: Guinefort, Healer of Children since the Thirteenth Century, tr. M. Thom (Cambridge Studies in Oral and Literate Culture, 8; Cambridge, 1983).

to resist, any but the lightest of feudal bonds with the neighbouring great magnates. Of these the most formidable were the counts of Savoy, whose lands bordered Dombes across the River Ain. Amadeus V of Savoy (1285–1323), through his marriage to the heiress of the Le Bâgé family in 1271, had annexed a substantial part of northern Bresse, and he and his sons threatened to encircle Dombes. But their efforts were checked by Humbert de la Tour du Pin, dauphin of Viennois, and his successors, who pressed up from the south, determined to contain Savoyard power within its traditional limits. Though there were periods of truce and even peace, the years 1275 to 1333 were largely consumed in a struggle between these two houses, with the archbishops of Lyons, who owned estates in the south of Dombes, occasionally intervening to prevent any outcome damaging to their own interests. Therefore the lords of Dombes, their goodwill constantly sought by one or other of their great neighbours, had only to play the parties off against each other to preserve their effective independence. The Dombes of Pierre's childhood, though war-torn, remained a haven for the individualist.

The La Palud lineage was distinguished. The Varembon lordship went back to at least the middle of the twelfth century, and probably far further—a warrior called Varembon de la Palud was said (in a late source) to have taken part in an Italian expedition around 1000.[3] Noble neighbours such as the count of Forez and the lord of Thoire and Villars were happy to testify to the exclusively noble stock of La Palud scions,[4] which was also upheld by the family coat of arms, 'gules with a cross of ermines', and by the title *miles* automatically accorded to the head of the family.[5] In accordance with aristocratic convention the lords of Varembon had married well and cultivated close connections with the neighbouring abbey of Chassagne. But the blueness of their blood was more striking than the extent of their lands. Although dowries, exchange, and inheritance had over the years increased their possessions beyond the bounds of the village on the Ain from whence they sprang, their lord-

---

[3] S. Guichenon, *Histoire de Bresse et de Bugey* (Lyons, 1650), 2. 2. 284. The unlikelihood of what is effectively a surname dating back to 1000 raises serious doubts as to the reliability of this evidence. But the individual concerned may have been identified in this way by his descendants.

[4] Ibid., p. 287. They guaranteed the nobility of Pierre's brother Perceval when he became a canon of Lyons.

[5] E. Révérend du Mesnil, *Armorial historique de Bresse, Bugey, Dombes, Pays de Gex, Valromey et Franc-Lyonnais* (Lyons, 1873), p. 491; *Obituarium Lugdunensis Ecclesiae*, ed. M.-C. Guigue (Lyons, 1867), p. 93.

ship remained relatively small until the second half of the thirteenth century, when luck or ambition began to visit the family.

If Pierre's military ancestors of the later twelfth and the early thirteenth centuries tended to be content with their lot, their ecclesiastical counterparts had displayed a rather different temper. The first signs of hunger for status within the church came with the elevation of Guillaume de la Palud to the bishopric of Aosta in 1159. Fifty years passed by before another Guillaume, son of Pierre de la Palud of Varembon and Clemence, established what became a family tradition by obtaining election to the chapter of Lyons.[6] Before his death in 1243 he had ensured that his nephew Gui, the most distinguished member of the family, would also become a canon of that cathedral. Gui's career, which included a spell in England as keeper of Queen Eleanor's wardrobe[7] (during which time he must have known the great canon lawyer Henry of Susa, who was similarly occupied in the royal household), culminated in his appointment as archdeacon of Lyons in 1254. Another Gui de la Palud, perhaps the uncle of our Pierre, also made a brief appearance as canon of Lyons in 1254-5. The importance of these promotions to the family's standing can hardly be overestimated. In the first place, the chapter of Lyons was exclusively noble; before acceptance a potential canon's ancestry had to be rigorously investigated; entry set a seal of approval on the whole lineage.[8] As might be expected, such an élitist group could afford to throw its weight around in ecclesiastical affairs; Matthew Paris caricatured this in his report that the canons threatened to throw into the Rhône any papal candidate for office in their chapter who dared put in an appearance.[9] Secondly, the La Palud sons mingled in the chapter with the clerical offspring of local magnates, the counts of Savoy and of

[6] J. Beyssac, *Les Chanoines de l'église de Lyon* (Lyons, 1914), p. 46; *Les Prévots de Fourvière* (Lyons, 1908), pp. 9-15.

[7] Beyssac, *Les Prévots*, pp. 16-21; *Les Chanoines*, p. 53. See *Henry III: Close Rolls, 1242-1247*, pp. 213, 228, 477, 506; *Patent Rolls, 1232-1247*, pp. 355, 356, 371, 408, 475; *Patent Rolls, 1247-58*, p. 466. See also B. Galland, 'Philippe de Savoie, archevêque de Lyon', *BEC* 146 (1988), 48. On the younger Gui see Beyssac, *Les Prévots*, p. 20, *Les Chanoines*, p. 56.

[8] Although the earliest capitular decree on the subject comes from 1337, Beyssac, *Les Chanoines*, p. xv, Pierre referred in 1315 to the strict demands of the Lyons chapter in his commentary on Book 4 of the *Sentences*, 36. 2, QSL fo. 175^r, where he stated that if the custom of Lyons were followed elsewhere, a king's bastard would need two dispensations, one for illegitimacy and the other for absence of nobility, for at Lyons all bastards were reckoned to be commoners.

[9] *Chronica majora*, ed. H. R. Luard (London, 1872-83), vi. 418.

Forez, the lords of Beaujeu and Thoire and Villars, and made the acquaintance of men who were subsequently to rule the church; Clement IV, Gregory X, and Clement V were all canons of Lyons before they became popes. Connections of this kind almost certainly opened doors for those members of the family who remained in the lay world. It was not surprising that, in his will dated 1299, Pierre's father Gerard left money for masses for the souls of Guillaume and Gui, his great-uncle and his uncle, who had shed lustre on his name.[10]

Gerard, son of Guillaume de la Palud, was first recorded, already an adult, in 1246.[11] During the course of his long life, he displayed conventional piety in patronizing the nearby abbey of Chassagne, and energy in acquiring Richemont, a four-sided, well-defended castle on the Ain some miles south of Varembon, where he and his family took up residence. Outsiders looked on him as a person of note in the area; Duke Robert of Burgundy, for example, sent him a private letter about the arrangements made for Revermont after the peace of 1287. And his neighbours were of the same opinion. Although necessarily sucked into the strife between Savoy and Viennois, Gerard apparently contrived to keep on good terms both with Amadeus V, whose court he visited, and with Albert de la Tour du Pin, from whom he acquired the guardianship of the Knights' Hospitaller Commanderie des Feuillées. While paying homage also to Louis de Beaujeu, he reserved his warmest friendship for the Thoire and Villars family, his immediate neighbours. Given the relentless strife surrounding him, it is most unlikely that Gerard maintained this web of relationships without tension or even intermittent fighting; but its existence is proof of his diplomatic skill. More remarkably, his status as vassal to all these magnates neither derogated from his control over his own lands nor diminished his social standing in Dombes.[12] Dues and services were apparently not part of the bargain. Yet he was able to persuade Amadeus V of Savoy in 1298 that, since the new bridge the count had built without his permission near Varembon had wrongfully reduced his

[10] Beyssac, *Les Prévots*, pp. 15, 21. Gerard also made lavish provision for masses for the soul of his son Jean, canon of Lyons, who died in 1298. See *Obituarium Lugdunensis Ecclesiae*, ed. Guigue, p. 93; and G. Guige and J. Laurent, *Obituaires de la Province de Lyon*, i (Paris, 1951), pp. 150–1.

[11] On Gerard see M. M. Valentin-Smith and M.-C. Guigue, eds., *Bibliotheca Dumbensis* (Trévoux, 1854–1885), ii. 65; Cox, 'Political and Social Institutions', p. 239; Guichenon, *Histoire*, 2. 2. 286; Beyssac, *Les Prévots*, pp. 15 and 21.

[12] Guichenon, *Histoire*, 2. 2. 286. That Gerard's homage did not diminish his control can be inferred from the treaty he made in 1287 with Louis of Beaujeu,

revenues, he must be adequately compensated. And he was chosen *per ami comunel des dites parties* as arbitrator in a dispute between the countess of Forez and the dauphin of Viennois in 1285.[13] Clearly his relationship with his lords was devoid of any legally enforced subordination such as usually characterized vassalage in contemporary northern France. And this explains why, in Bresse, the magnates' search for stable alliances continued to receive a courteous welcome from their social inferiors.

Gerard was married to Marguerite of Gex, a lady from the cadet branch of Joinville at Geneva,[14] an alliance which represented a social triumph for the La Paluds. In their castle at Richemont there were seven children, Gerard (probably the child of an earlier marriage) who succeeded his father in 1299,[15] Aimon who later inherited Varembon, Jean who became a canon of Lyons, Marguerite who married into the local aristocracy, Jean who became lord of Richemont, Perceval who also became a canon of Lyons, and Pierre, the future patriarch of Jerusalem. It was a brood any father could take pride in. But it was also a responsibility. Unlike his counterparts in later thirteenth-century England, Gerard was not constrained by a clearly defined customary law of primogeniture; provided he could arrange it amicably with his eldest son, he might share out his inheritance among those of his male children who were to remain in the lay world. His younger brother Guiges, whose offspring had died early, had in 1275 recognized Gerard, Gerard's eldest child, as his heir to Châtillon—nowadays known as Châtillon-la-Palud. This inheritance helped towards

by which each party agreed that if one of his men committed crimes on the lands of the other, he should be tried in the courts of the place where the crime was committed. No reference was made to any superior jurisdiction. L. Aubret, *Mémoires pour servir à l'histoire de Dombes* (4 vols; Trévoux, 1864-8), ii. 30.

13 *Bibliotheca Dumbensis*, i. 204–6.

14 Beyssac, *Les Chanoines*, p. 68, referring to her arms along with Gerard's on Jean's tomb. J. D. Levesque, *Les Frères Prêcheurs de Lyon: Notre Dame de Confort, 1218-1789* (Lyons, 1979), p. 103, says that Marguerite was daughter of Guillaume de Joinville. But du Mesnil, *Armorial historique*, p. 20, gives the date of Guillaume's marriage as 1294. If this was Guillaume's only marriage and if she was legitimate, then Gerard's wife cannot have been its offspring. I have been unable to fit her into the family tree in H.-F. Laborde, *Jean de Joinville et les seigneurs de Joinville* (Paris, 1884), pp. 230-1.

15 Although Guichenon believed the younger Gerard to have been Gerard's nephew, not his son, he is described as his son in the peace treaty they both witnessed in 1275 (Beyssac, *Les Prévots*, p. 21), and similarly in 1296 (see Aubret, *Mémoires . . . de Dombes*, ii. 37). Furthermore he was lord of Varembon in 1306 (see Guichenon, *Histoire*, 2. 1. 15).

the construction of a family settlement. The seventeenth-century historian Guichenon saw, but did not copy, an agreement made between Gerard the Elder and Gerard the Younger in 1295. If its terms can legitimately be inferred from what actually happened, Gerard the Younger was to succeed both his father and his uncle; but on his death, his children were to inherit only Châtillon, leaving the Varembon lordship to Aimon, his (half-?) brother; and Richemont was to be split from the Varembon lordship to make a separate estate for Jean the Younger. (Such generosity to younger sons suggests the father's preference for the children of a later, more aristocratic, marriage; it also demonstrates Gerard's freedom of action in relation to Richemont, his own acquisition.) The consequence of this far-sighted arrangement was that, by the second decade of the fourteenth century, three branches of the La Paluds flourished in close proximity, each eventually developing into a noble house of renown. Many years later, Pierre, searching for a metaphor to explain the gratitude Christians owed to Christ, lighted on the idea that true believers entered the kingdom of heaven as apanage-holders in virtue of their status as younger sons of God; therefore they owed total loyalty to Christ, God's first-born, through whose generosity they enjoyed this privilege (Clermont Ferrand, Bibliothèque municipale, MS 46, fo. 44ᵛ). Perhaps he had in mind, not the famous apanages of St Louis's brothers, already rather far from fourteenth-century memory, but those of his own brothers Aimon and Jean, conferred on them with Gerard the Younger's consent.

It is not likely that Pierre saw much of Gerard, Aimon, Jean, or Marguerite after his father's death in 1299. But he must have known that they continued to flourish and increase in possessions. In 1306 Gerard, described as lord of Varembon, Richemont, and Tossia, was enfeoffed by Humbert of Thoire and Villars with Bouligneux, and allowed to build a castle there.[16] In the same year Aimon married the heiress of the Asnière family, whose lands lay in and around St Julien-sur-Reyousse in the heart of Bresse.[17] When he succeeded Gerard around 1308 as lord of Varembon, he continued to concentrate on these northern estates, leaving his other brother Jean, now lord of Richemont and Tossia, to play the traditional family role in Dombes. As far as can be judged from the fragments of information that survive, relationships between the three

---

16 Guichenon, *Histoire*, 2. 1. 15.
17 Cox, 'Political and Social Institutions', pp. 183–4, 250.

branches of the family remained amicable. Pierre, in his commentary on Book 4 of the *Sentences* (33. 1, *QSL* fo. 165^v), took it for granted that natural friendship is founded on lines of kinship—'super communicationes consanguinitatis fundatur amicitia naturalis', and was to demonstrate the strength of his own family attachment by his assistance in the 1330s to Aimon's eldest son Pierre. But his abiding affection was doubtless reserved for his brothers Jean[18] and Perceval, the canons of Lyons, in whose company he passed much of his youth.

The surviving facts about his family offer little insight into Pierre's childhood environment. Yet there are two pointers which may with some imagination be taken as indicative of its quality. His sermons are unusually full of chivalric legends, of rich pseudohistorical accounts of the French monarchs and of other semi-legendary heroes, which his austere Dominican education did nothing to obliterate from his mind, and which sometimes intruded themselves unexpectedly into his scholastic exercises. It comes as a shock, in his commentary on Book 4 of the *Sentences*, to find in his discussion of incest an allusion to the legend that the Roland of Roncevalles fame was both Charlemagne's son and his nephew.[19] Or, in a serious analysis of papal power, to see him talking of a Baldwin who was emperor of Constantinople at the time Charlemagne was emperor of the west.[20] His sermons also demonstrate that his

---

[18] It appears to have been quite common in the La Palud family to use the same Christian name twice in one generation. Perhaps confusion was avoided by using the Latin form for the clerical son. The Joinville family attachment to Jean was natural; and if, as his clerical career suggests, the elder Jean was sickly in youth, the repetition of the name will have been intended to insure against the disappearance of a family tradition.

[19] 'Et in incestu Caroli magni cum sorore ex quo genuit Rolandum filium et nepotem. Ipse pater et avunculus, quia frater matri', 40. 1, *QSL* fo. 188^r. On this legend, see R. Lejeune and J. Stiennon, *La Légende de Roland dans l'art du moyen âge* (Brussels, 1967), i. 145–50. More original is the statement in the commentary at 3. 2. 5, found not in the printed version but in Oxford, Bodleian Library, MS Holkham Miscellaneous 10, fo. 13^v, 'Et Rolandus moriens herbam pro communione accepit; vel si erravit tunc hereticus non fuit.' This occurs in a discussion of the legitimacy of sacraments performed in unorthodox ways. Miss E. M. Rutson has called my attention to the similar description of William Rufus's death in Geffrei Gaimar, *L'Estoire des Engleis*, ed. A. Bell, pp. 200–1, 11. 6328–36.

[20] *DPP*, p. 119. A similar legend is to be found in J.-J. Smet, ed., *Recueil des Chroniques de Flandre*, i (Brussels, 1837), p. 36: 'Baldwinus Ferreus ... conquisivit Constantinopolim et Adrianopolim cum Ludovico Pio.' Pierre may therefore have had some acquaintance with Flemish sources. Alternatively the notion may have originated in a defective manuscript reading of *Les Grandes Chroniques*, ed. J. Viard, iii (Paris, 1923), bk. 3, ch. 169.

acquaintance with Geoffrey of Monmouth and Pseudo-Turpin was more than casual. Perhaps he acquired some of this knowledge in Lyons during the course of his early schooling; but it is probable that he first cultivated his taste for legend in his father's castle, as he passed the long winter evenings around the fire with the adults, listening to minstrels and jongleurs. Gerard the Elder's enthusiasm for such entertainment may be deduced from the name of his fifth son, Perceval, a choice which can only have been inspired by fondness for the grail literature.

The second and more speculative indicator comes in a sermon Pierre preached soon after his arrival in Paris. Here he compared the church in his own day, troubled by heretics and infidels, with a castle besieged by its enemies. He conveyed the sense of relief felt by the besieged when they heard that their lord had promised assistance; but until help actually came they were surrounded by enemies like a cloud of locusts, who erected catapults and attempted to climb in through all the windows. The defenders' plight was the worse because, as was quite common in those days, they had among them women and children, who could only hinder operations.[21] The vividness of the image suggests, though it can do no more, that Pierre was here drawing on a childhood experience, perhaps a siege of Richemont in his father's absence, which left a deep impression on his mind. Richemont as it was in Pierre's youth cannot be exactly reconstructed; but its defences were of the strongest, its four towers occupied only at their highest levels, its windows built tiny to withstand ferocious assaults.[22] Despite the beauty of its position, it offered its inmates few opportunities for gazing over the valley. The threat of attack was ever present in Pierre's childhood.

(b) Education

Because we have no direct evidence about Pierre's education, almost the whole of this section consists of deductions from his attested competences in various fields, filled out by hypotheses about where he acquired them. The ground is shaky. But we do know enough about normal patterns of aristocratic child-rearing in the late thirteenth century to be reasonably con-

---

[21] Worcester Cathedral, MS Q. 100, fos. 98ʳ and 102ʳ.
[22] Information, the present châtelaine.

fident that his initial introduction to the world of books took place at home. Teaching children to read and write, both in the vernacular and in Latin, was not thought to be a matter for professionals in the Middle Ages; if the lady of the house was too occupied with other matters, then any household clerk would be adequate to the task. According to the educational theorists, noble boys should be left in the care of women till around 7 years of age, and then be handed over to a knight or a tutor for instruction in adult concerns. But practice on these matters varied very widely.[23] Pierre was later to state in a sermon that a boy made his first appearance at his father's table as soon as he was weaned (Clermont Ferrand, Bibliothèque municipale, MS 46, fo. 41[r]: 'cum puer separabatur a lacte matris tunc primo admittebatur ad mensam patris'); so in his case the transition stage from female to male tutelage may have begun early and been prolonged. The young child was fortunate in that, although the French of Paris was a foreign language to the peasantry of Bresse, it was spoken in the La Palud household.[24] Perhaps his mother, with her distinguished family background, encouraged this. She would also have plied her children with stories of their Champagne and Geneva relatives and, above all, of the great Jean de Joinville's crusading exploits. The nursery at Richemont can be pictured as a stimulating environment.

As the youngest son in a noble family there is every sign that Pierre was intended from an early age for a clerical career. Only if Gerard, Aimon, and Jean of Richemont died without heirs and if the other Jean and Perceval both took orders might he inherit a knightly portion; and this had always seemed a remote contingency. Academic training will therefore have played a conspicuous role in his upbringing from a relatively tender age; as soon as he was capable of coping with the principles of Latin grammar, he will have joined Perceval—

[23] For a recent treatment of this subject in England, see N. Orme, *From Childhood to Chivalry: The Education of the English Kings and Aristocracy, 1066–1530* (London and New York, 1984), pp. 17–18, 146–7.

[24] For the distinctness of Burgundian from French, see the first miracle attributed by Geoffroi de Beaulieu to St Louis, *Acta sanctorum*, 25 Aug., v. 566, in which a hitherto deaf and dumb Burgundian was cured by the saint's relics in such a fashion that he spoke pure French, as if he had been brought up at St Denis. Pierre repeated this story in a sermon on St Louis recorded in Clermont Ferrand, Bibliothèque nationale, MS 46, fo. 192[v]. That French was spoken at Richemont can be deduced from the arbitration of Gerard de la Palud in 1285, recorded in French, Valentin-Smith and Guigue, eds., *Bibliotheca Dumbensis*, i. 204–6.

also destined for the church—in lessons from a tutor (perhaps the family chaplain). Nevertheless, during the time he remained at home, the atmosphere surrounding him was distinctly martial. Though only a watcher from the sidelines, Pierre was deeply affected by the preoccupations of his father and his elder brothers. Their defence of the castle, their testing of weapons and armour, their pursuit of high reputations among the knights of the surrounding countryside, provided him with a deep understanding of matters military and chivalric upon which, in the distant future, he was constantly to call in his sermons.

But sooner or later he must have left home, to acquire a proper grounding in grammar, rhetoric, dialectic, and at least some aspects of the *quadrivium*—arithmetic, astronomy, geometry, and music. His parents may have decided to send him away when he was relatively young. Much later, explaining the nature of implicit faith in the prologue to his commentary on the *Sentences*, Pierre cited the example of a small boy leaving home for school, who was told by his mother to trust his master in all things, because he would never lie to him; the boy therefore acquired implicit faith in his master, through the authority of his mother. This may well have been autobiographical. But the only scholastic practice he described in his sermons concerned a late arrival at the schools: a boy who spent too short a time in the classroom had to have a special tutor to go through his lessons with him, explain them, and make him understand.[25]

Before beginning his studies the young boy would have been tonsured as a clerk, would have accepted vestments regarded as suitable to his calling, and would have vowed himself to God's service (Bk. 4 of *Sentences*, 24. 3, QSL fo. 126^r). From now on he was expected to participate in the church services, to make the responses and lead the congregation; he might even be called on to read a lesson. Though he had taken no irrevocable step, entered into no lasting commitment, he had by this means put his foot on the bottom rung of the ecclesiastical ladder. Orders might follow later when he was old enough to take on responsibilities. Direct evidence on Pierre's reaction to

[25] On implicit faith see G. Groppo, 'La teologia et il suo "subiectum" secondo il prologo del commento alle Sentenze di Pietro da Palude O.P. († 1342)', *Salesianum*, 23 (1961), p. 257; for cramming, 'Notandum quod puer qui parum fuit in scolis necesse habet magistro speciali [sic] qui domini lecturam sibi repetat, exponat et difficilia intellegere faciat', Worcester Cathedral, MS Q. 100, fo. 98^v.

his father's plans for his career is lacking. But retrospectively he certainly did not resent his clerical fate.

As to Pierre's more advanced education, that it included a fairly prolonged study of canon and civil law is evident on every page of his *De potestate Papae* and of his commentary on Book 4 of the *Sentences*. His contemporaries regarded him as learned in Roman law, *jurisconsultissimus*; indeed one of them, an Italian lawyer Frederick de Senis, commenting on a legal opinion of Pierre's, described the future Patriarch of Jerusalem as a Doctor of Both Laws.[26] This description seems to have been the fruit of courtesy rather than knowledge. But the deference Frederick displayed indicates Pierre's standing in the legal profession. How and when did he acquire this considerable learning? If he had studied Roman law in depth, as Frederick's words suggest, then it must have been before he entered the Dominican order. For—as he himself reminded his reader—it was against canon law for any religious to read secular laws or medicine for more than two months (Bk. 4 of *Sentences*, 18. 3, QSL fo. 92^r). Had he merely studied the amount of Roman law necessary to qualify in canon law, then he might have done so after he became a friar.[27] But in fact the extent of his knowledge, both of Roman and of French customary laws, clearly outstripped that found in confessors' manuals, the usual Dominican textbooks for canon law. Therefore he was almost certainly trained in a law school. It follows that Pierre did not become a friar until his maturity, after he had already spent several years studying for the qualification that normally attracted men bent on high office in the secular church.

There can, I think, be little doubt that Lyons was Pierre's Alma Mater for his legal education, and perhaps also for his preliminary schooling. Three, if not four, generations of La Palud clerks had already been educated there; it lay only about 30 miles down the Ain valley from Richemont; and the young lad could be looked after there by his brother Jean, a canon of the cathedral from 1282 to 1298, who was in all probability already responsible for Perceval. Given the family tradition, it would have been eccentric for Gerard to have sent Pierre anywhere else. And Gerard was not an eccentric man. Consequently it is safe to imagine the young boy taking up residence in his

---

[26] Fournier, *HLF*, p. 40 n. 1; Naples, Biblioteca Nazionale, MS I. A. 4, fo. 59^v.

[27] W. A. Hinnebusch, *The History of the Dominican Order: Intellectual and Cultural Life to 1500*, ii (New York, 1973), pp. 245–7 on the attitude of the order to canon lawyers.

brother's house at the back of the cloister under the shadow of the great church of St Jean.

Lyons in the last decade of the thirteenth century was enjoying to the full the natural advantage of its situation at the confluence of the Rhône and the Sâone. It had first begun to revive commercially in the mid-eleventh century, when the Sâone bridge was built to link the two parts of the town and to facilitate access to the north. Technical difficulties still prevented the bridging of the Rhône in Pierre de la Palud's lifetime. None the less, traffic between Italy and France, between the Mediterranean and the northern lands, between the plains and the high Alpine valleys, flowed through the city. Caravans of merchants regularly wound their way through the narrow streets, while from time to time great crusading armies gathered there. Lyons had offered a safe refuge to Innocent IV when he was ejected from Rome, and two great church councils had been held within its walls. Lying on the fringes of imperial territory though within reach of Capetian pressure, it had some claim to regard itself as the crossroads of Europe. For a youth from Dombes, it must have provided an exciting and challenging environment.

Despite its growing commercial importance, for most of the thirteenth century the city had remained culturally and politically dominated by its cathedral, collegiate churches, and monasteries. Then in 1295 the bourgeoisie issued an effective challenge to the ancient clerical stranglehold, by establishing as a direct rival to the church school their own civic school for the liberal arts and both laws. Immediately the archbishop's official prohibited teaching within its walls. But in 1302 the Parlement of Paris recognized its right to exist and to teach the subjects it had chosen. So during Pierre's youth, Lyons tingled with intellectual excitement, as the two rival law schools applied all their talents in their own defence; and each appealed for support to the substantial number of scholars trained in Bologna who had begun to return to southern France in search of employment.[28] It was a period of conflict redolent with promise for the future. Yet that promise was not to be fulfilled. A combination of bad luck (Philip IV's annexation of the city)

---

[28] *Cartulaire municipal de la ville de Lyon*, ed. M.-C. Guigue (Lyons, 1885–93), i. 26, quoted in R. Fédou, *Les Hommes de loi lyonnais à la fin du moyen âge: Étude sur les origines de la classe de robe* (Paris, 1964), p. 23, which is the source for much of what is said here. On the impact of Bologna lawyers, see A. Gouron, *Études sur la diffusion des doctrines juridiques médiévales* (Variorum reprints, London, 1987), 'Les juristes de l'École de Montpellier', p. 15.

and rivalry from Avignon prevented the schools from acquiring the university status they clearly deserved in the first decade of the fourteenth century.[29]

Clerical jealousy of bourgeois pretensions, though sharp, was not well founded; for the church's law school was not very much older than its rival, owing its existence to Pope Innocent IV's residence in the city between 1244 and 1250. During those years Lyons was home to the *Studium Romanae Curiae* under the pope's special protection, which was renowned for its legal studies and was frequently visited by the famous canon lawyer Henry of Susa, known throughout Europe under his *nom de plume* Hostiensis, who was then bishop of nearby Sisteron. Although the *studium* went back to Rome with Innocent in 1250, a solid intellectual tradition survived within the cathedral of St Jean, which slowly took shape as an organized school of civil and canon law. While the new school maintained many links with the mother of all law schools at Bologna, its independence was recognized by Pope Nicholas IV in 1292, who stipulated that all the five professors in Lyons were to be born 'on this side of the Alps'. Pierre's teachers will have been among the chevaliers of Lyons, a group of distinguished doctors or bachelors of laws who had the duty of counselling the canons of the cathedral in all matters. He may well have sat at the feet of Barthelemy de la Rivière, who became professor in 1296.[30] But whoever his mentors, they clearly inculcated into him a profound respect for the opinions of Hostiensis, buried in the Dominican convent in Lyons in 1274, and regarded locally as the greatest of canon lawyers.

Gerard de la Palud's choice of law for Pierre's advanced education made sense if he harboured the ambition that both his youngest sons would become canons of the cathedral of Lyons. By the end of the thirteenth century, a training in civil and canon law (though not necessarily a degree, regarded as a teaching qualification) was a sound preparation for high office in the church. Noble fathers and ambitious sons saw the vocational advantages of a flexible course which either opened the door to a canonry or provided a means of earning a living through advocacy in the church courts.[31] But if Pierre began learning law from reasons of expediency, very quickly he was

---

[29] See A. B. Cobban, *Medieval Universities: Their Development and Organization* (London, 1975), p. 34.

[30] Fédou, *Les Hommes de loi lyonnais*, pp. 21–3, and p. 24 n. 26.

[31] Jean Dunbabin, 'Careers and vocations' in J. Catto, ed., *The History of the University of Oxford, i. The Early Schools* (Oxford, 1984), pp. 578–86.

drawn to it by temperament. Naturally argumentative, he thoroughly enjoyed the verbal tournaments of advocacy, as appeared two decades later in his stand against Jean de Pouilly. A digression in his Commentary on Book 4 of the *Sentences* (40. 1, *QSL* fos. 187^r and 187^v), where he discussed the greater logical cogency of canon than of civil law over the ways of reckoning kinship, suggests that he was also intellectually fascinated. His studies gave him a solid grounding in Roman law, above all in Justinian's codex, and an extensive knowledge not only of Gratien's *Decretum* but of the Decretists and Decretalists—he may even have attained the level of learning expected of a *doctor Decretorum*.[32] More significantly, his legal education had an indelible effect on his approach to problems, on his real interests, on the authorities he took seriously. His enthusiastic embrace of canon law affected him until the end of his life.

Yet he did not remain a lawyer. And here lies an intriguing problem—why did he abandon a thoroughly congenial career for another less rewarding in secular terms? For after what must have been a fairly extensive immersion in the law, Pierre entered the Dominican order, perhaps around 1300, and devoted himself to theology with the aim of becoming one of the Preachers' leading lights. His brother Jean's death in 1298 may have affected the timing of his decision; since for whatever reason Perceval did not obtain Jean's canonry—he did not become a canon till 1310—Gerard's hope that both his youngest sons might be promoted to the Lyons chapter may have seemed over-optimistic. Furthermore the loss of Jean's prebend, on which in all likelihood his two young brothers had depended for sustenance, would have been a serious blow to the family finances. It was an appropriate moment for Pierre to recast his future. It is possible that he had always wanted to become a friar but had met with family opposition, as had many other scions of noble families. (The sympathetic discussion in his commentary on Book 4 of the *Sentences*, 38. 1, *QSL* fo. 178^r, of the predicament of young boys who, on being sent to school, were required by their parents to promise solemnly neither to enter a religious order nor to go to lectures at the Dominican or

---

[32] Groppo, 'La teologia', p. 245 n. 1, commenting on 'Propter quod magis dicitur doctor decretorum baccalarius in theologia quam doctor decretalium', which he takes to reflect Pierre's standing. It could, however, simply be an expression of the usual Paris attitude towards the Decretals; see Rashdall, i. 433 n. 1.

Franciscan houses highlighted a familiar situation.[33]) If Gerard had opposed his wish, then his father's death in 1299 would finally have set him free to follow his own inclination. In his student years Pierre may have read with a sense of recognition Guillaume Peyraut's arguments against the evils of advocacy in his *Summa de virtutibus et vitiis* ((Lyons, 1585), ii, fos. 158–65), a book widely available in Lyons. This suggestion is compatible with the only hint he ever provided about his own feelings, in a sermon preached much later: he regarded it as impossible to combine well-paid advocacy for men with the rewards of advocacy for God: 'advocati mundi non expectant salarium Dei et advocati Dei qui fovent partem Dei contempnunt stipendia mundi' (Clermont Ferrand, Bibliothèque municipale, MS 46, fos. 30ᵛ–31ʳ; Worcester Cathedral, MS Q. 100, fo. 83ᵛ). He was perhaps a sensitive young man so strongly tempted by the sweets of the legal career as to be frightened for its effects on his character. But this cannot be substantiated; and even the date of his profession is unknown.

The Dominican house in Lyons, Notre Dame de Confort, second in age and dignity in the French province only to Paris, was founded two years after Pope Honorius had confirmed St Dominic's order in December 1216. The great Dominican master Humbert de Romans, who began his career as prior of Lyons, moved the convent to a new site, about half-way along a road leading from the Rhône to the Sâone, very close to the Templars' house. Its buildings, though austere in their simplicity, had grown sufficiently by 1316 to provide adequate room for the election of Pope John XXII. The church, consecrated by Pope Innocent IV in 1244, was probably enlarged during the latter part of the thirteenth century to allow sizeable congregations to enter and hear the preachers; its pillars were thin, its aisles wide, its ornament minimal.[34] The young Pierre must often have resorted here before he decided to enter the order; and in 1298 it gained new emotional significance for him when his brother Jean was buried in the cloister, with the family arms sculpted above his tomb.[35] Familiar though the place may have been, to become a novice there was a very

---

[33] 'Quarta conclusio est quod peccant parentes inducentes filios quos mittunt ad seculi scolas ad iurandum vel vovendum quod non intrabunt religionem nec ibunt ad predicatores vel minores nec ad audiendum sermonem, unde nec tenentur servare', 38. 1, *QSL* fo. 178ʳ.

[34] On the general principles of Dominican architecture see G. Meersseman, 'L'Architecture dominicaine au xiiiᵉ siècle', *AFP* 16 (1946), 136–90.

[35] Du Mesnil, *Armorial historique*, p. 491.

radical step indeed for a young man who had passed the previous few years amid the affluence enjoyed by the noble canons of Lyons. It was true that, once through the portals, he was not required to surrender his noble name or even all the privileges that went with it; true, too, that the deprivations he met with represented a considerable modification of those suffered by the original adherents of St Dominic. But the surrender of many personal possessions, the confinement to a rough habit, the loss of freedom and privacy, must have come as a grave shock to a system beginning to accustom itself to the comforts of life. Yet Pierre stuck out his novitiate, became a fully professed friar and eventually also a priest.

Everything in Pierre's later life suggests that his decision satisfied his deepest religious needs. He was later to record the opinion that every man who embraced the religious life in any of its manifestations merited a plenary indulgence for his sins, since he had done all he could to make satisfaction.[36] But his willingness to concede the claims of all religious orders was allied with the conviction that, for him at least, the Dominican way of life, dedicated to the spreading of the Gospel by teaching and example, and to the eradication of heresy by long, hard battles, provided the right path to salvation. The Preachers were *canes domini*, the dogs of the Good Shepherd, who gave their lives to safeguarding the flock and to chasing away its enemies. As Pierre later said in a sermon on St Dominic, dogs were quicker than shepherds in smelling wolves and running to capture them (Clermont Ferrand, Bibliothèque municipale, MS 46, fo. 170ᵛ). His first personal acquaintance with heresy may well have occurred in 1303, when the Dominican Inquisitor of Lyons, visiting his brother in nearby Nantua, found there a nest of doctrinal deviants who were strongly supported by their fellow townsmen against the Inquisitor's activities.[37] But highly though Pierre esteemed the inquisitors he was never to become one himself; nor did he consider that they had an exclusive claim to be the hounds of God.[38] His own personal

[36] *DPP*, p. 129. The high regard for all forms of religious life evident here seems characteristic of the Lyons house, and is well exemplified in Peyraut's *De eruditione religiosorum*.

[37] J. D. Levesque, *Les Frères Prêcheurs de Lyon: Notre Dame de Confort, 1218–1789* (Lyons, 1979), p. 89.

[38] Recent literature has tended to minimize the distinction between inquisitors and confessors, by portraying inquisitorial proceedings as arising out of acts of public penance. See e.g. E. Griffe, *Le Languedoc cathare et l'inquisition (1229–1329)* (Paris, 1980); A. Cazenave, 'Aveu et contrition: Manuels de confesseurs et interrogatoires d'inquisition en Languedoc et en Catalogne (xiiiᵉ-xivᵉ

commitment within the order was to prevention, not cure, to expounding Christianity from the pulpit and absolving from sin in the confessional. The challenge of the task was to occupy his adult life. And in this he followed the precepts of Humbert de Romans, whose works were much read in Notre Dame de Confort, where almost all had been written between 1263 and 1277.[39]

The lives of the senior friars of Notre Dame in the early years of the fourteenth century will still have resembled those described by Étienne de Bourbon in his delightful *Tractatus de diversis materiis praedicabilibus*.[40] He portrayed them on excellent terms with the local aristocrats and important officials, travelling through the countryside to preach and teach, constantly on the look-out for manifestations of God's will and attempting to descry the inner Christian meaning behind the most mundane of events. Their mobility, their sociability, and the relevance of their message will all have appealed to an extrovert like Pierre. But before he could join in their activities he had to undergo a rigorous training within the convent. His instruction in the trials, temptations, and sweets of the religious life would have been derived from a work like Guillaume Peyraut's *Liber eruditionis religiosorum*, a patchwork of quotations from Scripture, from the Fathers, and from more recent writers, joined together by a commentary on the relevance of each to the life within the cloister.[41] Pierre would also have learned the exacting requirements of the divine office and of the chapter. He may even have demeaned himself by performing some of the manual tasks necessary for the community's functioning. All this was a preliminary to the long hours spent in the schools, where he had the advantage of combining maturity with a well-trained mind. Hardly surprisingly his intellectual abilities were soon recognized and he was picked to undergo higher education in theology.

Toulouse university has traditionally been suggested as the place at which Pierre acquired his bachelor's degree in

siècles)', *Actes du 99ᵉ congrès nationale des sociétés savantes*, i (Paris, 1977), 333–52.

[39] S. Tugwell, ed., *Early Dominican Writings* (New York, Romsey, and Toronto, 1982) and E. T. Brett, *Humbert of Romans: His Life and Views of Thirteenth-Century Society* (Toronto, 1984).

[40] Ed. de la Marche in *Étienne de Bourbon*.

[41] A. Dondaine, 'Guillaume Peyraut: Vie et oeuvres', *AFP* 18 (1948), 162–236; cf. R. Creytens, 'L'Instruction des novices dominicains du XIIIᵉ siècle', *AFP* 20 (1950), 114–93.

theology.[42] Since Toulouse was the nearest university to Lyons, this is a perfectly possible hypothesis. But the one piece of evidence on which it rests, the incorporation of his name among the scholars of Toulouse in a seventeenth-century list drawn up by J. J. Percin,[43] involves a misreading. The Pierre de la Palud there mentioned has late sixteenth-century dates. That our Pierre's name does not occur in the reasonably full lists of the late thirteenth- or early fourteenth-century masters argues rather against him having been at Toulouse. Furthermore, neither in his sermons nor in his polemical writings did he show any trace of personal knowledge of that part of southern France. Friars were not always sent short distances to be educated—Oxford and Cambridge were common enough destinations for young Dominicans. But on the other hand residence at a university was not compulsory for theological study. According to the papal privileges of Alexander IV and Clement IV, theology could be taught in *studia particularia* in each province;[44] it was only necessary to go to a university in order to obtain a degree. Pierre may possibly have spent one year at a university at some time after his novitiate, as his contemporary, Meister Eckhart did at Paris.[45] But Pierre is not named in any Paris document before 1311.

If Toulouse is not a strong candidate and there is no evidence for Paris before 1311, where did Pierre begin learning theology? As with his legal training, Lyons is a plausible answer. According to the 1337 capitulary of the General Chapter, the canons of the cathedral of St Jean undertook to provide the money for regular lectures on theology in their cloister and refectory, normally to be given by a master from the nearby Dominican house. But this was no innovation in 1337. The great Humbert de Romans was probably a lector at the cathedral before he became prior; after him Hugues de St Cher had taught there, as

[42] Although Mortier regarded Lyons as his place of education, ii. 522 n. 2, R. Chabanne in 'Pierre de la Palu', *Dictionnaire de droit canonique*, vi (Paris, 1957), col. 1481, and J. A. Weisheipl, 'Peter of la Palud', *New Catholic Encyclopaedia*, ii. 220, clearly favoured Toulouse.

[43] *Monumenta Conventus Tolosani Ordinis FF Praedicatorum* (Toulouse, 1693), p. 197.

[44] M. W. Sheehan, 'The Religious Orders, 1220–1370', in Catto, ed., *The Early History of the University of Oxford*, i. 193, 199; A. de Guimaraes, 'Hervé Noël († 1323): Étude biographique', *AFP* 8 (1938), 28–9.

[45] Eckhart came as a bachelor in theology from Cologne to Paris in 1293–4; he then became lector at Erfurt, and returned to Paris in 1302 as Master in Theology for his year of necessary regency; see E. Z. Brunn, Z. Kaluza, A. de Libera, P. Vignaux, and E. Weber, *Maître Eckhart à Paris: Une critique médiévale de l'ontothéologie: Études, textes, et introductions* (Paris, 1984).

had Guillaume Peyraut and Pierre de Tarentaise, the future Pope Innocent V; Étienne de Bourbon may have done so; and in 1287 a certain Hugues de Lozanne was also described as lector of the cloister.[46] Despite the occasional interruption of teaching implied by the capitulary of 1337, St Jean had a tradition to be proud of. Consequently Pierre would have had no reason for leaving in order to cover the syllabus as a *baccalaurius biblicus*.[47] And if he remained, the similarity between his style of commenting on the Bible (see Ch. 5a) and that of Hugues de St Cher would be explained, since Hugues had established the exegetical tradition of Notre Dame. On this hypothesis, Pierre passed some years after 1300 in Lyons, learning the mysteries of exegesis; he attained the status of *baccalaurius biblicus* perhaps by 1306, and then devoted at least two years to expounding systematically the literal meaning of a book of the Old and a book of the New Testament, before the critical gaze of his master and his fellow students.

There are in any case grounds for postulating that Pierre was in Lyons in the years 1308–9. When he gave evidence before the pope's commission of inquiry in Paris in April 1311 (see next section) he declared that he had sat in on the examination of many Templars. There is no sign of his name on any of the documents relating to the examinations in Paris;[48] and the independent judgement he offered on the Templars' possible innocence argues strongly against his having been in the city when the university masters were consulted by the king in 1308. On the other hand, he can plausibly be connected with the Archbishop of Lyons's commission. The archbishop, like other bishops, had received—though belatedly—a papal bull first sent out in August 1308, ordering him to set up a body consisting of himself, two canons of his cathedral church, two Dominicans, and two Franciscans, to investigate whether the

---

[46] J. Beyssac, *Les Lecteurs et théologaux: Notes pour servir à l'histoire de l'église de Lyon* (Lyons, 1926), pp. 6–10; Levesque, *Les Frères Prêcheurs*, pp. 43–4 and 273–6; R. E. Lerner, 'Poverty, Preaching and Eschatology in the Revelation Commentaries of "Hugh of St. Cher" ', in K. Walsh and D. Wood, eds., *The Bible in the Medieval World* (Oxford, 1985), p. 161 n. 2; J. Dunbabin, 'The Lyon Dominicans: A Double Act', in J. Loades, ed., *Monastic Studies: The Continuity of Tradition* (Penarth, forthcoming).

[47] I have assumed that Pierre did become *baccalaurius biblicus* because he went on to acquire a Paris D.Th. But it has been suggested that not all Dominicans who went on to be Masters of Theology did so; see M. H. Laurent, *Le Bienheureux Innocent V (Pierre de Tarentaise) et son temps* (Vatican, 1947), p. 40.

[48] H. Finke, *Pappstum und Untergang des Templarordens* (Münster, 1907), ii. 307–12; CUP, pp. 125–7, no. 664. On this see Guimaraes, 'Hervé Noël', p. 55.

allegations made against the Templars were true of those in his archdiocese.[49] In the course of 1308 Pierre de Savoie, nephew of Amadeus V, count of Savoy, was elected archbishop, and it fell to him to implement the pope's orders. It would have been natural for him to promote Pierre de la Palud, from a family of proven loyalty to his, to a commission for which his legal training made him peculiarly fitted. While it cannot be proved that Pierre's experience of Templar examinations was gained in Lyons, a later connection with Pierre de Savoie (see next section) makes it probable.

The arrest of the Templars, their near neighbours, must have alarmed and excited the Lyons Dominicans considerably. Although there had been small sources of friction between the two houses—should the nuts that fell from the trees in the Templar garden on to the Dominicans' path belong to the friars or to the Templars?[50]—relations had normally been good, as indeed they were throughout Europe and especially in the mission fields of the Middle East.[51] What Pierre had to say about the order's probable innocence suggests that the brothers met with an open-mindedness in Lyons usually denied them in France. The city's tradition of legal study may have protected them from some of the horrors experienced by those who fell into the clutches of the king's men; and Archbishop Pierre was not inclined to make things easy for Philip IV, with whom he was already in conflict. But the absence of evidence against the Templars in Lyons is only surprising when taken against the wealth of unbelievable confessions the Grand Inquisitor of France managed to extort in northern France.

The records of the Templar commission prove that by April 1311 Pierre had recently left Lyons for Paris. It was almost inevitable that a Dominican of his scholarly ability would be sent at some time to the great convent of St Jacques, to complete his theological education among those regarded as the cream of West European intellects. But the date of his first attested appearance in that city is suggestive. It opens the possibility that he originally journeyed there in the company of Archbishop Pierre, who was forced (by an armed guard under the command of Prince Louis) to visit the caital in 1310 and submit to a humiliating peace with King Philip IV, by the terms

[49] B. Barbiche, ed., *Les Actes pontificaux originaux des Archives Nationales de Paris*, iii. *1305-1415* (Vatican, 1982), p. 42, no. 2333. For the papal commission sent to Lyons during the vacancy see p. 46, no. 2345.

[50] Levesque, *Les Frères Prêcheurs*, pp. 74-5.

[51] Mortier, i. 153.

of which Lyons lost its age-long independence.[52] This tentative speculation is only supported by the fact that it was apparently in the archbishop's Paris residence that the papal commission heard of Pierre and his knowledge of the Templars. But whether or not Pierre arrived with that historic mission, it remains true that a turning-point in his life strikingly coincided with a milestone in the history of the city in which he had grown up, and to which he was never, as far as we know, to return.

Pierre's departure did not, however, extinguish his fierce loyalty to the town on the Rhône and the Sâone. Despite his exposure to Parisian intellectual traditions, the great men of Lyons, Hostiensis, Hugues de St Cher, and above all Humbert de Romans, remained his guiding stars throughout his life. And he even continued to fight the city's political battles. In his most systematic work, *De potestate Papae*, finished by 1317, he took up its cause in a rather unexpected context. Having devoted himself whole-heartedly to proving the king of France's sovereignty within French territory, he then pointedly commented that the strongest pillar of the royal position, prescription, also legally protected from royal encroachment those cities which had long been outside the kingdom.[53] By implication, Philip V could not enjoy the benefits of independence from pope and emperor without also according to Lyons a similar independence. It was a brave stand. But unsurprisingly it was ineffective in moving Philip, who proved as obdurate as his father. Lyons was forced to be French, though Pierre was no longer there to see the consequences.

(c) The Templar Commission

By the time Pierre emerged from obscurity into the historical records, he was in his early- or mid-thirties, a man of wide experience and self-confidence. The episode in which he first figured offers an invaluable insight into his complex personality. It occurred in the context of Philip the Fair's violent onslaught against the Temple, which had begun in 1307 with the sudden arrest by royal officials of all French Templars, and was followed by relentless demands that the ecclesiastical

---

[52] See G. de Valoux, *Le Patriciat lyonnais aux XIIIe et XIVe siècles* (Paris, 1973), pp. 34–5.
[53] *DPP*, p. 154.

authorities condemn them for heresy. The king's motive in acting thus is still a subject of controversy among historians; but if the allegations produced against the brothers have generally failed to impress twentieth-century readers, contemporaries were unsettled by the rich store of crimes to which the knights and sergeants confessed before the Paris inquisition.[54] The royal initiative deeply embarrassed and angered the pope, not only because Clement V clearly believed that the charges had been trumped up, but also because he resented the king's manipulation of ecclesiastical procedures. Therefore in 1308 he took the matter into his own hands, halting the Paris inquisition's hearings and appointing both a papal commission of inquiry and local examining boards to investigate the charges. This move was for a while effective in stalling the trials. But then those knights who had at first spoken up in the Temple's defence either disappeared in suspicious circumstances or were persuaded not to testify before the commission. And in 1310 the king's impatience burst forth; on 11 May fifty-four Templars were burned at the command of the archbishop of Sens.

The effect of this brutal action was to silence almost all the voices that had once been tentatively raised in support of the order. The papal commission of inquiry became little more than a farce. Of its seven members, its chairman the archbishop of Narbonne was absent as often as not, the bishop of Bayeux had been called to Avignon to negotiate with the pope, and the archdeacon of Maguelonne was excused on grounds of illness. The remaining four members, the bishops of Limoges and Mende, Matthew of Naples, and the archdeacon of Trent, had to bear the brunt of testing the allegations made by King Philip's counsellors, although all chance of obtaining unbiased testimony from witnesses had by now been destroyed. Those Templars who did appear before the commission were far too cowed to attempt anything more than their own disassociation from the party that had appealed to the pope against Philip's violent and cruel onslaught.[55] In any case the commissioners, who had originally been chosen to propitiate the king, were not over-anxious to bolster the defence. Still, they did conduct the inquiry in accordance with proper forms and resisted blatant

---

[54] For recent treatments of the problem see J. Favier, *Philippe le Bel* (Paris, 1978), pp. 426–80; M. Barber, *The Trial of the Templars* (Cambridge, 1978); and P. Partner, *The Murdered Magicians: The Templars and their Myth* (Oxford, 1982).

[55] Barber, *Trial of the Templars*, pp. 154–77.

royal bullying as far as possible; but this was not enough.
Without any positive support the Templars were clearly a lost
cause. It therefore demanded very considerable courage to behave
as Pierre de la Palud did when he was called to testify. That he
was called at all is surprising, since very few non-Templars
gave evidence. A clue to his appearance may lie in the fact that
on 19 April 1311 the commission was sitting 'in domo . . . domini
Petri de Sabaudie', the house of Archbishop Pierre de Savoie.[56]
The friar's doubtless unwelcome summons may conjecturally
be explained by a servant in the archbishop's *hôtel* informing
the commissioners of Pierre's heated words championing the
Templars, spoken when he had stayed there in the early part of
1310; that something like this occurred is perhaps implied in
Pierre's careful denial at the beginning of the interrogation
that he knew anything more than what he was about to say. No
resident of Paris, however recent his arrival, could risk a
whole-hearted defence of the order in April 1311. Merely to
whisper disbelief in the charges laid was to incur the dangerous
wrath of King Philip. Pierre therefore chose his words circum-
spectly. Nevertheless his speech is striking for its honesty and
integrity. He had, he said, been present at the examination of
many Templars, had heard some confess to the charges and
others deny them; yet 'from the many arguments it seemed to
him that more faith was to be attached to those denying than
to those confessing'.[57] This reference to confessions extorted
by force or by torture, oblique as it was, cast doubt on all
the previous testimonies submitted. Only a man prepared for
a rough ride would have said it. Having demonstrated his
courage, Pierre did backtrack just a little, for since coming to
Paris he had met and learned to respect many men who did not
agree with him on the matter—his mentor and friend Hervé de
Nédellec among them.[58] He therefore gave it as his opinion
that the allegations concerning blasphemy and homosexual
practices committed at reception ceremonies—to some of

---

[56] J. Michelet, *Le Procès des Templiers*, ii (Paris, 1851), p. 191; I am most
grateful to Professor Barber for giving me this reference.

[57] Lizerand, *Le Dossier de l'affaire des Templiers* (Paris, 1923), pp. 192–4.

[58] Guimaraes, 'Hervé Noël', *AFP* 8 (1938), 55 and n. 121 on Hervé's
participation in the affair. Hervé clearly regarded the Templars as guilty of the
sins to which they had confessed, even though he was not, as Guimaraes rightly
points out, an avid supporter of Philip the Fair. His attitude towards the whole
affair was probably that expressed by the Masters of Theology in Paris in 1308;
see Lizerand, *Dossier*, pp. 62–70.

which the Visitor of France, Hugues de Pairaud, had confessed[59]—might be true in some cases, though not in others. A modern reader may perhaps regret that Pierre felt impelled to add these words. Yet given the sheer bulk of confessions relating to the reception ceremonies, it would have taken some arrogance to assert that the accusations were always false.

Up until this point, Pierre had spoken like a level-headed canon lawyer scrupulously evaluating evidence. Then suddenly he became a credulous teller of tall stories. This transformation could perhaps be ascribed, given the occasion, to the subtle methods of interrogation used. But a taste for legend is too much a feature of Pierre's personality to require sinister explanation; his later sermons and even his polemical writings contain just such Jekyll and Hyde leaps from the learned to the popular. To the benefit of his reputation, Pierre did not vouch for the truth of either of the stories he told. He did, however, offer a warrant for the first—it was connected with a picture in which two Templars were depicted riding the same horse. (What he had in mind was probably the Templar seal, which showed a shared mount in commemoration of the order's primitive poverty;[60] as knowledge about early Templar conditions had passed into oblivion, the seal had started to pique men's curiosity.) Pierre's explanation for this unusual equestrian feat was that the man riding behind was the Devil in disguise, using his position to tempt into blasphemy the knight holding the reins. It was commonplace in Dominican sermons to offer congregations hypothetical explanations of the paintings they could see on the church walls; but a technique that produced telling exempla in the pulpit was singularly inappropriate to legal testimony. The second story was about a former Grand Master of the Temple who, imprisoned by the Saracens, was later released on condition that he introduce evil practices into the order.[61] The friar did not attempt to give verisimilitude to these tales by providing names, places, or dates; they were simply rattling good yarns, such as might have been told one evening around the fire. As legal evidence for guilt they were valueless; if the commissioners believed them, they could not exploit them in any useful way. From the historian's perspective, Pierre's words attest to a widespread belief among those outside the order that the Templars' early purity had somehow

[59] Barber, *Trial of the Templars*, pp. 66–7.

[60] Lizerand, *Dossier*, p. 194; Barber, *Trial of the Templars*, p. 279 n. 61.

[61] This story was also recounted in the confession of the Templar Receptor of Aquitaine; see Barber, *Trial of the Templars*, p. 69.

become soiled. But this was so common a sentiment about all religious orders, and even about the church herself, as to be quite unremarkable.

Neither Pierre's courageous stand nor his colourful addenda had any effect whatever on the commission's work. When it finished its hearings on 26 May 1311, it ordered its lengthy proceedings to be copied out and sent to the pope. The affair ended at the Council of Vienne on 3 April 1312, when Clement V announced the suppression of the order of the Temple, 'though not by way of a judicial sentence'.[62] But Clement's decision was a response to immediate political pressures, not the result of carefully considering the weighty documents forwarded to him by the papal commission. In fact the huge mass of records languished unread in the papal archive until it became the hunting-ground for historians. So unless he told them himself— which would have been a dangerous thing to do—Pierre's contemporaries in Paris can have known nothing of what happened on 19 April.

[62] Ibid., pp. 228-9.

2. Bachelor

(a) Pierre at St Jacques

By the time Pierre arrived there, the university of Paris had
fully evolved from a group of distinguished but relatively
ephemeral schools, usually centred on the cathedral cloister
and the local monastic houses, that had been its core in the
twelfth century, into a recognizable institution with a permanent site on the Left Bank and a growing number of buildings.
In the long battle the masters had fought during the early
thirteenth century for independence against the chancellor
and the bishop of Paris they had carried most of their points.
Consequently they had become a privileged body, subject to
their own jurisdiction, enjoying a high degree of freedom of
speech, and capable of defending their rights by reference to a
formidable bulk of charters. Nevertheless their hard-won
academic autonomy was still vulnerable to infringement by the
papacy and by the king of France, especially when violent
disagreements broke out among the masters themselves. Papal
prohibitions on the discussion of certain topics—for example,
on mendicant privileges, enforced by the legate Benedict Gaetani
(the future pope Boniface VIII) in 1290—could seriously limit
their freedom of debate. Less visible but probably more in-
trusive was royal pressure. This grew in intensity during the
reign of Philip the Fair, assisted by the rebuilding of the royal
palace on the Île de la Cité which brought the court into regular
contact with the schools. During the first three decades of the
fourteenth century, under royal influence the university grew
steadily more French in composition, until the point when its
status as the most prestigious centre for higher education in
northern Europe began to be challenged by English and German
schools, to which non-Frenchmen increasingly resorted.

The university was composed of four faculties, later described by Pierre as the four columns supporting the corners of
the church (Clermont Ferrand, MS 46, fo. 63^r). Two of these,
Medicine and Canon Law, were small and relatively insignificant, Medicine because it was new and in competition with
more famous centres, Canon Law because Paris scholars had
been prohibited since the early thirteenth century from studying Roman Law, which most canonists regarded as an essential

foundation for the discipline, and also because it was tightly subordinated to the powerful Theology faculty. The Arts Faculty, in the thirteenth century notably active and intellectually adventurous, was by the early fourteenth century in decline, its reputation permanently impaired by the controversies of the 1270s. The Theology faculty therefore reigned supreme within Paris, and was held in high regard throughout the western church. The masters of theology explored the Scriptures in search of fine definitions, examined the practices of the contemporary church to ensure that belief and action ran parallel, and tried to reconcile differences of opinion on matters of belief by cogitating deeply on the mysteries of the faith. Corporately they saw themselves as a bastion of the catholic church, a body of experts to be consulted automatically by the papal curia on all contentious issues. But the pope and cardinals, though initially willing to listen respectfully to the Paris theologians' opinions, began during the pontificate of Boniface VIII to suspect their impartiality on questions that had a political dimension. This encouraged them to resort increasingly to the theological advisers resident at the curia, who were specially picked for their knowledge and experience.[1] As a consequence, by the early years of the fourteenth century the papacy viewed the Paris faculty as little more than a think-tank, powerless to impose its decisions. Pierre was, in the 1330s, to lead the first challenge to this view of its relative insignificance.

From their initial appearance in the city the mendicant orders had played a major role in the evolution of theological learning in Paris, and as a result had cornered for themselves a privileged position in the Theology faculty. In 1254 the seculars claimed, though unjustifiably, that the mendicants held all but three of the fifteen chairs in theology.[2] The anger that lay behind this distorted perception was the fruit of jealousy; whereas the friars were able regularly to cream off to their Paris *studia* the intellectual talent from all their European houses, the secular masters, their mobility limited by lack of money, had to rely on more sporadic recruitment. The 1250s and 1260s were rent by bitter feuds, in which the mendicants

---

[1] R. W. Southern, 'The Changing Role of Universities in Medieval Europe', *BIHR* 60 (1987), 139–40.
[2] G. Leff, *Paris and Oxford Universities in the Thirteenth and Fourteenth Centuries* (New York, 1968), pp. 38–47. For the actual, as opposed to the perceived, situation, see W. J. Courtenay, *Teaching Careers at the University of Paris in the Thirteenth and Fourteenth Centuries* (Notre Dame, Ind., 1988), p. 28.

scored victories both through papal assistance and through the brilliance of their greatest thinkers, of whom Albertus Magnus, Thomas Aquinas, and Bonaventura were the most notable. But in the 1280s and 1290s the seculars were helped by the growing number of hospices and colleges providing them with subsidised accommodation, and able men (particularly from the Low Countries) began to attract ecclesiastical patronage adequate to finance them for the long periods of study necessary for the doctorate. The Theology faculty therefore became rather better balanced, if only marginally less strife-ridden.

By 1310 Pierre de la Palud was in residence in St Jacques, the largest of all the Dominican houses, founded at St Dominic's command to educate the Preachers for their mission. Within its walls it catered for three different categories of student: those from houses in the Paris region for whom it was the natural choice of ordinary *studium*; others from houses throughout Europe, chosen at provincial chapters to enjoy the privilege of three years' more advanced study;[3] and a small group of intellectually outstanding friars, nominated each year by the master general of the order to read the *Sentences*. These men aimed to obtain doctorates in theology, to spend two years as regent masters of the University of Paris, and then to teach in the various Dominican *studia* or administer the order. It was this select body of advanced students that Pierre joined, to work under the master in the chair of the French, one of the two chairs attached to the house.

The first decade of the fourteenth century had not been particularly easy for the inhabitants of St Jacques. Hervé de Nédellec, regent master in the chair of the French in 1307–9 and a powerful influence on Pierre, had been among the Dominicans who had signed the notorious appeal of 1303 launched by Philip IV and Guillaume de Nogaret against Pope Boniface VIII. But the non-French friars had left the city; and others, including some of the more eminent, apparently refused to sign and had been obliged to quit.[4] Since the Dominican order had been founded to reinforce papal authority, those who demonstrated their loyalty to King Philip by remaining in Paris must have suffered a serious crisis of nerve, especially after the news of Boniface's treatment at Agnani filtered

---

[3] A. Dondaine, 'Documents pour servir à l'histoire de la province de France. L'Appel au concile (1303)', *AFP* 22 (1952), 384.

[4] Ibid., p. 384. On foreign friars being required to leave Paris, see *The Register of John de Halton, bishop of Carlisle, 1292–1324*, i, ed. W. N. Thompson and T. F. Tout (London, 1913), p. 211.

through to them. And Nogaret's determination to secure Boniface's posthumous condemnation as a heretic kept the issue on the boil long after the original crisis. But by 1310 the commotion was slowly dying down, as Enguerran de Marigny successfully persuaded the king towards a relatively conciliatory policy.[5] Foreigners had reappeared at St Jacques, the two best known of Pierre de la Palud's contemporaries being Jacques de Lausanne, soon to be a famous preacher, and John of Naples (Giovanni Regina di Napoli). Still the oppressive closeness of the court, once demonstrated, could not be forgotten. The mutual respect that had characterized the relationship between the king and the Dominicans in the age of St Louis was now subject to strains of an unpredictable sort. Pierre, brought up at Lyons in an atmosphere inimical to the government of Philip IV, automatically sided with the king's critics as soon as Philip's death in 1314 made it safe to express his true feelings; but in the later years of his career he was to learn dexterity in attracting royal goodwill. Like other Frenchmen, he came to appreciate that he could not afford the luxury of neutrality towards the court.

At St Jacques political uncertainty was compounded by intellectual challenge. In 1277 the bishop of Paris, Étienne Tempier, had issued a list of 219 propositions (many of them restricting the freedom of God and affirming the necessity of the laws of nature) which he condemned as unsuitable to be taught in schools. Although the Paris articles, unlike those issued by Kilwardby in Oxford in the same year, did not directly attack Thomas Aquinas's major theses, they were drafted by known opponents of his views. As a result, the Dominican order rallied to the defence of Aquinas (who had died in 1274), binding itself in 1286 to teach and defend his doctrines. This is not the place to summarize Thomism nor to describe its debt to earlier theological thinkers. But in order to understand some of the problems Pierre de la Palud discussed, it is necessary to sketch—albeit by over-simplification—the outlines of Thomas's teleology, which became very controversial. According to Thomas, God endowed man with reason in order that he might attain to the good life. By following the natural law, in accordance with which all created things were intended to operate, man could fulfil his potential here on earth. In so doing he acquired virtues that bore some direct relation to the

[5] J. Favier, *Un Conseiller de Philippe le Bel: Enguerran de Marigny* (Paris, 1963), pp. 129–37.

theological virtues attainable through God's grace; in Thomas's most famous phrase, 'Grace does not abolish but perfects nature.' Man's other guides towards heaven were first the divine law contained in Scripture, and secondly the eternal law, God's plan for creation as a whole; these two laws perfectly complemented each other. Although the eternal law transcended human reason, a devoted and learned man might, by constant dedication, discover its outlines (Thomas's *Summa theologiae* contained his own description of aspects of the eternal law). Therefore, guided by the natural, the eternal, and the divine laws, the elect would march along the road to salvation.

Behind this splendid vision Thomas's critics, led by Henry of Ghent, discerned two basic assumptions: that human reason was the prime spur to man's moral improvement; and that, although initially free to create as He wished, once He had created God had apparently obliged Himself to operate in a consistent fashion (the eternal law). They therefore believed that Thomas (and the tradition he represented) underestimated the part played by will in man's activities, and that he had failed to see the difficulties inherent in his analysis of God's freedom of action. The opposition, divided on many points of principle, acquired in the first decade of the fourteenth century a leader of brilliance in the Franciscan Duns Scotus, whose opinions were to prove as controversial as those he attacked. According to Scotus, since God's omnipotence necessarily went hand-in-hand with total freedom of will, His actions must sometimes transcend laws observable by human beings. His *potentia ordinata* which normally operated in accordance with natural and eternal law (though it did not need to do so) was fortified by a *potentia absoluta* that in theory permitted divine action outside and against the established law. But even when acting through ordained power, God could and did vary the rules: a simple illustration of this was the permission He granted to the patriarchs of the Old Testament to practise polygamy, although this was in clear defiance of the natural law.[6] To respond to Thomas's critics, the Parisian Dominicans

---

[6] On the Dominican order's short-lived fight in defence of Thomism, see W. J. Courtenay, *Schools and Scholars in Fourteenth-Century England* (Princeton, NJ, 1987), pp. 178–82. In describing the arguments about God's freedom of action, I have used the same author's 'The Dialectic of Omnipotence in the High and Late Middle Ages', in T. Rudavsky, ed., *Divine Omniscience and Omnipotence in Medieval Philosophy* (Dordrecht, Boston, and Lancaster, 1985), pp. 243–69 (though any misunderstandings are mine alone). For the question of the

led by Hervé de Nédellec were obliged to engage in controversy on a very broad front. When Pierre de la Palud began to read the *Sentences* at St Jacques, he found himself on a battlefield.

(b) *Bachelor of the* Sentences

Pierre will have been told in 1308 or 1309 that he had been selected by the master general to start reading the *Sentences* in Paris, apparently in 1310. If I am correct in thinking that he was still in Lyons during the Templar inquiry of 1308–9, he will not have been given long to become acclimatized to his new environment. But while he was doubtless sad to move far from his family and the city he now knew intimately to a place much more distinctly northern in climate and style, when he arrived there he did at least have the comfort of finding other men from Bresse at the Paris houses of Count Amadeus of Savoy[7] and of Archbishop Pierre. And it is perhaps worth conjecturing that the change permitted a meeting with his famous relation Jean de Joinville, by now a very old man, who had finished his Life of St Louis before the end of 1305, but was still capable of writing letters in 1315. If the two did indeed have an opportunity for conversation, the effect on the future Patriarch of Jerusalem's subsequent development can be imagined.

Within St Jacques, Pierre was fortunate to be counted a French friar (the Lyons convent having always been part of the Dominican French province), because it shielded him from the undoubted resentment felt by many inmates of St Jacques against the foreign students they were obliged to support. Of his first master, Laurence de Nantes, nothing is known. But Pierre must have faced a sizeable problem in the classroom, in being required to adapt to a tradition more philosophical, more scholastic, than the one in which he had apparently been brought up. To judge by the sources quoted in his scholarly works Aristotle had played only a very minor part in his education; though he must have had some philosophical grounding at Notre Dame de Confort, it seems not to have penetrated very deeply into his consciousness. On the other hand his companions from the northern and the Italian *studia*

patriarchs, see H. de Gandillac, in A. Fliche and V. Martin, eds., *Histoire de l'Église*, xiii (Paris, 1951), pp. 344–5.

[7] *Syllabus (in English) of the Documents Relating to England and Other Kingdoms Contained in the Collection Known as 'Rymer's Foedera'*, ed. T. D. Hardy (London, 1869), i. 4. 115.

were thoroughly familar with all the Stagirite's logical works and with the *libri naturales*. And by tradition lectures on the *Sentences* provided the opportunity for a plunge into speculative theology, for which a sound philosophical training proved invaluable. Pierre may therefore have found his duty intimidating, an unusual experience for him. By the time he began lecturing in Paris he was treading a path well worn for more than 150 years by others, some cleverer than himself, many better equipped. It says much for his nous that he eventually harnessed his own assets to the task and created something original. But he spilt much ink before achieving this.

The prologue to his commentary on the *Sentences*, probably written when he had finished the whole work, compared the value of canon law to theology with that of naval astronomy to pure astronomy; although primarily a product of man's reason while theology was a divine science, canon law was a worthwhile ancillary subject.[8] This contention Pierre was successfully to demonstrate in his work on Book 4 of the *Sentences*. But the first three books offered little material suited to a legalistic exposition. In fact the most important academic exercise of his career dragged him into a world of abstraction that he was later conspicuously to eschew, perhaps because he found it alien both scholastically and temperamentally. And there are signs of strain in his diffuseness. While it was normal for each new bachelor to comment on the problems his immediate predecessors had found in the text (which has the consequence that the commentaries of any particular decade offer the historian a reasonably exact insight into the intellectual preoccupations of the day), Pierre carried this habit to excess. In one of his early sermons he caricatured himself when he described how (Worcester Cathedral, MS Q 100, fo. 81^v) a newly incepted Master in Theology at Paris would continue his disputation until he had attacked all the errors he had ever heard of in relation to his chosen subject. His own huge sprawling commentary contained a wealth of conflicting opinions on every thesis, but was distinctly weaker on resolving than on finding difficulties. In Pierre's hands the analytical framework of scholastic discourse became less an instrument for reaching conclusions than for stating problems.

To take an example: in his commentary on Book 2 of the *Sentences*, Pierre asked the question 'utrum Deus agat propter

---

[8] G. Groppo, 'La teologia e il suo "subiectum" secondo il prologo del commento alle sentenze di Pietro da Palude, O.P. († 1342)', *Salesianum*, 23 (1961), 261.

finem' (Vatican, MS Latin 1073, fo. 7^r), whether God acts in accordance with a predetermined end.[9] Following precedent, he gave superficial arguments both in favour of and against the proposition. The next step began: *respondeo*, but instead of answering the problem, he set out the steps he intended to take: first he would give the opinion of Thomas Aquinas; then of Thomas's opponents; then he would reply to the opponents; then he would deal with their objections to Thomas's propositions; and finally he would try to reach some conclusion of his own. In fact he simply copied the first four sections *in extenso* from earlier disciples of Thomas. And although the final conclusion was in his own words, it was the standard Thomist one that God indeed operated 'propter finem'. When the problem was more open to debate, such as whether the stars only moved like other movable objects or whether they had a motion of their own, he was more prolific. As before, his *respondeo* simply described the next steps he would take: first he would state the opinion of certain men on three central questions, the replies made to these opinions, and the responses to these replies. Then he would recapitulate and put forward another opinion expressed in five conclusions. This sounds decisive. But when, after a very lengthy exposé of other men's views, he reached his five conclusions, although all relevant to points made earlier they did not constitute a reply to the original question (Vatican, MS Latin 1073, fo. 58^v). On other problems he did offer solutions of sorts, though they were less straightforward answers than determined compromises between the differing opinions he had summarized. As he said when discussing the question of heavenly influences on earthly life, 'I reply that I shall first state the opinion of certain men. Then I shall raise questions about their views. Thirdly I shall put together another opinion from all that has been said.' (Vatican, MS Latin 1073, fo. 72^r; 'Respondeo primo ponetur opinio quorundam. Secundo inquiretur de dictis in ea. Tertio confabuletur alia opinio ex dictis.')

To the reader accustomed to the older and more sharply analytical framework employed by thirteenth-century theologians, the structure of Pierre's questions is unsatisfying. And it certainly risked confusing his listeners; since modern readers with the manuscript in front of them often find themselves

---

[9] This question also circulated independently of the commentary. See M. Grabmann, 'Petri de Palude O.P. († 1342) Quaestio: "Utrum Deus immediate agat in omni actione?"', *Acta Pontificalis Academiae Romanae S. Thomae Aq. et Religionis Catholicae*, 1939–40, pp. 41–58.

baffled by the sheer quantity of opinions cited and the incon-
clusiveness of the conclusions,[10] it is a fair supposition that
those who only heard what he had to say were on occasion
uncertain as to whether he was reporting the opinions of
others, criticizing them, or putting forward his own views. On
the other hand, his style accorded with the latest trend in
presentation. The complexity of the problems facing early
fourteenth-century theologians had led them to distrust quick
or neat answers. They needed a format that would permit
consideration of a larger range of opinions and sub-arguments,
that aimed to fit into a continuing dialogue, that sought to
identify small nuggets of truth instead of offering large conclusions. Pierre was among the earliest of practitioners of the
new type of question; he should therefore be credited with
giving his audience and readers what they wanted.[11]

It was an aspect of this new approach to theological discourse that original formulations of problems surfaced only
occasionally. Nevertheless they occurred, as in the final
conclusion of Pierre's lengthy treatment of original sin, which
is remarkable for its common sense and clarity. Characteristically he offered a neat and familiar analogy: let us suppose
that a king gives two sources of income to a faithful soldier, the
one a gift in perpetuity, the other a stipend drawn from the
royal treasury. The first would be inheritable by his son,
the second would not unless the king chose to grant it. If the

[10] This explains why scholars, basing their researches on the commentary on
Book 3 of the *Sentences*, 19. 5, are still unable to be sure whether or not Pierre
supported the Immaculate Conception; see W. A. Hinnebusch, *The History of the
Dominican Order* (New York, 1973), ii. 172. But it is in fact clear from the
sermon in Clermont Ferrand, MS 46, fos. 14ʳ–20ʳ (preached on the feast-day of
the Conception) that he did so, and that he thought Thomas Aquinas agreed with
him. He set out the two sides of the controversy and then remarked: 'Queque
istorum opinionum sit verior nolo determinare ad presens, quia quamvis opinio
que ponit eam conceptam in oribili sit antiquorum doctorum et sanctorum sicut
beati Bernardi, contrarium et beati Thoma de Aquino et michi probabilior
videtur. Tamen nolo eam asserere contrariam condemnendo seu assertive
reprobando quia etiam illa est multorum et magistrorum et catholicorum
doctorum modernorum. Et quamvis necesse sit alteram esse veram et alteram
falsam que sunt contradictorie, tamen possibile est utramque esse probabilem.'
This is perhaps another indication that Pierre's knowledge of St Thomas's
theological positions was inadequate. His own adherence to the doctrine may
reflect his Lyons background, since the canons there were among its earliest
supporters. Nevertheless, the question of whether or not the Virgin's conception
was actually immaculate was irrelevant to most of the arguments he put
forward for recognizing the feast. In this his sermon accorded with what he had
said in the commentary on the *Sentences*.

[11] I am most grateful to Professor Courtenay for pointing this out to me.

soldier were later to commit a crime against the king, he would be deprived of both sources of income.

Thus the son would lose both grants through the fault of the father, although he would not have received both from him. This is our present case. Adam because of his sin has transmitted to us both the privation of grace and the privation of original justice, although had he remained faithful he would have transmitted only the latter; but each of his descendants would have received grace from God.[12]

What made Pierre unusually incisive on this occasion was that, as a trained lawyer, he knew himself to be an expert on inheritance. He could therefore speak on original sin with an authority he lacked elsewhere.

Similarly he offered a canonist's rather than a theologian's angle on God's freedom of action, the tenet central to Duns Scotus's theology. God's justice is above the rules, He can remit the punishment for sin as and when he wishes, because He does not hold His justice in fee from any other source. This was a lawyer's view of jurisdictional right. God's omission of punishment for the patriarchs guilty of polygamy reminded Pierre of the king's power to pardon a homicide: a sovereign king can pardon a murder on impulse without injuring any third party other than God; not even the pope can normally excommunicate him for a failure to do justice in this way. But it remains true that rules define the circumstances in which a king may forgive a homicide; and so it is with God's power to remit punishment for sin.[13]

It was perhaps these insights, the fruit of an unusually concrete mind operating on abstract theological speculation, which attracted one of Pierre's pupils to produce, around 1320, a digest of his master's teaching on the first three books of the *Sentences*, including in the margins references to Pierre's

---

[12] C. O. Vollert, 'The Doctrine of Hervaeus Natalis on Primitive Justice and Original Sin', *Analecta Gregoriana*, 42 (1947), 112. Vollert says of his treatment of original sin that it is 'in many details the clearest and soundest presentation of Thomistic teaching contributed during the debate against Durandus', p. 269. It must, however, be admitted that a less elegant form of the same argument can be found in Giles of Rome's *De ecclesiastica potestate*, ed. R. Scholz (Weimar, 1929), 2. 8. 4 and 5.

[13] 'Sicut rex si a nullo homine tenet iustitiam suam, nulli homini facit iniuriam si homicidam dimittit; sed erga deum a quo tenet delinquit si sine causa hoc facit. Nec forte papa propter hanc iniustitiam potest excommunicare si ab eo non tenet, plus quam officialis prepositum dimittentem homicidam laicum nisi forte quia ledit reipublicam.' *Scriptum super tertium Sententiarum*, ed. Peter of Nimeguen (Paris, 1517), 20. 1, fos. 98[r-v].

sources.[14] The existence of this compilation in Barcelona, Arch. Corona de Aragòn, MS Ripoll 77 bis is proof that, little though they have appealed to some modern critics, Pierre's views were reckoned to be of value in the schools of his own day.

(c) Pierre and Durand de St Pourçain

Pierre's commentaries on the first three books of the Sentences have a value additional to their author's insights, in that they contain evidence about how the Dominicans preserved the theological inheritance of their most distinguished doctor. Since the death of Thomas Aquinas in 1274 and the condemnation of some of his doctrines in Oxford in 1277, Paris-based Dominicans had been engaged in a lengthy digestion of the huge bulk of work he had left to them. Aware, as few others yet were, of the coherence and moderation of Thomas's stand on major theological issues, they had striven to answer his critics, to clarify the points that were still obscure, and to come to grips with the difficult problems raised above all by his intellectualism and his belief in the unity of forms. Their mission as 'second generation Thomists' was blessed by the general chapter of Saragossa in 1309, which decreed that Thomas's teaching should become standard throughout the whole order. Deviation from it was not to be tolerated.

This order restricted the freedom of those Dominicans who remained unconvinced, particularly on points where Thomas had been criticized by Henry of Ghent or Duns Scotus. The leader of this group when Pierre first arrived in Paris was Durand de St Pourçain, an able friar who found it impossible to agree with Thomas on a wide range of principles, among them that there was a real distinction between the will and the intellect, that the act of knowing was an absolute accident inhering in the soul, or that immortality could be demonstrated rigorously. Durand began lecturing on the Sentences in 1307–8. His lectures were both brilliant and provocative. Taking further a point about relation first made by Duns Scotus, he propounded an original solution to the unanswerable question of how the three persons of the Trinity were related. From the same starting-point he argued that the quantity of Christ's body was

---

[14] A. Maier, Ausgehendes Mittelalter: Gesammelte Aufsätze zur Geistes-geschichte des 14 Jahrhunderts, i (Rome, 1964), p. 141.

not present in any way in the Eucharist—a contradiction of Thomas Aquinas's opinion.

Then he went on to challenge the very basis of Thomas's psychological system, in the process of which he rebutted the views that grace was an infused quality and that original sin was a sin in the normal sense of the word.

The disputatious method of teaching in Paris encouraged toleration of a wide range of views on abstract theological questions; provided a proposition was not palpably in contravention of the Scriptures or of defined articles of faith, it was fit to be discussed. Though original, Durand's ideas had affinities with the teachings of men held in the highest respect at the university; consequently scholars at large were loath to criticize him ruthlessly. Furthermore he presented his more innovative ideas with a skill that made him difficult to attack. For example, he introduced one under the rubric *opinio singularis*, remarking at the end of his sympathetic discussion that 'although this opinion seems quite probable, because it is unusual I do not adhere to it'.[15] Should the contention later meet with condemnation, he could hardly be regarded as heretical for having propounded it, since heresy is characterized by intransigence, and he had decisively demonstrated his flexibility. According to the normal conventions of academic debate, Durand was a cautious and responsible theologian.

But the reaction of the Dominican order was rather different. By criticizing Thomas Aquinas's views, Durand was deliberately flying in the face of the capitular decision at Saragossa in 1309. Indeed he implicitly challenged that decision in his claim at the beginning of his commentary on the *Sentences* that the proper procedure in speaking and writing of things which did not touch the faith was to rely on reason rather than on the authority of any doctor, however famous and revered he might be.[16] Furthermore Durand was alleged to have published the

---

[15] J. Koch, 'Die Jahre 1312-1317 im Leben des Durandus de S. Porciano', *Studi e Testi*, 37 (1924), 275 n. 2. Koch's views in this article are somewhat updated by Vollert, 'The Doctrine of Hervaeus Natalis', pp. 289-303. For the dates see A. de Guimaraes, 'Hervé Noël († 1323): Étude biographique', *AFP* 8 (1938), 45. On the general significance of Durand's teaching, J. Koch, 'Durandus de S. Porciano O.P.: Forschungen zum Streit um Thomas von Aquin zu Beginn des 14 Jahrhunderts', *Beiträge zur Geschichte der Philosophie des Mittelalters*, 26. 1 (1927) remains fundamental. For a brief summary, see E. Gilson, *A History of Christian Philosophy in the Middle Ages* (London, 1955), pp. 473-6.

[16] Durand de St Pourçain, *In Sententias theologicas Petri Lombardi Commentariorum Libri Quatuor* (Lyons, 1587), p. 3: 'Nos igitur plus rationi quam cuiuscumque auctoritati humanae consentientes, nullius puri hominis auctoritatem rationi praeferimus.'

first version of his commentary before it had been examined and approved by the master general of the order, despite ancient (though in practice almost obsolete) prohibitions on such conduct going back to 1254 and 1256.[17] His opponents raised an outcry. In 1311 the bachelor therefore produced an expurgated version of the work, toning down several conclusions without altering its basic orientation. This was enough to secure him the regent mastership in the chair of the French at St Jacques in 1312, a promotion probably owed to external influences;[18] and in early 1313 his high reputation in the outside world brought him a call to Avignon, to become master of the school (*lector sacrii palatii*) at the curia.

Far from stilling the storm, Durand's departure for Avignon left the Paris stage dominated by his adversaries, led by Hervé de Nédellec, prior provincial of France since 1309.[19] Hervé, who wrote a regular stream of pamphlets against Durand until his own death in 1323, was not one to be overawed by Clement V's approval of Durand's innovative theology. At the Metz general chapter of 1313, he persuaded the assembled friars to renew the Saragossa declaration on the order's rigid adherence to Thomism, to institute censorship procedures which would in future prevent dissenters from obtaining the public hearing Durand had enjoyed, and to nominate a commission to inquire into Durand's errors. Among the nine members of the commission appointed were the two senior bachelors of the *Sentences*, John of Naples and Pierre de la Palud, on whom the real responsibility for enumerating the errors fell. It was Pierre's first experience of a role he was often in the future to play.

John and Pierre, in accordance with instructions, tackled the task from two different angles. First they drew up a list of 93 articles from Durand's commentary on the *Sentences* that were, in their view, either of doubtful orthodoxy or potentially dangerous because they might be understood in a heretical way. This list was subsequently forwarded by the next general chapter to Durand, who produced in response his *Excusationes*, a series of self-justifications which did include some retractions.[20] Secondly they—in fact chiefly John of Naples—compiled

---

[17] But in this connection see his own much later remark that his first edition had been put into circulation secretly and against his will; Durand de St Pourçain, *In Sententias theologicas*, p. 951.

[18] Guimaraes, 'Hervé Noël', p. 5.

[19] Koch, 'Die Jahre 1312–1317', p. 282.

[20] These are known through Hervé de Nédellec's *Reprobationes excusationum Durandi*, contained in Bibliothèque de Reims, MS 502, fos. 112^v–116^v, 128^v–131^v.

a list of 253 unThomistic propositions from the same source.[21] The friars were still discussing what use should be made of this list when, in 1317, Pope John XXII released Durand from obedience to the order by promoting him to the bishopric of Limoux. He took advantage of his immunity to produce a third version of his commentary, completed in 1327, in which he reaffirmed at least some of the views he had eliminated in his expurgated version of 1311, though in general his tone was calmer and less controversial.

Pierre had the misfortune to be lecturing on the first three books of the *Sentences* during the bitterest years of this dispute. Some conflict of loyalties was almost inevitable for him, especially during the months of 1312 when Durand was his own regent master. His admiration for Durand's intellect sometimes led him to express his criticism with caution; for example, commenting on Durand's thesis that Christ's body in the Eucharist lacked quantity, he concluded: 'Although this opinion is very subtle and plausible, it contains some doubtful elements.' Hervé de Nédellec, reading this remark after Pierre's work was circulated, appended a marginal note: 'This seems to me not only insufficient but also largely false.'[22] In one of his pamphlets Hervé, after systematically refuting Durand, somewhat scornfully remarked: 'On this question you can look at another solution provided by Pierre de la Palud, consider it and rebut it if you wish to.'[23] All the pressure the prior provincial could exert was inadequate to prevent Pierre from explicitly defending Durand on one matter at least, the status of marriage. Although his thesis that marriage was not a sacrament in the fullest sense had shocked the Paris theologians, Pierre pointed out that here Durand was effectively taking the same line as Gratian and the canonists, and therefore what he said deserved serious consideration, even if in the end it must be rejected.[24]

However, these very fragmentary expressions of respect for Durand were easily lost in a morass of intended criticism.

---

[21] Koch changed his opinion on the authorship of these articles when he had access to the Barcelona manuscript. See 'Zu codex 35 des Archivo del Cabildo Catedral de Barcelona', *AFP* 13 (1943), 106–7.

[22] Koch, 'Durandus', p. 267.

[23] Ibid., p. 262.

[24] For the earlier history of the argument over grace in marriage, in particular for Olivi's contribution, see D. Burr, 'Olivi on Marriage: The Conservative as Prophet', *Journal of Medieval and Renaissance Studies*, 2 (1972), 183–204; Maier, *Ausgehendes Mittelalter*, ii. 247–9.

Though Pierre was not a mere echo of Hervé, his sympathies lay firmly with the supporters of the Thomist line. Indeed his commentary on the first three books of the *Sentences* was planned as a point-by-point examination and refutation of Durand's great work. The result was singular, perhaps even counter-productive. For Pierre's training as a canon lawyer had accustomed him to stating fully and scrupulously his opponent's position, if possible in his own words, before attacking it. Therefore he copied out verbatim huge tracts of Durand's commentary, a reproduction which apparently contains excerpts from the unexpurgated version of that work.[25] If both useful to twentieth-century historians, and a proof of Pierre's intellectual honesty, this habit was a distinct drawback in a controversialist. It forced him to write at quite inordinate length (Durand's commentary was itself substantial), and to publicize his opponent's views more extensively than their refutation. Had his own rebuttals been conclusive, his prolixity might not have mattered; but they were not.

As only one example of his inability to pierce Durand's intellectual armour, let us examine Pierre's handling of the gifts of the Holy Spirit.[26] Thomas Aquinas had held that man submits to two principles of action: an interior principle, based on reason, which requires human virtues to operate; and an exterior principle, based on God, which operates through the gifts of the Holy Spirit. In an endeavour to determine the relationship between virtues and gifts, he refuted two opinions: that while virtues are given us so that we may do good, the gifts of the Holy Spirit save us from temptation; or an alternative version of the same proposition, that while the virtues help us to evade sin, the gifts cure us from the consequence of sin. Both these, he said, did not adequately differentiate between the two. Therefore he put forward the belief that virtues relate to a human way of comporting oneself, but the gifts of the Holy Spirit relate to a divine or superhuman way. Durand copied out

---

[25] Koch, 'Durandus', pp. 22–31, claimed that almost the whole unexpurgated version could be recovered from Pierre's work; but O. Lottin, *Psychologie et Morale au XIIe et XIIIe siècles*, iv (Gembloux, 1954), pp. 709–10 n. 2, showed that Pierre used the expurgated version of Book 3; and this has also been demonstrated for Book 4 by V. Heynck, 'Zur Datierung des Sentenzenkommentars des Petrus de Palude', *Franziskanische Studien*, 53 (1971), 326–7. As far as I know, the problem of Books 1 and 2 has not yet been tackled; though for the difficulty of so doing, see A. Maier, *Ausgehendes Mittelalter*, i. 466.

[26] This relies on O. Lottin, 'La Théorie des dons du Saint-Esprit au début du XIVe siècle', *Mélanges Ghellink* (2 vols.; Paris, 1951), ii. 849–54.

Thomas's treatment and added to it a fourth view derived from Duns Scotus, that virtues and gifts are much the same, differing only in that all virtues are comprised in gifts, while not all gifts are virtues. He then recorded his own belief that it was impossible to be certain which of the two views—Thomas's or Scotus's —was true. Pierre copied out the whole of Durand's argument including the final words, adding no criticism or comment. But after this he offered what he described as a fifth theory, though in reality it was only a development of Thomas's view: he distinguished gifts of the Holy Spirit from theological virtues, from infused moral virtues, and also from acquired moral virtues, distinctions effectively irreconcilable with the Scotist argument he had just apparently endorsed. It was characteristic of Pierre's approach that he left the Scotist position unassailed when he recorded his own position; and that he was clearer on what something was not than on what it was. But his readers must have been left in some perplexity as to what they ought to think.

In sum Pierre's attempt to expose Durand's weaknesses was like a man trying to trap a rat by throwing a duvet at it. The sharp-nosed philosopher had no difficulty in evading the soft mass of predigested second-hand opinions or the brief and often ill-focused refutations Pierre provided at the end of each question. Perhaps Durand detected his opponent's great weakness, his sketchy knowledge of Thomas Aquinas's writings other than the commentary on the *Sentences*. Joseph Koch, who first examined the whole episode, even suggested that Pierre's ignorance led him sometimes to rely on Durand's summary of Thomas's views for information about what the orthodox Dominican line was.[27] Here Pierre paid the price for years of study in the law; and as a hounder of anti-Thomists he consequently cut a somewhat uncertain figure.[28] The Dominican order had to wait for Durandellus's *Evidentiae contra Durandum*[29] of c.1330 for a work that actually achieved Pierre's objective. Nevertheless, his commentaries on the first three books of the *Sentences* at least set out the problems that had to be grappled with; they were a starting-point. And this no

[27] Koch, 'Die Jahre 1312–1317', p. 282.

[28] Koch, 'Zu codex 35', p. 103, explains how it came about that a later editor of the MS mistakenly described the list of propositions as Jacques de Lausanne's criticisms of Pierre.

[29] For manuscripts of this work see T. Kaeppeli, *Scriptores Ordinis Praedicatorum Medii Aevi*, i (Rome, 1970), pp. 337–8.

doubt accounted for the degree of interest they aroused in contemporaries.[30]

(d) Canon Law and Theology

In his commentary on the first three books of the *Sentences* Pierre's sources are easily discovered because he quotes *in extenso* from his contemporaries, Durand, the Carmelite Gui de Terreni, Hervé de Nédellec, and some anonymous tracts. The few original elements are inconspicuous to the casual reader of that formidable bulk. But the commentary on Book 4 is rather different.[31] Although Pierre will have lectured on this before he became a doctor in May 1314, the extant version, which was circulated after examination by the master general of the order, was probably not finalized before the beginning of 1315 at the earliest.[32] The subject of Book 4 is the sacraments, a theme on which canon lawyers had much to contribute to the standard theological exposition. From the beginning, Pierre seemed more

[30] e.g. Pietro Falaco of Genoa in 1315 copied out part of his commentary on Book 1. See Kaeppeli, *Scriptores Ordinis Praedicatorum*, iii (Rome, 1980), p. 255.

[31] I have used the second edn. of *Quartus Sententiarum liber* by Vincent Haerlem (Vincent of Haarlem) (Paris, 1514); on this see L. Vereecke, 'Les Éditions des oeuvres morales de Pierre de la Palu († 1342) à Paris au début du XVIe siècle', *Studia Moralia*, 17 (1979), 270. I have also made extensive use of Oxford, Bodleian Library, MS Holkham Miscellaneous 10, a 14th-cent. MS which has been very carefully corrected, and which has fuller readings on some occasions.

[32] On the dating of the books see V. Heynck, 'Zur Datierung', pp. 317-27. Heynck mistakes a reference to the king of France's election to the Roman senate for a comment on Louis X's accession to the throne of France (p. 325), which destroys his argument that the work must be later than the end of 1314. (What Pierre had in mind here is not clear; but on the suggestion by Pierre Dubois that the king of France should be made Roman senator, see D. Waley, *The Papal State in the Middle Ages* (London, 1961), p. 301 n. 2.) There is a clear indication that the question on mendicant privileges was written in the lifetime of Pope Clement V, and therefore before Pierre became a master. On the other hand Heynck is surely correct in emphasizing that the extant version of Pierre's commentary on Book 4 is not a report of his lectures but a fully finished work intended for publication, which must have taken time to produce. In this connection it is worthy of note that Oxford, Bodleian Library, MS Holkham Miscellaneous 10, apparently an early MS, has been systematically corrected and checked before being put into circulation. Given the order's insistence on vetting books, and the fuss over Durand's unvetted commentary, it is reasonable to assume that polishing his lectures on Book 4 was Pierre's first occupation as a master, and therefore that the work cannot have been completed before the beginning of 1315.

confident, more incisive in his handling of the material. At last he was able to fulfil the promise he had made in the prologue: to embed into the abstract cogitations of sacramental theology the canonists' more practical concerns. And here he must be judged to have succeeded, since what he had to say was appreciated by his contemporaries and read in the schools for many long years afterwards.

Modern theologians have placed Pierre's commentary within Dominican tradition, identifying the individual elements in his theological thinking and measuring them in terms of their compatibility with the teaching of St Thomas Aquinas. They usually conclude that he was a very modified Thomist.[33] Ecclesiastical historians have shown some interest in his handling of penance and the taxation of satisfactions; and recently in his teachings on sex and marriage have attracted wider attention. But to get the flavour of his whole work we have to go back to a fifteenth-century critic, St Antoninus of Florence, who said, 'I believe there can be found no other commentary on the Fourth Book of the *Sentences* which descends so far to practicalities.'[34] St Antoninus recognized Pierre's contribution, not as a philosophical treatise for sheltered academics, but rather as a handbook for field-workers. In this light, its historical interest lies both in its biting comments on contemporary affairs and in its summary of the church's teaching on practical morality in the second decade of the fourteenth century.

Pierre's response to the question, should heretics be extirpated? (13. 3, *QSL* fos. 56ᵛ–57ʳ) provides a characteristic example of his approach. As he saw it, the issue was one of law, not ethics. Quoting from the decree *ad abolendam*, he reaffirmed the canonical doctrine that recalcitrant heretics ought to be handed over to the secular arm as quickly as possible in order to prevent them from spreading their poison. If not caught red-handed, they could be convicted by the testimony of witnesses or by their own confessions—though here he noted that confessions extracted through torture or fear of

---

[33] 'Pierre est le représentat le plus qualifié du thomisme au début du XIVᵉ siècle', A. Michel in *Dictionnaire de théologie catholique*, under 'Pénitence', xii, col. 1004. See also A. Duval in *Dictionnaire de spiritualité*, xii. 2, col. 1632, and F. J. Roensch, *Early Thomistic School* (Dubuque, Iowa, 1964), pp. 124–31.

[34] Quoted by Vincent Haerlem (Vincent of Haarlem) in his prologue. Similar preoccupations were common in works specifically compiled as confessors' manuals, in the tradition of John of Freiburg; Pierre must have had a deep acquaintance with such literature. But the problems he discussed were not identical with those found in such manuals.

torture did not always inspire confidence, a canonical caveat the force of which had been brought home to him in the Templar episode. The punishment of the convicted should be commensurate with the gravity of their offence. But, despite the pope's anxiety that condemnation should not be purely on the basis of suspicion, no procedure was necessary for the relapsed. Consequently relapse needed careful definition. Pierre's words are obscure at this point, but he seems to be referring to a precise case (that of Jacques de Molay, the Grand Master of the Temple?) in which an individual confessed but then relapsed before abjuration, an act which would not have counted as true relapse under the older understanding of canon law, but now did. Reference to concrete example to pin down the law's meaning was characteristic of his teaching method; he repeated it in the following conclusion where, speaking of the punishment of *credentes*, the supporters of heresy, he included in this category both those who regarded the Cathar perfects as good men and those who intended to be fully hereticated before their deaths; to explain the latter, he cited a man arrested in the company of a Cathar perfect who had expressed the wish 'to die in the faith of the lord Guillaume Autier [Lantieri]';[35] the allusion to a leading Cathar preacher, active in Sabarthès and the surrounding area in the first decade of the fourteenth century, will have been familiar to all Pierre's listeners. (It is perhaps interesting that he chose to cite two forms of commitment to the heretics, belief that they were good men, which was widespread in Languedoc, and the promise to receive the *consolamentum*, a much more binding involvement. His definition was thus very wide. His familiarity with Dominican inquisitorial practices was, as would be expected, great.)

Similar references to topical or everyday incidents could be quoted from most sections of the book (except distinctions 43–50, devoted to the world to come). To demonstrate vividly the stigma illegitimacy might confer in some circles, Pierre pointed out that if a royal bastard wished to join the chapter of Lyons, where the rules of noble descent were strict, he would need a dispensation not only for illegitimacy but also for lowly birth (36. 2, QSL fo. 175^r). On the pope's powers to dispense from a

---

[35] Guillaume Autier was captured towards the end of 1309 and subsequently put to death by the inquisitors. The words 'I wish to die in the faith of lord Guillaume Autier' are exactly those recorded by Raymond Autier as spoken by his sister at her heretication; see A. Pales-Gobilliard, *L'Inquisiteur Geoffroy d'Ablis et les cathares du comté de Foix* (Paris, 1984), p. 126.

religious vow where the common good demanded it, he cited
the case (though not the name) of Ramiro II of Aragon, who was
allowed to leave his monastery to father an heir to the throne
(33. 1, *QSL* fo. 165^r). Pierre's contemporaries will have understood at once the force of these examples; as they listened
canon law principles acquired for them a new specificity.
The practical bent of the author's mind was everywhere
evident. Not content with enunciating principles, he went on
to draw out their everyday applications. For example, when
dealing with dowries (42. 2, *QSL* fo. 195^r), he considered the
plight of a woman whose dowry was confiscated along with all
her husband's property after he had been convicted of treason.
While the friar saw the sense in confiscating the dowry,
because to give it to the wife would make her a gainer by her
husband's crime, nevertheless he insisted that the royal fisc,
which acquired it, had thereby inherited the husband's obligation to provide for the wife's necessities during his lifetime, and
on his death ought to return the dowry to her. If only we knew
whether Pierre had an actual case in mind and, if so, whether
the king's servants shared his view of their obligation!

Sometimes Pierre created hypothetical situations to clarify
principles. Defining the jurisdictional rights of bishops, he
asked what would happen to a doctor with a medical degree
from Montpellier, were the bishop of Paris to excommunicate
all practitioners who were not masters of Paris? (18. 2, *QSL*
fo. 91^r.) Though the bishop was unlikely actually to take such
a draconian step, checking on the qualifications of medical
practitioners in the city was a thorny problem,[36] which would
have interested an early fourteenth-century class of budding
theologians. Pierre's answer was the legally correct one that
unless the Montpellier doctor chose to practise in the diocese
of Paris he was not subject to that bishop's authority and
therefore could carry on his good work without concern. By
raising the issue in this form the lecturer impressed indelibly
on his audience's memories the geographical limits of episcopal
jurisdiction.

Granted this turn of mind, it seems acceptable to set some of
Pierre's more dogmatic statements of principle against the
background of the events of 1314 and 1315, and to interpret
them as his personal responses to the situation. Indeed some of
them could hardly be anything else. What he had to say in 17. 4

---

[36] See e.g. Pope John XXII's letter of Jan. 1330 to the bishop of Paris, *CUP*
ii. 336, no. 900.

and 5 (*QSL* fos. 81ᵛ-85ʳ) on the burning question of friars' rights to hear confessions and on the implications of the Council of Vienne's decree *Dudum* was obviously a rejoinder to the secular master Jean de Pouilly. But since refuting Jean was to be a major preoccupation of Pierre's regency, it makes sense to postpone discussion of this until the next chapter. Similarly, Pierre's support for the proposition that popes could commit simony (25. 4, *QSL* fos. 134ʳ-135ᵛ),[37] his very careful definition of simony in relation to canonries, and his insistence that a man who bought a benefice from the pope should not automatically be required to resign, were clear responses to the policies of Boniface VIII and Clement V. On the one hand he sought to dam the flood of wild accusations,[38] particularly against those whom the popes had legitimately dispensed, while on the other he remained adamant that canonries which constituted a man's title to clergy could not be sold without sin. In the same spirit he denied the pope's right to permit the holding of more than one benefice unless there was good cause, because pluralism was in breach of the natural law (38. 4, *QSL* fo. 183ᵛ). Such outspokenness may indicate that he was writing the final draft of his commentary after Clement's death in April 1314.

Not all Pierre's criticism was aimed at ecclesiastics. He was energetic in denouncing royal self-enrichment at the expense of those Jewish moneylenders who had nothing to live on except the interest they charged their debtors. If the king seized the profits of usury, it should be with the intention of returning the money to those from whom it had been wrongfully taken or, if the owners could not be found, of giving it to the poor. Only if the defence of the realm necessitated it—and then preferably with the licence of the bishop—was it licit for the king to retain it himself. Otherwise there could be no justification for appropriating it to the royal fisc (13. 3, *QSL* fo. 57ᵛ). Since the Jews had been expelled from France in 1306 (though they were readmitted in 1315), it is likely that Pierre was actually concerned to protect their debtors, whose debts the king and his agents continued to collect as royal revenue for several years

[37] It was alleged against Pope Boniface VIII that he had denied the pope could commit simony, Augustinus Triumphus, *Tractatus contra articulos inventos ad diffamationem sanctissimum patrem Bonifaciem sancte memorie*, Paris, Bibliothèque nationale, MS Latin 4046, fo. 20ʳ, also ed. H. Finke, *Aus den Tagen Bonifaz' VIII* (Münster, 1902), pp. lxxiii-lxxiv.

[38] e.g. Guillaume de Plaisians's fulmination, P. Dupuy, *Histoire du différend d'entre le Pape Boniface VIII et Philippes le Bel, roy de France* (Paris, 1655), 'Preuves', p. 103.

after the expulsion.[39] These words were proof that the court could not completely gag its critics in the schools—though their publication after Philip IV's death in November 1314 occurred during a period of violent discontent, when it was relatively safe to express anger at royal misdemeanours.

The link between Pierre's teaching on adultery and the crisis of Louis X's marriage is more speculative, but sufficiently plausible to be worth pursuing. In the last months of Philip IV's reign, the royal family had been hit by scandal. Two of the king's daughters-in-law, Marguerite of Burgundy, wife of Louis le Hutin, and Blanche, wife of Charles, were both declared guilty of adultery. With the very minimum of legal formality, the knights accused of being their lovers were executed in a barbaric fashion, and the ladies divorced, then imprisoned. It was a sign of the fear rampant by 1314 that contemporaries had very little to say on the matter. But after the old king's death, the subject could hardly be ignored. Louis was crowned king in his stead; by Marguerite he had had one daughter, Jeanne, whose legitimacy had been called into question by her mother's behaviour. In order to secure the succession the king must be free to marry again. His brother Charles had a similar though less pressing interest in the matter. But the church prohibited a second marriage during the lifetime of the first wife.

Pierre's treatment of adultery in his commentary on Book 4 of the *Sentences* (35. 1 and 2, *QSL* fos. 171ᵛ–174ʳ) seems to relate to this affair. He agreed that a man whose wife was guilty of adultery was justified in repudiating her. But this was the only crumb of comfort he offered Louis. Since divorce did not cancel marriage, 'vinculum matrimonii non solvitur per sententiam divortii' (fo. 173ʳ), there could be no possibility of another marriage. Earlier he had proved that not even the pope could dispense against natural law to allow a man to marry twice (33. 1, *QSL* fo. 165ʳ); the precedent of the Old Testament patriarchs was invalid. If therefore a man chose to divorce his wife, he did so on the understanding that he would remain continent for the rest of his life. If he could not, then he should not divorce. In no circumstances might the husband kill his erring partner,[40] either at the time he caught her in *flagrante*

---

[39] On Philip IV's policy on Jews see J. Strayer, *The Reign of Philip the Fair* (Princeton, NJ, 1980), pp. 54, 84, 162.

[40] In this connection it is suggestive that the corrector of Oxford, Bodleian Library, MS Holkham Miscellaneous 10 added a note to the bottom of fo. 161ᵛ, derived from Guillaume Durand the Elder's *Speculum iudiciale*: 'si vir interfecit

delicto or later—nor might he kill the man involved, unless the law of the country so prescribed and a proper trial was held (fo. 173ʳ). If later the wife repented, there would be no harm in resuming the married state; indeed, there might even be a duty to do so. Pierre admitted that the teaching of the church on whether a penitent wife must be received back by her husband was contradictory; while Raymond of Pennafort held that his priest should compel him to readmit her, Godfrey of Trano denied this. Pierre resolved the contradiction by what he called the middle way, that though there was no ground for compulsion, nevertheless a wronged husband should in conscience take back his penitent wife (fo. 173ᵛ).⁴¹

On the fundamental teaching that dissolution of a marriage did not permit remarriage, Pierre was, of course, simply stating the standard position in canon law. Yet the details he added and the problems he raised—particularly the question of slaying the adulterer without trial—fitted the circumstances of the royal family in 1314 to 1315 so well as to create a prima-facie presumption that he was addressing himself to them. If this was so, then he appeared sharply critical of what had been done, offering no means out of Louis's dilemma that did not involve a radical change of direction. The Dominican order showed courage in permitting these decisive words to be published in the university of Paris, at a time when Louis's wife Marguerite was languishing in prison in a chamber open to all the winds, crying and desperately pleading for forgiveness.⁴² But in addition to a general sense of outrage over the treatment meted out to her, the friars of St Jacques had reason to feel personal bitterness, since one of their number had been unjustly accused of having concealed the adultery, and had had to be sheltered in the convent from torture.⁴³ However Pierre's bold stand against cruelty in fact achieved nothing. Marguerite

uxorem vel machinatus est in mortem eius ad hoc ut haberet aliam, non potest umquam illam habere, et si contraxerit cum ea non tenet matrimonium.'

⁴¹ Cf. Guillaume Peyraut: 'if [a wife] commits adultery, and should afterwards repent, she should be received with mercy by her husband'; see D. d'Avray, 'The Gospel of the Marriage Feast of Cana and Marriage Preaching in France', in K. Walsh and D. Wood, eds., *The Bible in the Medieval World* (Oxford, 1985), p. 215.

⁴² For this plausible explanation of her mysterious death, see J. Favier, *Philippe le Bel* (Paris, 1978), pp. 527–9. Marguerite was imprisoned in Chateau Gaillard.

⁴³ Continuation of *Chronique latine de Guillaume de Nangis*, ed. H. Géraud (Paris, 1843), p. 406.

died of cold on 30 April 1315, freeing Louis to take a second wife, Clemence of Hungary.

Pierre's direct comments on the disputes of his own day, fascinating though they are, occupy only a small part of his lengthy work; and for the historian they are transcended in importance by his full and precise statements of current ecclesiastical opinion on moral issues. Like all would-be confessors, he was interested in sexual ethics within marriage. Indeed, one modern commentator has been so struck by his handling of the subject as to claim that Pierre rewrote marriage theory.[44] But this exaggerates the changes he made, which amounted to little more than small concessions on particular issues. He continued to subscribe to the standard patristic opinion that intercourse could only be justified by the desire to procreate or by the need to avoid fornication (31. 2, *QSL* fo. 159^v). Though he relaxed the demand for total abstinence in Lent (32. 1, *QSL* fo. 161^v), precedents for this softening of disciplining go back to the twelfth century. He was more liberal in arguing that foreplay was sometimes sinless, in other cases only venial; and that illness excused departure from the approved positions for intercourse (31. 3, *QSL* fo. 161^r). But only one of his propositions was at all daring: his declaration that *coitus interruptus*, if practised to prevent the births of children a man was too poor to support, was not a mortal sin (31. 3, *QSL* fo. 160^v). However, he followed this radical statement with the usual endorsement of continence as the proper means of birth control. Pierre did, then, exhibit a certain sympathy with some aspects of laymen's problems; but he was no trail-blazer in the cause of sexual liberation.[45] And towards women he was harsh, particularly in his treatment of marital sexual obligation in the event of one partner contracting leprosy; whereas the wife continued to owe her leprous husband intercourse, a husband was not

---

[44] According to A. Burgière in J. Le Goff and P. Nora, eds., *Constructing the Past: Essays in Historical Methodology*, English trans. with an introduction by C. Lucas (Cambridge, 1985), p. 106 and n. 23, the Belgian demographer E. Hélin made this claim. Since it does not appear in the text of Hélin's contribution to *La Prévention des naissances dans la famille: Ses origines dans les temps modernes* (Institut national d'études demographiques, handbook 35; Paris, 1960), pp. 235–51, he must have said it during the conference debate.

[45] I have not read *Lucubrationum opus quartum Sententiarum*, ascribed to Pierre in the 1552 edn. of Andreas a Portoneriis, Salamanca, because it is not referred to in any early Dominican list of his writings. (It is, however, mentioned as widely known in Baluze-Mollat, *VPA*, ii. 188.) But the kernel of *Lucubrationum* is to be found in the authentic text of the commentary on Book 4 of the *Sentences*. On the significance of its sexual teachings, see J. A. Brundage, *Law, Sex and Christian Society in Medieval Europe* (Chicago and London, 1987), pp. 430–43.

similarly bound to a leprous wife, because medical opinion held that he was more likely to be infected than she was (32. 1, *QSL* fo. 161^r).

Another serious concern of Pierre's was arranging for people to confess regularly, even when they were away from home. He considered the plight of those who attended a university for only one year, and therefore still counted their home parish priest as their proper confessor; of those who departed from their towns and villages to attend the Parlement of Paris; those who changed from winter to summer residences (Oxford, Bodleian Library, MS Holkham Miscellaneous 10, fo. 78^r); and those who journeyed to Rome (17. 4, *QSL* fo. 81^v). Since none of these must lack the saving grace of confession and absolution, arrangements should be made to accommodate them. He emphasized the duty of a confessor to encourage the return of all stolen or misappropriated goods as a necessary part of the sinner's satisfaction. Within the principle of restitution—according to him a specifically Dominican one—he introduced various calculations on the extent to which an individual member of a community that charged interest or seized goods by violence was personally liable for the damage caused (15. 2, *QSL* fo. 66^r). Here the connection between the confessor and the lawyer was at its closest. There was similar exactness in his discussion of goods seized by usury, where restitution was particularly difficult to enforce if the goods had come into the hands of an innocent third party (13. 3, *QSL* fo. 57^v). On this issue it later became clear that he was particularly keen to justify Dominican alms-taking from usurers or others who had profited from their sins (15. 3, *QSL* fo. 68^r).

Pierre appreciated that pious men's good intentions were frequently frustrated by uncertainties about their duties in canon law. In his discussion of the first tonsure, he did sterling work in clarifying the clerk's as opposed to the cleric's status and obligations (24. 3, *QSL* fos. 126^r–126^v). By the beginning of the fourteenth century, the difference between acquiring a clerical tonsure and entering an order of the church had long been appreciated. But Pierre integrated canon law into his own interpretation of the clerk's purpose in life, thus clarifying the category.[46] Of at least 7 years of age, sufficiently literate in Latin to make responses in a church service, a clerk received his first tonsure from his bishop, as an outward sign of his

---

[46] On the implications of this, see Jean Dunbabin, 'From Clerk to Knight: Changing Orders', in C. Harper-Bill and R. Harvey, eds., *The Ideals and Practice of Medieval Knighthood* (Bury St Edmunds, 1988), pp. 26–39.

desire to serve God by reading the Psalms and chanting in the choir. A sensible preliminary to a career within the church, the first tonsure marked the new clerk out from other men, though not irreversibly; he could not later be forced to take holy orders. His status obliged him to study and prohibited him from engaging in trade or business, in surgery, in fighting whether in war or in tournament, or in any judicial process involving mutilation or death. He might marry, though only once and to a virgin. So long as he kept his tonsure and wore a clerical habit, he could enjoy exemption from tallages (the mark of a free man) and benefit of clergy (judgement in ecclesiastical courts), with the added advantage that his attackers would incur automatic excommunication.

Having defined, Pierre then cogitated. The old law that clerks should not receive payment for any medical treatments they might give was no longer recognized in practice; it was also incompatible with the current behaviour of clerical lawyers, who sold their skills like laymen. Indeed, the pope himself encouraged clerks to take payment for giving professional advice, not just to ensure their survival, but to improve their standard of living. Given this example from the top of the hierarchy, ordinary clerks could hardly be expected to maintain the old rules (*QSL* fos. 126ᵛ–127ʳ). This sharp dig at curial practice under Pope Clement V formed the codicil to an important discussion which had thrown much light on both the enduring and the changing characteristics of clerks. It was particularly appropriate for a Paris audience, since at that university all students were required to be clerks, yet relatively few had sufficient knowledge of canon law to feel confident of fulfilling their obligations.

Therefore the popularity of Pierre's commentary on Book 4 of the *Sentences* was hardly surprising. By introducing his extensive knowledge of contemporary canon law into the corpus of theological speculation, he had related practical ethics to enduring principles in a fashion his more rarefied colleagues were quite incapable of imitating. The university of Paris produced few doctoral dissertations of equal importance to the man in the street. As a consequence it was copied time and again in the next two centuries, printed among the earliest of theological works, and plagiarized extensively.[47] Its

---

[47] For the manuscripts and editions see Kaeppeli, *Scriptores Ordinis Praedicatorum*, iii (Rome, 1980), pp. 244–5. Among the plagiarists was the influential 15th-cent. theologian Capreolus, who drew very extensively on Pierre; see Fournier, *HLF*, p. 59.

publication brought to a triumphant conclusion the four years
of hard, often unsatisfying, and always intimidating lecturing
that had filled Pierre's bachelor years.

In addition to their courses on the *Sentences*, bachelors were
required to preach within their convents. By good fortune John
of St Germains, a monk from Worcester Cathedral, was
present in Paris during the period 1310 to 1311, and recorded
for the edification of his fellow inmates at Worcester a large
number of sermons preached in Paris during that year, including four of Pierre's, probably his earliest efforts in the pulpit.[48]
Already his sermons illustrated the qualities later to make him
a famous preacher: vivid images, clear moral lessons, a rich
store of random information to stimulate his audience's
interest. On one occasion he pursued the image of an army
besieged within the castle of faith by the devil and all his
demons; another time he talked of a farmer checking on a
delinquent serf who had failed to root out the thistles, break up
the sods, and plant good seed. He discussed the inter-relation-
ships of the planets, the art of catching hares, the means
whereby schoolboys could catch up on lost lessons, the appor-
tionment of advocates' salaries; and each of these gobbets of
rarefied knowledge was chosen to illustrate a clear moral
point. Above all, he hammered home the lesson that while
perdition was easy, salvation was the fruit of tireless dedication. Thus he tried to rouse in his audience the same furious
energy in the pursuit of good that he devoted to preaching at
them (Worcester Cathedral, MS Q 100, fos. 81^v–84^r, 84^r–86^v,
86^v–90^r, 98^r–105^r).

---

[48] The information comes from a note written by A. G. Little, in the fly-leaf of
Worcester Cathedral, MS Q. 100. On John of St Germains, see P. Glorieux, 'Jean
de Saint-Germain, maître de Paris et copiste de Worcester', in *Mélanges
A. Pelzer* (Louvain, 1947), pp. 513–29.

3. Master

(a) Disputations

On 13 June 1314 Pierre, in company with Guillaume de Laudun, incepted as a Doctor of Theology of the university of Paris, and began his period of necessary regency in the chair of the French attached to St Jacques. He was fortunate to be allowed to do so only four years after his arrival there, for although the rules prescribed this for bachelors, in practice there was usually a queue of qualified men for the two Dominican chairs (the second of which was the chair for foreigners, i.e. non-French friars). Patience was therefore required of those who aimed for the pinnacle of academic achievement. Whether Pierre's swift promotion was due to his noble birth or to Hervé's patronage, we do not know. In any case it consolidated his position within the Dominican hierarchy and offered him the opportunity for a more public role since, while bachelors performed only within their master's school, regent masters were required to lecture and dispute publicly. The office thus exposed its holder to the gaze of the whole university, perhaps even to that of a section of the educated laity in Paris. There is no sign that Pierre shrank from that gaze.

In a sermon of much later date preached on the feast of St Gregory the Great, Pierre expounded the privileges and responsibilities of a Doctor in Theology (Clermont Ferrand, Bibliothèque municipale, MS 46, fos. 71^r–72^r). A doctor is privileged in that he alone has an unimpeachable warrant to preach to the people; this warrant is granted after due inquiries by the chancellor of the university, acting on behalf of Christ, the one authority who never promotes an unworthy candidate nor denies promotion to a worthy one. The doctor must heal and preserve the souls of his flock; in pursuit of this end he should never sell his knowledge for money or honours. He will have his reward if he edifies himself and others: 'Sunt qui scire volunt ut edificent, et caritas est; et sunt qui scire volunt ut edificentur, et prudentia est' (fo. 72^r).[1] No doctor can hope to inherit an aureole in heaven unless he preaches at least sometimes; indeed, the doctor who fails to make use of his

---

[1] Quoting from St Bernard, *Song of Songs*, Sermon 36.

talents in the pulpit is to be compared with a servant who absconds with the money his master was intending to bestow on others. The shepherd who does not feed his sheep does not love them. But the faithful doctor must be Mary as well as Martha; he must seek the truth through contemplation, he must learn with his intellect and his soul the things that are necessary for salvation. In combining these two activities, he should follow the example of St Gregory, who taught and advised all day long, then devoted his nights to spiritual exercises. Lastly, a true doctor must cultivate the moral and theological virtues, so that he may overcome original sin with constant repentance, thus fortifying the grace he earned in his baptism. A man who succeeds on all three planes is truly worthy of the raised chair, the *cathedra*, on which all doctors sit. As can be seen, Pierre was not one to set his sights low.

Only one of his surviving sermons can be indisputably dated to the period of Pierre's regency, 'Tempus tribulationis est' (Paris, Bibliothèque nationale, MS Latin 14799, fos. 251^v-252^r), preached during the famine of 1315–17, probably in the summer of 1316 when the harvest was completely blighted by endless rain and the situation was made more dire by the imminence of war in Flanders.[2] Pierre made no attempt to minimize the sufferings of the people. Far from it. Predictably he interpreted them as punishments for sin, like the plague Rome had endured before Gregory the Great was elected; less predictably also as a means to salvation, 'per multas tribulationes oportet nos intrare in regnum celorum'. Though the weather was appallingly unseasonal, it was serving God's purpose: 'Modo licet tempus estivum in quo sumus ratione sui debeat esse serenum et calidum non frigidum et pluviosum sicut est, tamen ratione nostri debet esse quale est.' As St James, who feast day it was, had been beheaded, and St Louis had been imprisoned by Saracens, so the French were being tested by God. Pierre compared them in their afflictions with grain which has to be ground before it can be baked and grapes which are trampled to make them into wine. He exhorted his countrymen to think about the difference between wild animals like boars and harts which destroy the crops and the vines, and domestic animals like horses, oxen, and asses which assist the harvest by ploughing and carting. If the people were patient under God's scourgings, they too might become domesticated to

---

[2] H. Lucas, 'The Great European Famine of 1315, 1316, 1317', *Speculum*, 5 (1930), 343–77.

His will and contribute to His harvest of souls. Apparently anticipating that some of his listeners would regard themselves as innocent of the sins that brought so terrible a retribution, Pierre quoted, 'Many are called but few are chosen'; then he pointed out that even the elect must, like good citizens, bear the punishment for the offences of the whole body. He therefore called on them all to repent and to pray to the saints, who had the power to save them from the flood.

This sermon shows Pierre the preacher in characteristic mood. He offered no temporal comfort to his audience—starvation was a far better fate than consignment to hell. On the other hand he did try to make sense of what was happening, to see events within the Augustinian framework of God's design for man's salvation. And he expressed his meaning in vivid similes, derived on this occasion from his childhood memories in Bresse, where wild boars were commoner than they were in Paris. What he had to say was easily comprehensible, but also thought-provoking, particularly perhaps for a city audience which prided itself on its sophisticated superiority over all rustics. The ox and the ass once again became models of good behaviour. The patient slave who did his master's bidding in the end earned his reward, while those who railed against discipline incurred yet heavier punishment. Rebellion was dangerous. Yet God's justice was real. Pierre's final confident assurance that the saints could divert the rain and clear the heavens of clouds provided at last some measure of soothing relief from the inexorable chords of disaster he had sounded.

The chief academic task of a newly qualified doctor was to lecture *per modum questionis* on the Scriptures, normally on a book of the Old and a book of the New Testament, after the *baccalarius biblicus* assigned to him had construed the texts.[3] Pierre will have found this congenial, for his practical mind was easily assured of its utility, and he had grown used to the question form in lecturing on the *Sentences*. But those of his Biblical commentaries which are still extant contain no questions; they therefore would appear to date either from his very early days in Lyons or from a later period in his life. Therefore the major undertaking of his doctoral years escapes the historian's eye. (There is nothing unusual about this, for medieval masters, like modern university lecturers, rarely

---

[3] B. Smalley, *The Study of the Bible in the Middle Ages*, 3rd edn. (Oxford, 1983), p. 276 and n. 1.

published their lectures; none the less it is indicative of
the Paris schools' real interests that far more commentaries
on the *Sentences* than on the Scriptures were put into circulation.)

The daily grind of exegesis was interrupted from time to time
by disputations. Of these none can have been more formidable
for Pierre than his first (and only extant) quodlibetal discussion, dated to Advent 1314. Quodlibetal disputations were
intended to be a form of penance for the masters who undertook them; hence they occurred only in the penitential seasons
of Advent and Lent. Questions *de quodlibet*, about anything,
usually highly contentious issues, were proposed by the audience, often made up of pupils of rival masters; the bachelors
assembled offered arguments for or against the proposition
under examination; then the master was given time to deliberate on his reply. When the audience reconvened, he had to give
his considered verdict on the issue, along with his refutation of
the arguments that did not please him. There could be no
evasion. Unlike other forms of academic exercise the quodlibetal disputation did not permit of hiding behind other men's
opinions or hedging one's bets.[4] A straight answer was called
for. Granted his normal instinct for obscuring his own views in
a morass of other people's, Pierre must have found the experience very trying, which may explain why he apparently only
underwent it once.

Pierre's Quodlibet is found in Toulouse, MS Bibliothèque
municipale, MS 744, fos. 75^r–118^v, a manuscript largely devoted
to his works. Of the eleven questions, ten are concerned with
matters of speculative theology: first the relations of the
persons in the Trinity with created creatures, involving a
series of problems inspired by Duns Scotus. In one of Pierre's
sermons, he mentioned a certain master so subtle that his
pupils could not understand him, who had to employ an inter-
mediary to explain his ideas in simpler language (Clermont
Ferrand, MS 46, fo. 135^v). Pierre may have felt like the pupils
when faced by Scotist problems, for in his hands the complic-

[4] P. Glorieux, *La Littérature quodlibétique* (2 vols.; Paris, 1925–36); G. Leff,
Paris and Oxford Universities in the Thirteenth and Fourteenth Centuries (New
York, 1968), pp. 171–3; J. F. Wippel, 'The Quodlibetal Question as a Distinctive
Literary Genre', in *Les Genres littéraires dans les sources théologiques et philosophiques médiévales* (Louvain, 1982), pp. 67–84; and id., in *Les Questions
disputées et les questions quodlibétiques dans les facultés de théologie, de droit
et de médecine: Typologie des sources du moyen âge occidental*, ed. L. Genicot,
xliv (Brepols, 1985), pp. 153–222.

ated concept of relation seemed to boil down to little more than the old universal. He was also asked in the course of the disputation about the difference between reflexive and ordinary acts, about whether all angels belonged to the same species, and about the nature of heavenly happiness. Considering the abstract nature of these questions, his replies were clear and commonsensical, though hardly innovative.

But the fourth question: 'utrum episcopus possit committere audientiam confessionum sine licentia curatorum' (fos. 84^v–98^v), whether a bishop can permit a man to hear confessions who has not been licensed by the parish priest, was exactly the sort of issue Pierre had been hoping for. His response to it was very lengthy and, for him, incisive. The problem was one of immediate significance for the mendicants, who had found themselves in an extremely embarrassing position in the aftermath of the Council of Vienne in 1312. The complicated arguments on the friars' right to hear confessions had their root in varying interpretations of *Omnis utriusque sexus*, the decree of the Fourth Lateran Council in 1215, accepted by both sides as the immutable law of the church, which had laid down that all Christians must confess to their own priests at least once a year. The seculars translated 'own priests' as 'parish priests', and regarded subsequent papal privileges to the mendicant orders to hear confession, in particular the bull *Ad fructus uberes* of Pope Martin IV in 1281, as disruptive of proper order in the church. The friars naturally disagreed, translating 'own priests' more liberally. Although this difference of opinion provoked only occasional trouble throughout most of Europe, at the Paris schools where the underlying intellectual issues were debated a storm arose, causing such scandal that in the end Pope Boniface VIII was forced to intervene. 'For the sake of the peace of the church', he produced in February 1300 the bull *Super cathedram*, requiring friars to obtain the permission of parish priests before preaching in parish churches, limiting the right to hear confessions to a small group of friars specially licensed by the bishops, confining their activities to the areas for which they held licences, and ordering them to pay parish priests a quarter of their earnings from funerals and associated offerings. The mendicant orders, accustomed to look to the papacy for protection, greeted this bull with bitterness and resentment, a resentment increased when the seculars drew from its wording the implication that, in order to comply both with *Omnis utriusque sexus* and with *Super cathedram*, parishioners who had confessed to the friars must confess the same sins again to their parish priests—double confession.[5]

The friars' chance to overturn *Super cathedram* came immediately on Boniface VIII's death, with the election of Benedict XI, a former master general of the Dominican order. In February 1304 Benedict promulgated *Inter cunctas*, which annulled *Super cathedram*, reinstated mendicant privileges in the pulpit and the confessional, and specifically denied the seculars' contention that double confession was necessary. Predictably, *Inter cunctas* not only infuriated the seculars but raised serious constitutional issues for the church. Clement V wisely delayed his consideration of the question until the Council of Vienne had been convened; then, in the presence of all the prelates, the pope advocated a return to *Super cathedram*, which was formulated in the decree *Dudum*. Unfortunately, because Clement wanted the constitutions proposed by the council to be debated in the schools before they were promulgated, and because his death in April 1314 occurred before there had been time for that debate, the status of *Dudum* was to remain uncertain until October 1317, when Pope John XXII formally issued the constitutions of Vienne under the title of the Clementines.

But it could not be expected that the secular masters at Paris would patiently await the promulgation of *Dudum* before expressing their glee at the council's decision. Their leader, Jean de Pouilly, a Paris Master of Theology and an old opponent of Hervé de Nédellec,[6] used the occasion of his quodlibetal disputations in 1312 and 1314 to contend that, now that *Inter cunctas* had been revoked, the provisions of *Super cathedram* were once more in force, and therefore any lay man who had confessed to a friar must repeat his confession to his parish

---

[5] The text of *Super cathedram* can be found in *Corpus iuris canonici*, ed. E. Friedberg (Graz, 1955), Clementines, bk. 3, 7. 2. For the popular view of its contents see *Les Grandes Chroniques*, ed. J. Viard, viii (Paris, 1934), p. 181, 'et fist son decret ycelui pape, que celui qui se confesseroit à ces freres, confessast et repeti ist yeés meismes pechiez à son propre prestre'. There is an extensive literature on the subject of mendicant privileges. The seminal article is by Y. Congar, 'Aspects ecclésiologiques de la querelle entre mendiants et séculiers dans la seconde moitié du xiiie siècle et le début du xive', *AHDLMA* 28 (1961), 35–151. For the argument on hierarchy see D. E. Luscombe, 'Thomas Aquinas and Conceptions of Hierarchy in the Thirteenth Century', *Miscellanea Mediaevalia*, 19 (1986), 261–77.

[6] P. T. Stella, 'Intentio Aristotelis, secundum superficiem suae litterae: La "replicatio contra magistrum Herveum praedicatorem" di Giovanni di Pouilly', *Salesianum*, 23 (1961), 481–528. For Jean de Pouilly's stand on the Templars, see M. Barber, *The Trial of the Templars* (Cambridge, 1978), pp. 150–3.

priest. Those who denied this were pitting their own authority against that of the church universal, and therefore deserved to be excommunicated. Furthermore he alleged that the friars had illicitly claimed privileges equal to those of papal penitentiaries; and—a charge particularly hurtful to the mendicants —that the Council of Vienne had recognized Benedict XI's promulgation of *Inter cunctas* as erroneous. Jean believed this to illustrate the principle that while conciliar decrees were reliable, the decrees of one man were not. In 1313 Jean persuaded a synod of the Reims diocese held at Senlis to accept the return to the practices laid down by *Super cathedram*. Then the fat was in the fire. Both Franciscans and Dominicans rushed into the attack, leading an onslaught on the seculars that maintained its violence until 1321, and that was to be of particular concern to Pierre de la Palud for several years to come (see Ch. 4*b*).

Pierre's Advent Quodlibet occurred after Clement V's death and during the bitterest period of the controversy. From the Toulouse Manuscript, it can be deduced that many supporters of the seculars were present in the school of St Jacques on the day the new master was to debate—in his published Quodlibet Pierre reported their arguments, introducing them by 'dicunt quidam'. Jean de Pouilly was certainly there in spirit, if not in the flesh; he is presumably to be identified with the 'bolder soul' who had dared to assert that *Inter cunctas* had never been valid, cited by a certain doctor in the course of the proceedings (fo. 89^r); and Pierre quoted verbatim from his opponent's quodlibets. Therefore the first day of the disputation was tense. The new master was doubtless distinctly apprehensive when he resumed his seat to begin his lengthy solution of a problem, in any case provocatively phrased, which had in the course of the debate expanded far beyond the bounds of the original question. The anonymous questioner, starting from *Super cathedram*'s stipulation that a friar must have the permission of the parish priest before preaching in his church, had hoped to extend that permission to the hearing of confessions. Pierre was bound to reply that since *Dudum* had not yet been promulgated, friars' privileges under *Inter cunctas* still obtained; therefore neither licence from the bishop nor permission from the priest was yet necessary; and secondly, since no parish priest was ever entitled to go against the wishes of his bishop, he must always accept any friar the bishop licensed. But far more was expected of him than this simple answer. He had to defend the whole mendicant position.

Nervousness made him play relentlessly to his strongest suit, knowledge of the law. He tried to confound his opponents by references to the *Institutes* and to the ways in which emperors promulgated legislation. He compared parishioners with a duty to confess to debtors trying to pay back their creditors, and to accused men exercising their right to choose the most favourable court in which actions against themselves should be heard. He argued that, just as the losing party in an arbitration was bound to surrender only the rights specified by the arbitrators, so the friars, who would lose by the reimposition of *Super cathedram*, were entitled to regard all those privileges unmentioned in the bull as tacitly endorsed by the Council of Vienne. His opponents seem to have been unimpressed by these analogies. But, discarding the legal parallels, Pierre's case boiled down to three points: mendicant privileges were compatible with the proper ordering of the church; a free market economy in confessions was desirable; and to postulate the necessity for double confession was to insult the Roman church.

The first argument necessitated acceptance of his opponents' point that Christ had instituted the apostles and disciples, and subsequently their successors the bishops and parish priests, to care for the souls of Christians: 'Concedo ergo quod soli episcopi et curati sunt successores apostolorum et discipulorum' (fo. 97^r). It would therefore indeed be a violation of divine law if the pope tried to upset this arrangement by abolishing the offices of either (fos. 87^r-87^v). But mendicant privileges did not have this effect. The parishioner who chose to confess to a friar rather than to his parish priest remained bound to respect his priest, to accept other sacraments from him, and to contribute to his income by tithes (fo. 91^v). The pope had merely permitted, in accordance with Christ's intentions, a small dispensation from human law in the interests of the common good (fo. 97^v). Nor should bishops and priests glory in their Christ-given status to the point of denigrating those other orders instituted later in time. The constitution of the primitive church was a sure guide to the divine will, but not a complete statement of it. Deacons, secular canons, monks, hermits, and martyrs were all, like the friars, later evolutions to serve God's purposes. That the church had once been able to get along without them was no argument for regarding them as either evil or superfluous now. In particular it ill became a Master of Theology—surely a dig at Jean de Pouilly—to take this line, since more than a thousand years of ecclesiastical history

had rolled by before university doctors first emerged, yet no
one denied that nowadays they played an indispensable role
(fo. 97^r). Thus Pierre's view of 'natural order' of the church
was a complicated, evolutionary concept, not the static one in
which Jean de Pouilly and his followers purported to believe.
But even arguing on their premisses he denounced his questioner, who implicitly undermined the bishops' sole right to
license friars, as himself guilty of subverting the natural order.
Indeed, it was absurd to regard the bishop, a ruler, as more
obliged to consult the parish priest, his subject, than vice versa
(fo. 92^r). The seculars were therefore vulnerable to their own
accusations.

More significantly, his opponents' case depended on a misreading of *Omnis utriusque sexus*; a man's 'own priest' was not
only his parish priest, but any of that priest's superiors in the
hierarchy; that is, his bishop or the pope or by extension
anyone delegated by them to perform sacerdotal functions in
their stead (92^v). 'Unde cum deus in ordinando quod peccator
confiteretur proprio sacerdoti non posuerit curatum tantum
sed immo principalius posuerit alios' (fo. 91^v)—a point Pierre
owed to Hostiensis. Jean de Pouilly and his followers accepted
this in relation to papal penitentiaries (licensed by the pope to
hear the confessions of those whose sins only he could absolve),
for papal legates, and even for some episcopal officials. Yet
they denied it for the friars, who enjoyed a general, not a
special, dispensation. In Pierre's eyes, although the friars
differed from papal penitentiaries in that resort to them was
voluntary, the essential difference was minimal (fo. 96^r), and
the pope was undoubtedly competent to issue both special and
general dispensations. The friars' general dispensation was
not unique; many religious orders and secular colleges benefited from a general exemption from episcopal control (fo. 97^v);
and parish priests sometimes lost their right to perform sacraments by uncontentious local traditions, like that at Avignon,
where four canons monopolized extreme unction (fo. 90^v).[7]
Mendicant privileges were therefore lawful, and as a consequence priests had no right to prevent friars from hearing
confessions. To convince his audience of this, Pierre drew a
parallel between a friar confessor working in a parish in virtue
of a papal dispensation and a royal *missus* operating within a
duchy of which he was an inhabitant, who, by virtue of his

---

[7] This reference raises the possibility that Pierre had already visited Avignon
at some time before he became a master.

royal office, was exempt from ducal jurisdiction. If even the duke could not prevent this man, though one of his subjects, from carrying out the royal will, the duke's servants were totally powerless against him (fo. 98^r). Similarly curates were powerless against a friar armed with a papal dispensation. (Perhaps the point of this analogy was to convince royal clerks that upholding the interests of the mendicant orders was effectively to promote centralized government in other spheres.)

Pierre's stance left the choice to the parishioner. Although the priest's obligation to provide confession on demand was not affected by mendicant privileges, the parishioner's to resort to him was. A father must provide food for his son, but his son is not forced to eat it if he can find something better (fo. 92^v). Just as under Roman law scholars could choose to answer charges brought against them before the bishop, before their own master, or before the civil courts (fo. 94^r), so the parishioner was privileged to choose his confessor from among those who could claim to be 'his' priest. This was Christian liberty. Pierre's confidence that parishioners would in practice prefer a friar as confessor was apparently well founded, for Jean de Pouilly reluctantly accepted this; though the explanation he preferred was that it was less embarrassing to confess to a travelling friar than to a priest who was a permanent neighbour. Pierre on the other hand maintained that what the friars had to offer was of better quality. He agreed—it would have been heretical to deny—that an ignorant priest could absolve a sinner as effectively as a learned one. But in order to earn absolution a sinner had to feel true contrition; to confess without contrition dispensed a man from the need to confess again, but from nothing else. 'Quia licet ignorantia vel malitia sacerdotis non auferat ei potestatem absolvendi, sicut dixerunt aliqui heretici, tamen frequenter [contingit] quod illorum aufert fructum penitencie' (fo. 90^v). It was here that the learning of a mendicant confessor was invaluable, because he could recognize at once the true nature of the sin and therefore award the appropriate penance.[8] Pierre's advice to the layman was that should he entertain any doubts about his parish priest's morals or competence, he would do well to search out a friar for his confessor (fo. 90^v); to the priests he issued this challenge: 'Show yourself to be as good and as learned as a friar, and you will have nothing to fear' (fo. 96^v). So long as it

---

[8] This fits in with the importance Pierre attached to the taxation of satisfactions in his commentary on Book 4 of the *Sentences*, 20. 2, *QSL* fos. 109^r–110^r.

remained true that of any twenty parish priests only one at the most had any instruction in theology (fo. 90^v), priests had no more ground for complaint that their task was being usurped than had stall-holders at a market when all the customers favoured the one stall with quality goods (fo. 96^v). In the meantime, the superiority of the friars, both as confessors and as preachers, justified the pope in subtracting a little from the function of parish priests in the interests of Christian welfare (fos. 87^r–87^v).

Despite its cogency, part at least of this argument was beside the point, since Jean de Pouilly and his supporters, taking their stand on their own reading of *Dudum*, insisted that parish priests' right to give or withhold permission overrode their parishioners' right of choice. Furthermore, since in their opinion *Inter cunctas* had been revoked and *Super cathedram* had automatically come into force again, so also had the (unspoken) stipulation that parishioners who confessed to friars must confess again to their parish priests. How could Pierre respond to this interpretation of the Vienne decree? In the first place he pointed out that *Inter cunctas* was still the law of the church. His opponents' view, which had prevailed at the provincial synod of Reims, had not found favour anywhere else (fo. 92^v) because it was legally void. Canon law resembled Roman law in that, although its decrees might be formulated by men other than the pope, only the pope could promulgate them (fo. 91^r). Clement had not promulgated *Dudum* before his death; and Boniface VIII, long dead, could not repromulgate *Super cathedram* (fo. 91^v). Therefore the situation remained as it was before the Council of Vienne. Since Jean de Pouilly was wrong in thinking *Inter cunctas* had been revoked, he was also wrong in criticizing the constitution and Benedict XI its maker (fo. 91^r).[9]

[9] Jean criticized Benedict for producing *Inter cunctas* without proper consultation. Pierre declared this to be untrue; Benedict had consulted 'all his brothers' (fo. 92^r)—which meant the cardinals, not the Dominicans, as Jean somewhat maliciously inferred. (Here the influence of Hostiensis on Pierre's thought is apparent.) It was perhaps in relation to this statement that Pierre was later asked whether it represented adequate consultation if the pope merely referred to two cardinals; he replied that it did not. See the testimony of the 15th-cent. cardinal Julian of Torquemada; C. Piana, 'Scritti polemici fra Conventuali ed Osservanti a metà del '400, con la participazione dei gurristi secolari', *AFH* 71 (1978), 375. Nevertheless it seems to me that on this occasion Pierre's emphasis on the cardinals as essential to a statement of faith arose more from a need to respond to Jean than from a clear commitment to the local Roman church (rather than the church universal) as the fount of inerrancy.

This argument was technically correct. But Pierre also recognized that, once a general council of the church had pronounced on a matter, its decree was not likely to suffer substantial alteration before promulgation. Fulminating against Jean de Pouilly for jumping the gun was therefore petty-minded. On the other hand there was a great deal of point in challenging the need for double confession, on which the council had said nothing, since no parishioner would ever freely confess to a friar if he knew he was obliged to repeat that confession to his parish priest. Pierre correctly pointed out that the seculars' inference from *Omnis utriusque sexus* that double confession was necessary had never been formally endorsed by the church; but since some men of authority had concurred in it, it needed to be combated. He brought forward two stock mendicant responses: first that friars, as priests, had indisputable power to absolve sinners; if they performed that sacrament correctly then even the pope could not prevent the consequence ordained by divine law, absolution (fo. 89^r). And a man who had been absolved was no more bound to reconfess than a debtor who had paid off his debts. Secondly, Cardinal Jean le Moine's claim that *Super cathedram* necessitated double confession, not because the sacrament offered by the friars was deficient but because a parishioner was indebted to his own priest, was wrong (fo. 88^v).[10] Repetition of a sacrament automatically cast doubt on the efficacy of the first occasion; the issue was too important to be subordinated to the requirement of deference to parish priests, who in any case ought to be more concerned with their parishioners' salvation than with their own honour (fo. 96^v).

But Pierre strengthened the traditional case with a more original and legalistic argument. In matters of dispute where learned doctors, after earnest debate, could not agree, the Roman see might adjudicate, and once it had given its verdict all were bound by it (fo. 89^r). In the case of double confession, this had already happened; Benedict XI had specifically denied that it was necessary. Therefore all were now bound to accept his judgement. His opponents' response, that *Inter cunctas* had been revoked, was technically incorrect, and furthermore fundamentally misconceived. If a future pope were to promulgate *Dudum*, then those provisions of *Inter cunctas* which were negated by the reimposition of *Super cathedram* would become

---

[10] On this see G. Le Bras, *Histoire du droit et des institutions de l'église en Occident, vii. L'Âge classique, 1140-1378* (Paris, 1965), p. 329.

null; but the parts of the bull which were unaffected by *Super cathedram*, in particular the denial of the necessity for double confession, would remain intact (fo. 91^v). This should not be dismissed as a lawyer's casuistry; it involved an important principle on the nature of revocation. And it may have been intended for the ear of those responsible for the final drafts of the Vienne decrees: if they did their work properly they might avoid further trouble.

Pierre went on to state his opinion that legislation endorsing double confession would be of dubious value as human law, because it was irrational. Furthermore it would cast doubt on the Roman church's authority, since either the new law or *Inter cunctas* must be wrong, and therefore the church had either erred in the past or was erring now—'cum Romana ecclesia semel positionem declaravit non potest oppositionem declarare quin constet ipsam errare vel primitus erravisse' (fo. 94^r). This at first sight seemed to contradict what he had said about *Dudum* validly negating certain propositions in *Inter cunctas*. But the contradiction was only apparent. Pierre made a distinction between matters of faith, which could not be altered, and matters of human convenience, which obviously could. He chose to classify Benedict's denial of double confession as a matter of faith, the rest of *Inter cunctas* as purely expedient.

Then—in an argument that has recently been much quoted —he asserted that it had never occurred and through God's grace it never would occur that the Roman church retracted a declaration of faith, for this would be tantamount to confessing either that she had erred in the past or that she was erring now:

Et quamvis statuta romana ecclesie sepe mutantur quia quod iustum est aliquando mutatione aliqua temporum vel personarum sit iniustum, tamen quia veritas fidei est immutabilis numquam auditum est nec per dei gratiam audietur quod ecclesia romana retractaret declarationem a se alias factam in talibus quia tunc confiteretur se aliquando errasse vel tunc errare. (fo. 92^r)

This brief statement has earned for Pierre in some circles a reputation as the earliest non-Franciscan upholder of papal infallibility.[11] (It should be emphasized that, in his opinion, it

---

[11] T. Turley, 'Infallibilists at the curia of Pope John XXII', *Journal of Medieval History*, 1 (1975), 75–8. 'Infallibilist' is here defined as a believer in the inerrancy of the local Roman church, inerrancy being understood in an 'ultramontane' sense; see B. Tierney, *The Origins of Papal Infallibility, 1150–1350* (Leiden, 1972). For a critique of this approach see J. Heft, *John XXII*

was the Roman church which was inerrant, not the person of the pope—he willingly ascribed errors to past popes (fo. 89ᵛ).) His position allowed for plenty of argument over what was meant by the Roman church, and even more over which statements were matters of faith. But he palpably went further than most of his contemporaries in asserting that if all other churches upheld one doctrine and the Roman church the opposite, it was to the latter than a man should adhere—'Si tota ecclesia residua tenet unum et romana ecclesia oppositum ipsi est adherendum' (fo. 94ᵛ), a statement that might be interpreted as anti-conciliarist.[12]

In the immediate context of 1314, Pierre was simply turning the heat on his opponents. In response to Jean's declaration that those who refused to accept the authority of the Council of Vienne deserved to be excommunicated, Pierre exhibited equal self-righteousness in finding the upholders of double confession guilty of casting a slur on the church. Both sides were now quits. But it would be unwise to dismiss his statement of the church's inerrancy as nothing more than an advocate's trick. Throughout his life Pierre interpreted Christ's prayer for Peter that his faith be made strong (Luke 22: 32) as a promise to protect the Roman and universal church from error in matters of faith. But both before and after this he broadened the composition of the church's inerrant body (see Ch. 5c). On this occasion he stated his interpretation in unusually stark and

and Papal Teaching Authority (Lewiston and Queenston, 1986), pp. 167–201. Although it does indeed sound from the quodlibet as if Pierre was asserting the inerrancy of the local Roman church, I doubt if he meant to be either as clear-cut or as innovative as Turley thinks. In his commentary on Book 4 of the *Sentences*, 18. 3 (*QSL* fo. 91ᵛ) he had said: 'non ergo est excommunicatus a iure qui tenet illud quod una ecclesia particularis iudicat esse hereticum sed qui firmiter adheret ei quod ecclesia universalis vel romana diffinivit esse hereticum . . . quia quamdiu homo adheret fidei ecclesie romane quecumque alia ecclesia tenens oppositum numquam est hereticus . . . quia illa non potest errare sed omnis alia sic, sicut tota ecclesia Grecorum.' Here he identified the universal with the Roman church, and contrasted it with the Greek church, as he was again to do in his tract *De paupertate* of 1328–9 (see Ch. 5c). It therefore seems safer to interpret his words in the quodlibet, taken from canonical texts, as upholding the standard theological opinion that ultimate authority in matters of faith rested with the universal church.

[12] Pierre had earlier dealt with the problem of conflicting church authorities in relation to the bishop of Paris's 1277 condemnation (commentary on Book 4 of the *Sentences*, 13. 3, *QSL* fo. 56ᵛ), where he had denied that excommunication automatically befell anyone propounding one of the condemned articles, since they had not been promulgated by the pope. His apparently radical statement of the Roman church's authority in the quodlibet may have been inspired by this in fact traditional contrast between individual churches and the church universal.

exclusive terms—it was the pope and the cardinals who were inerrant. Leaving aside the question of who was competent to make declarations of faith, his insistence that such declarations were infallible sprang from his conviction that the point he was arguing against Jean was vital to the health of the church. In line with the Anselmian tradition he knew God to be incapable of contradicting Himself; consequently the statement of faith in *Inter cunctas* could not be both true and untrue. That Benedict XI's condemnation of the necessity for double confession was a statement of faith was for him certain because it was based on the very nature of absolution—a point Jean de Pouilly would not concede. Therefore Pierre was bound to see Jean de Pouilly's attack on *Inter cunctas* and on Benedict XI for issuing it as a potential threat to all authority in the church.

Behind the noise and clamour of the controversy there lay another and more general issue which was to dog Pierre for the rest of his life. Like all later medieval canon lawyers, he had to take on board the Roman law underpinnings of canon law. On the one hand, since Roman emperors were clearly entitled to alter or abrogate the laws of their predecessors, the popes, as the fount of legislation within the church, ought to have the same right. On the other hand, some laws of the church represented the will of God and were therefore eternal and immutable. How could any particular law or clause of it be indisputably consigned to this category?[13] Giving guidance on the status of particular decrees was to be a recurring occupation of Pierre's later years. On double confession he could speak with complete conviction, and ultimately prevailed over his opponent. But he was apparently to take the opposite line on *Exiit qui seminat* of 1279 in his advice to Pope John on Franciscan poverty (see Ch. 5c). Differences of opinion on these issues were heated. And it must often have seemed to critical observers of the Paris Theology faculty in the second decade of the fourteenth century that discrimination between human ecclesiastical law and divine will depended not on absolute standards but on particular interests—Dominicans regarded one clause of *Inter cunctas* as a matter of faith,

---

[13] The problem went back to Hugoccio's gloss on the canon *sunt quidam*: 'In those things which pertain to salvation, such as what is contained in the Gospels and the Prophets, it is not possible to change. In like manner it is not possible to dispense in those things which pertain to the status of the church as in the sacraments and in the articles of faith; but there are many statutes which it is possible to change.' Translated by Heft, *John XXII and Papal Teaching Authority*, p. 141.

Franciscans all of *Exiit qui seminat*, and seculars *Omnis utriusque sexus* as expanded in *Super cathedram*. In this atmosphere, it was perhaps not surprising that the radical thinker Marsilius of Padua, who had returned to Paris by 1319 and was preparing to study theology by 1326,[14] should in his *Defensor pacis* cut the Gordian knot and treat all canon law not directly based on Scripture as purely human legislation.

This question in his only extant quodlibetal disputation displayed Pierre at his most formidable. He had remoulded the traditional mendicant response to criticism into a coherent and forceful defence of the friars at a particularly difficult point in time for the orders. Clearly impressed by his down-to-earth tackling of the contentious points, other clerics, including important seculars, began to ask the new Master for advice on tricky practical problems with a canon law dimension, particularly those involving an overlap of ecclesiastical and secular jurisdiction. In Toulouse, Bibliothèque municipale, MS 744, immediately after the record of Pierre's disputation, Marcuzzi found a lengthy opinion on the subject of usury, which he more than plausibly identified as Pierre's. On internal evidence he dated it to the second half of 1314;[15] but I would narrow the time to December 1314, which would make it contemporaneous with the Quodlibet. My reason is that the questions to which Pierre was responding were highly critical of Philip IV's ordinance of 8 December 1312, expanding and explaining that of July 1312,[16] and that such criticism is not likely to have been voiced during the lifetime of the formidable monarch. But on Philip's death in November 1314, a head of steam burst forth. The nobles formed leagues demanding a restoration of their privileges, Philip's chief servant Marigny was imprisoned then executed, and Louis X was besieged with demands that he abandon his father's evil ways. To date Pierre's discussion of usury to just after Philip's death is to see it within the framework of widespread criticism of the past reign. Though he may himself have invented the questions as part of a scholastic exercise, Marcuzzi's assumption that they were put to him by members of the higher clergy is inherently more probable.

[14] Testified by his servant Francis the Venetian: Baluze-Mansi, *Miscellanea*, ii. 281.

[15] 'L'Usura, un caso di giurisdizione controversa in un *responsum* inedito di Pietro di la Palu (1280–1342)', *Salesianum*, 40 (1978), 245–92; on the date, see pp. 270–3. For *responsiones* edited with quodlibetal questions see T. Turley, 'An Unnoticed Quaestio of Giovanni Regina de Napoli', *AFP* 54 (1984), 285.

[16] *Ordonnances des roys de France*, i. 494–6.

The burden of the prelates' complaint at that time was that the king, in order to enrich himself, was competing with ecclesiastical jurisdiction in a sphere which was traditionally out of bounds to lay justice. The Council of Vienne's condemnation of the defenders of usury had encouraged Philip IV to punish usurers himself, to the great benefit of the fisc. The thirteen questions Pierre faced were devised to elicit precise limits on royal jurisdiction in the area. Churchmen were particularly upset by the ordinance of 8 December 1312, which they read as declaring the king's intention of proceeding against all usurers, not only those who charged excessive rates. Furthermore they alleged that in carrying out this ordinance, royal officials were preventing usurers from effecting restitution of their ill-gotten gains, the traditional first step in the ecclesiastical process. The opposition therefore hoped not only to safeguard the church's jurisdiction but also to facilitate the sinners' contrition.

Pierre's sympathy with the ends of his respondents cannot be in doubt. Yet he was extremely cautious in supplying them with ammunition. Trained in Roman law, he was familiar with Justinian's legislation against usury, issued six centuries before that of Pope Gregory X at the Second Council of Lyons; he could not therefore accept the incompetence of lay rulers in this field. Nevertheless he limited their right to cases of immoderate usury, on the ground that excessive interest rates clearly harmed the common good with which rulers were automatically concerned, while moderate rates could confer benefits —a surprisingly open statement of a lesson learned from experience in the marketplace. It followed (though he did not explicitly state it) that usurers who set rates at or above the limits laid down in Philip's ordinance of July 1312 could be prosecuted in royal courts; but that others were immune, despite the December 1312 claim. There was, however, a serious complication: this general principle was deduced from civil law; but in the northern two-thirds of France, the *pays de coutûme*, civil law did not run. Was the king free to disregard it? In Pierre's view he was not, because the political distinction between moderate and immoderate usury could be apprehended rationally; civil law only stated what any man who thought about it might come to understand. Furthermore, the king could not interfere in cases of moderate usury without infringing the liberties of the French church—though ultimately he might develop a custom which would permit it. If in the meantime he chose to intervene, then he ran the risk of excommunication.

Since immoderate usury fell within royal jurisdiction, could the king suddenly introduce a fine for the crime when he had never exacted one before? According to Pierre, by customary law the only circumstance which would prevent it was if the church had as a matter of course imposed monetary penalties on usurers; in which case it would have acquired a prescriptive right to do so, and the king could not encroach on this. Otherwise, since offenders ought not to be left unpunished, he could do as he wished, at least with those immediately subject to his jurisdiction. Those under the authority of other lords would normally pay fines to those lords. Only in exceptional circumstances—above all, war—were there precedents for kings punishing the subjects of other lords. Nor had the king the right to fine a usurer so heavily as to prevent him from making restitution; restitution must come first, fines second. This meant that the king could not tallage those Jews who had nothing to live on other than interest; if he did so, he became a participant in the sin of usury.

The argument was complex, the difficulties raised numerous. Yet Pierre contrived here to make distinctions that were probably workable. The king himself had defined what immoderate usury was. Over those limits he had the right to punish, though he should take care in so doing, and should remember that the church also had jurisdiction in these cases. But below those limits, the state could not interfere. Royal officers enforcing literally the ordinance of 8 December 1312 risked excommunication. If King Philip's enemies had hoped for less moderate and well-considered opinions than Pierre's, at least they could not accuse him of fudging the issue. Equally the king's servants knew just where they now stood. It took courage to be as plain as this; and Pierre's reputation within the university no doubt grew as a result of this exercise.

(b)   *De potestate Papae*

Like his commentary on Book 4 of the *Sentences*, Pierre's *De potestate Papae*[17] shows him working on a theme that caught

---

[17] Ed. P. T. Stella, (Zurich, 1966). I do not accept the argument of V. Heynck in *Franziskanische Studien*, 49 (1967), 171-2 that the attribution is incorrect because Pierre put forward rather different ecclesiological opinions in his case against Jean de Pouilly. Slight inconsistency between a position taken in a literary work and one in a legal case seems to me normal. See also V. Hunecke, 'Die Kirchenpolitischen Exkurse in den Chroniken des Galvaneus Flamma O.P. (1283–c.1344): Einleitung und Edition', *DA* 25 (1969), 145–7 for the early attribu-

his imagination and led him towards positions to which he adhered for the rest of his life. As always, his concerns were intensely topical. He therefore faced the task of fitting the solutions demanded by canon law and immediate papal problems into a pattern of thought he would be prepared to defend in the abstract. If this committed him to the occasional serious inconsistency and to many distinctions easier to appreciate on paper than in life, he nevertheless achieved what he sought: a definition of papal power compatible with the maintenance of most contemporary ecclesiastical practices, including the friar's privileges, yet also with the temporal sovereignty of the French crown. Following in the footsteps of Thomas Aquinas and Jean Quidort de Paris, Pierre gave new specificity to the doctrine that both the temporal and the spiritual powers derived from God, at the same time as he affirmed the consequences of papal judicial primacy within the church. Energetically rebutting the papal hierocratic thinkers, particularly Giles of Rome in his *De ecclesiastica potestate*, he also denied the pretensions of Jean de Pouilly and his episcopal supporters to a church in which jurisdictional power was equally diffused throughout the episcopate. On his analysis, while within the church the pope was supreme judge, his sacramental position had much in common with that of all other bishops, and his lordship over ecclesiastical temporalities, though extensive, was strictly defined; over lay temporalities he had only accidental rights. In practice any pope who sought to justify his behaviour by Pierre's principles would have had to compartmentalize his activities very rigidly.

Some characteristics of *De potestate Papae*, the reference to Pierre's advice on a case heard in the ecclesiastical courts (*DPP*, pp. 166–9), the raising of topical issues (e.g. whether it was licit to baptize an infidel child against the will of its parents (*DPP*, pp. 99–103)), and the apparent response to another debater's points (as *DPP*, pp. 105–7) suggest that the tract originated in a scholastic exercise undertaken in Pierre's years as a master. A. Maier has shown that a version of the

tion of this tract to Pierre. On *De potestate Papae* literature, see J. Miethke, 'Die Traktat *De potestate papae*: Ein Typus politik-theoretischer Literatur', *Les Genres littéraires dans les sources théologiques et philosophiques médiévales: Actes du colloque international de Louvain, 1981* (Louvain, 1982), pp. 193–211. For general background see most recently J. A. Watt, 'Spiritual and Temporal Powers', in J. Burns, ed., *The Cambridge History of Medieval Political Thought* (Cambridge, 1988), pp. 367–423. In my discussion I have not cited the canons on which Pierre based his statements, because Stella has identified them in the edition.

first part must have been in circulation by late 1314 or 1315.[18] But the work as a whole was a substantial one, on which Pierre will have laboured for some time after he finished his commentary on Book 4 of the *Sentences*. And since I am convinced that the final version addressed itself to the problems faced by Pope John XXII on his accession in August 1316, I would date the completion of the whole to the months following that event.[19]

Pope John XXII may well have met Pierre soon after his election, heard that he had disputed at Paris on papal pre-eminence, and asked the famous regent master in theology to write an extended treatise for him on the subject. That one lawyer should welcome advice from another would be natural. But even if there was no request, the tract was a clear response to John's situation. Whether the papacy should continue to be based in Avignon (*DPP*, pp. 187–90), how papal rights in the disputed imperial election should be defended (*DPP*, p. 217), on what conditions the pope could legitimately make grants of ecclesiastical tenths to princes (*DPP*, p. 172), whether he could assign lands conquered in Palestine to victorious crusaders (*DPP*, p. 123), these were major issues for John XXII in the first year of his pontificate, as he struggled with the consequences of the long papal interregnum before his accession, and attempted to enforce the crusading vows made to Clement V. Verbose and tortuous though his prose was, Pierre gave precise answers on all these matters, and a great many more besides. The effectiveness of his advice cannot be measured; but it may have been considerable.

De potestate Papae falls into two parts. The first answers the question 'whether the pope's preeminence in power, which he enjoys in the church in respect of all things, was conferred on him immediately by Christ or simply ordained by the church' (*DPP*, p. 98); the second, 'whether it is necessary to be subject to the pope in temporalities as well as in spiritualities' (*DPP*,

---

[18] A. Maier, *Ausgehendes Mittelalter: Gesammelte Aufsätze zur Geistesgeschichte des 14 Jahrhunderts*, ii (Rome, 1967), p. 509. J. Miethke, 'Eine unbekannte Handschrift von Petrus de Paludes Traktat *De Potestate Papae* aus dem Besitz Juan de Torquemadas in der Vatikanischen Bibliotheke', *QFIAB* 59 (1979), 469, 474, has strengthened the case for regarding the two questions as originally separate.

[19] Stella, introduction, pp. 19–21. Stella's *terminus a quo*, an apparent reference to Philip V (which would place the completion of the work after 6 January 1317) is not beyond question. But Pierre's concern with papal rights in imperial elections confirms for me the correctness of placing the work towards the latter part of the period March 1314 to October 1317, the termini Stella identified by quotations from canon law.

p. 202). Each question is divided into *articuli*, the first into three, the second into five; each article is then divided into chapters. The framework is therefore logical and scholastic. But it leaps to the eye at the first reading of the text that it has been stretched out of shape by Pierre's relentless determination to stuff between its supports discussion of all his favourite secondary problems in the contemporary church. Under the weight of his discursiveness, what should have been a knapsack has become a rucksack. Nevertheless the extra weight contains much of historical interest.

In so far as *De potestate Papae* has attracted the attention of historians, it has been treated either as a narrow response to Jean de Pouilly or as a contribution to Dominican ecclesiology.[20] Taken in the first way, the tract determinedly sought to undermine Jean's contention, explicitly made in the course of 1314 or 1315, that the pope was bound by conciliar decrees. The value of Jean's argument to the seculars was obvious: if true, the pope was obliged to enact *Dudum* (on mendicant privileges) as soon as possible, because it had been passed at the Council of Vienne. According to Pierre, this was to put the cart before the horse. In fact it was the pope who gave conciliar decrees their validity—'lex concilii, cui papa dat auctoritatem, est lex pape et per consequens papa illi non subditur' (*DPP*, p. 201). Pierre accepted that the pope might not alter conciliar decrees such as those of the first four Ecumenical Councils which defined the faith (a point agreed on all sides since the days of Gregory the Great). But it was their essential truth, not their character as conciliar decrees, which made these eternally binding. Other conciliar decrees dealing with purely human arrangements should be equated with papal bulls in that they had no more power to bind the pope's successors than any of his own statutes (*DPP*, p. 201). This was a point of view which Pierre consistently upheld, but which he did not elaborate here.

On ecclesiology *De potestate Papae* took a notably moderate stand. The debate had divided theologians for about fifty years, and had broad practical implications. All parties accepted the distinction that had emerged in the course of the thirteenth century between the sacerdotal powers of priests, conferred on them by ordination, in which all priests shared equally, and

---

[20] C. A. Zuckerman, 'Dominican Theories of the Papal Primacy, 1250–1320', unpublished Ph.D. (Cornell University, 1971), appendix 1; W. D. McCready, *The Theory of Papal Monarchy in the Fourteenth Century: Guillaume de Pierre Godin, 'Tractatus de causa immediata ecclesiastice potestatis'* (Toronto, 1982), introduction, pp. 20–33.

their jurisdictional powers, of which in practice popes and bishops had more than simple priests. The question was whether Christ had given priests the jurisdictional powers they enjoyed, as Godfrey of Fontaines and then Jean de Pouilly maintained, or whether He had bestowed all jurisdictional power on St Peter, who then delegated it to his inferiors, as Hervé de Nédellec held. On Jean's assumption, the church was a constitutional monarchy, the papacy its elected head; on Hervé's, the papacy was God-given, therefore supreme. These positions were based on different interpretations of the Petrine commission, of Christ's commission to the apostles and the disciples, and of Christ's last words to Peter before His ascension. Neither side could convince the other; nor could they agree to differ. If Godfrey and Jean were right, then the pope could not legitimately intrude upon priests' jurisdictional rights; if Hervé was correct, then no criticism of papal action could be justified. Though the issue far transcended that of mendicant privileges, it was bound to be debated each time that thorny issue raised its head.

Pierre's choice of question, whether papal primacy was a direct gift of Christ or had emerged in the course of ecclesiastical history, showed his willingness to engage in the controversy. His final solution (DPP, pp. 176–83) steered a middle course between Jean's claims for the original equality of the apostles both in sacramental matters and in jurisdiction, and the belief, here ascribed to Pope Innocent IV, that only the pope received power directly from Christ. Pierre's conclusion, dependent on a distinction between potestas and preeminentia, conceded far more to Jean than he was later to do:

The third opinion, which seems to me truer, is that the powers of the pope, the bishops and the priests all derive from Christ, as does the pre-eminence of the bishops over parish priests and unbeneficed priests, and the preeminence of the pope over all. (DPP, p. 182)[21]

This apparently secured for the lower members of the ecclesiastical hierarchy at least some measure of power, apart from sacramental power, independent of delegation from the pope. Pierre's inconclusive discussion on the point earlier (DPP, pp. 126–7) was compatible with this viewpoint. In taking so un-

---

[21] Pierre was here close to Thomas Aquinas, Sentences, bk. 4, 24. 3. 2, 'Although the power of binding and loosing was given to all the apostles in common, nevertheless to signify that there is some order in this power, it was first given to Peter alone to show that this power ought to descend from him to the others.'

provocative and traditional a stance, he was perhaps influenced by his great respect for Hostiensis, who had repeatedly insisted that bishops enjoyed a measure of jurisdictional independence of the papacy.[22]

Pierre's moderation here was in line with the main ecclesiological emphasis of the *De potestate*, concerned as it was with the pope's pre-eminence, with his greater rights and capabilities, rather than specifically with his plenitude of power, his monopoly of rights. In fact his chief avowed opponent was not the Paris theologian Jean de Pouilly, but the 'schismatical and heretical' Greeks who refused to accept papal primacy. He therefore set himself the task, drawing on Thomas Aquinas's *Contra errores Grecorum*, of demonstrating from Greek sources that they were wrong (*DPP*, p. 184). In so doing he aspired to be useful to the Dominican missionaries among the Greeks, the Cumans and the Armenians, whose activities he regarded as even more worthy of papal support than a crusade to recover the Holy Land (*DPP*, p. 141). (Here he probably betrayed Berengar of Landorra's influence, for Berengar was well known as a vigorous reformer and encourager of the Peregrinantes, the missionary arm of the order.) In addition, he presumably hoped to help the pope cow the Greeks in negotiations for the union of the churches;[23] and also to provide ammunition against the legitimacy of the Greek empire in order to justify a Latin reconquest of Constantinople. He was nothing if not ambitious in seeing potential applications for his ideas.

At the core of Pierre's case for papal primacy lay, inevitably, the Petrine commission, interpreted as Christ's exclusive gift to Peter. But he departed from the Dominican platitude by regarding that gift as similar to a father's recognition of his eldest son's rights, 'Ita, etiam Deus primogenituram apostolatus dedit Petro, quem solidiosum fecit in fide et dilectione, licet ipse non fuerit primus in vocatione' (*DPP*, p. 184), a comparison which left intact the status of other bishops, who were implicitly recognized as the younger sons of God (*DPP*, p. 185). Because Christ conferred the power of binding and loosing on all the apostles (Matthew 18: 18), Pierre even thought there was no great harm in regarding all the apostles as equal by special privilege, although he himself did not favour this opinion (*DPP*,

[22] K. Pennington, *Pope and Bishops: The Papal Monarchy in the Twelfth and Thirteenth Centuries* (Pennsylvania, 1984), p. 148.

[23] Mortier, ii. 496; J. Richard, *La Papauté et les missions d'orient au moyen âge* (Rome, 1977), pp. 126–38; *Acta Ioannis XXII (1317–1334) e registris vaticanis aliisque fontibus collectis*, ed. A. L. Tautu (Vatican, 1952), passim.

p. 186). But such a concession might have led to the corollary that since the difference in status between the successors of Peter and the other bishops was a later development, papal supremacy must be man-made. Pierre naturally could not entertain this. Therefore he argued, from Christ's prayer to strengthen Peter's faith (Luke 22: 32), that the pope's right of making rules for the conduct of the sacraments and defining dogma on all doubtful issues must derive directly from God: 'Quia igitur Petrus a Christo est in fide solidatus, ideo in sacramentis et pertinentibus ad fidem factis est regular aliorum' (*DPP*, p. 191). Theologically speaking the proof hardly seemed solid enough to support his denunciations of the Greeks for refusing to accept it. But in his opinion papal primacy was powerfully reinforced, not only by early conciliar authority (*DPP*, p. 136), but also by the practices of the fourteenth-century Roman church. Because the popes had in fact altered the marriage law of the church, did issue indulgences, exempt individuals from rules that bound everyone else, and accepted appeals from churches everywhere, they were clearly entitled so to do (*DPP*, pp. 190, 191). (Pierre was obviously incapable of envisaging the Greek reaction to such a claim.) He underlined his point with the firm assertion that since the papal primacy could not legitimately be altered or undermined by the church, it must have been established by God. Unlike the Templar order, which the pope had instituted and suppressed, papal primacy lay above all human intervention (*DPP*, p. 183). Those who refused to submit to it were inexcusable.

However, Pierre's major preoccupation in the *De potestate Papae* was less defensive than clarificatory. Here what excites a twentieth-century reader's interest is not Pierre's philosophical presuppositions—though occasionally they were thought-provoking—but his determination to be as concrete as possible. Not content with making theoretical statements, he sought to provide precise, practical guidance for John XXII's own needs. He began by accepting the standard thirteenth-century canon lawyers' distinction between the powers conferred on the pope by his ordination and his judicial powers. Since the pope was by ordination a priest and bishop, he naturally possessed a *potestas ordinis* identical with that of other priests and bishops, through which he performed all sacraments. But in addition he had exclusive sacramental rights: he could license a mere priest—usually in practice a cardinal priest—to confirm or ordain to the four minor orders; and he could change by legislation the prohibited degrees of kinship in marriage. Therefore even in relation to sacraments, although Christ had bestowed powers equally on all the apostles, the pope had acquired a valid primacy.

One of the sacraments, that of penance, in practice inconveniently associated the powers of ordination and the judicial powers which might be needed to make it effective. Pierre, following Aquinas, separated the two aspects as far as possible: while penance was sacramental, the power to excommunicate was purely judicial.[24] This was evident from the fact that non-priests, such as bishops' officials, could excommunicate and even absolve from minor excommunications (though not from heresy, schism, and notorious or serious crime which necessarily demanded a priest) (DPP, p. 105). Once more the ecclesiastical practice of his own time furnished proof for him of the correctness of an intellectual distinction. What was and what should be were inextricably linked in his mind—as, indeed, in the mind of any canon lawyer who believed in the authenticiy of the church's evolving tradition.

Within the church, jurisdiction was of two kinds, voluntary and contentious. Pierre angled his discussion of voluntary jurisdiction to air his opinion on plenary indulgences, a topical question since Boniface VIII's Jubilee indulgence of 1300 had considerably extended their traditional bounds. He interpreted Christ's words to Peter, 'Who then is that wise and faithful steward, whom his lord shall make ruler over his household, to give them their portion of meat in due season?' (Luke 12: 42) as justifying and restricting to the heirs of St Peter the plenary indulgence (DPP, p. 191). But the pope could not use this supreme power at will, as Christ himself had done while on earth; for were he competent to absolve everyone from the pains of hell and purgatory, then it would be cruel of him not to do so. He could neither entirely annul purgatory nor remit satisfaction without destroying God's justice (DPP, p. 128). It was therefore wrong to grant indulgences to the great of this world; the grantor incurred sin by so doing, the grant was likely to be ineffective, and the faith was brought into disrepute (DPP, p. 129). This sharp and very personal comment shows Pierre in his guise as a committed and unrepentant reformer. Perhaps his sojourn in Paris, among the many critics of Pope Boniface VIII, had given him the courage to speak so plainly. And his words seem to have fallen on receptive ears; for Pope John XXII did his best to restrict plenary indulgences to those

24 Zuckerman, 'Dominican Theories', p. 37.

who actually went on crusade, sometimes only to those who had died for the Christian cause.[25]

The next issue was the pope's contentious jurisdiction, its origin and extent. Pierre made a clear distinction between spiritualities and temporalities. To take spiritualities first, while the power of binding and loosing was bestowed by Christ on all the apostles, it was bestowed unequally on Peter by the Petrine commission. The pope therefore could exercise his contentious jurisdiction in spiritualities on all men everywhere. All men could appeal to him for failure of justice in a lower ecclesiastical court; yet beyond him there was no appeal. Christ's gift of the power to bind and loose placed the whole world under Peter's coercive power and competence. This was so self-evident a proposition that Pierre saw no need to dwell on it, at least in relation to Christians (*DPP*, pp. 191–2). For him, the point of Christ's coming was to reorder the world by subjecting it to papal spiritual authority (*DPP*, pp. 139–40). Therefore to deny papal spiritual jurisdiction would be the utmost folly.

But papal authority over non-Christians was less clear-cut. Boniface VIII's claim in *Unam Sanctam* that submission to the papacy was essential to the salvation of all men provided a justification for the subjection of pagans, Saracens, and Jews to papal spiritual authority.[26] In the case of Jews, Pierre called in support the Mosaic law obligating them to submit to the high priest (*DPP*, p. 129), but without referring to the Jewish interpretation of that text. He conceded, in accordance with patristic teaching, that the pope might not order the forcible baptism of the Jews; but he endorsed the practice first authorized by Pope Gregory IX of requiring them to attend Christian sermons. All three categories of non-Christians were then made to suffer from his interpretation of 'Go forth into the world and preach the gospel to all creatures'—'By these words he subjected every man to those preaching by the authority of St Peter, for simple admonition is appropriate for equals or betters, but preaching by authority only for those subjected to the person or persons sent' (*DPP*, p. 130). Attendance at friar's sermons thus became part of political obligation for all non-Christian peoples.[27]

[25] N. Housley, *The Avignon Papacy and the Crusades, 1307–1378* (Oxford, 1986), pp. 132–3.

[26] Pierre's words support J. Muldoon's reading of the bull as a statement of the ground for missionary activity; see *Popes, Lawyers and Infidels: The Church and the Non-Christian World, 1250–1550* (Liverpool, 1979), pp. 70–1.

[27] He was influenced by Hostiensis; see B. Z. Kedar, *Crusade and Mission: European Approaches toward the Muslims* (Princeton, NJ, 1984), pp. 169–70.

The pope's rights of contentious jurisdiction over temporalities naturally provided more of a problem in a period when they remained intensely controversial. Pierre took for granted papal absolute rulership of the papal patrimony (*DPP*, pp. 130, 159), without even considering the challenge to this point of view mounted by the citizens of Rome—an illustration of his relative ignorance of matters Italian. Beyond the patrimony, however, there was a mass of conflicting customs and claims virtually impossible to sort out. As a lawyer, Pierre knew well the clause in the Theodosian code that allowed all bishops to hear appeals from secular courts, and the debate over whether Justinian had abrogated that clause (*DPP*, pp. 131-2). But on balance he was inclined to think that the church had lost through non-use the right to hear appeals from lay courts, except in some specific cases where the pope had regularly exercised it and where it had therefore remained intact. There was, then, no general papal or ecclesiastical right of contentious jurisdiction over temporalities, except during a vacancy in the empire, when a decretal of Gregory X had secured this for the papacy. Nevertheless the pope might entertain supplications against lay jurisdiction even where he thought appeals inappropriate (*DPP*, p. 134). Just what this would mean in practice Pierre did not say. And at this point he dropped the investigation, with the intention of resuming it when he had cleared up one major difficulty in his path.

This was the problem of ownership of property, *dominium* in the Roman law term. Giles of Rome in his *De ecclesiastica potestate* of 1302 had argued that since legitimacy derived from justice and true justice was vested only in the righteous, the church, acting through its head the pope, was the only channel through which legitimate ownership of property might be conferred.[28] Giles's claim constructed the coping-stone on the great edifice of papal hierocratic theory; now papal power in this world was apparently unlimited. Hardly surprisingly his tract met with immediate rebuttals. Of these the most thoughtful was the *De potestate regia et papali* of Jean Quidort de Paris, written in 1303, which contended that legitimate ownership derived from natural law; the true owners of property were those by whose labour it was made fruitful. *Dominium* was therefore vested in the laity, who might make gifts to the church as they thought fit. On this premiss papal *dominium*

---

[28] Ed. R. Scholz (Weimar, 1929), bk. 2. Here Giles seems to echo the early 13th-cent. canonist Alanus Anglicus.

was limited to such possessions as the papacy had acquired by lawful donations.[29]

Entering the lists as a disciple of Jean, Pierre faithfully echoed on this point the substance of the *De potestate regia et papali*. But he avoided Jean's syllogisms and deductions from Scripture in favour of his own proofs derived from history. For example, take his response to the Waldensian (and also Spiritual Franciscan) assertion that the church ought not to own private property; according to which Pope Sylvester I was responsible, by his acceptance of the Donation of Constantine, for abandoning the practice of communal property established by St Peter, and thus for laying the whole church open to corruption. Pierre indignantly replied that this contention was founded on a misunderstanding of early Christian history. In fact private property-holding derived from the ancient customs of the newly converted Christian peoples, that is, from below, not from an error of the rulers. The Roman emperors merely sanctioned the *fait accompli* and provided material goods to supply the needs of the church and of the poor. The popes, in accepting this change, showed a proper concern for the welfare of the imperfect among their flock (*DPP*, p. 116). Here Pierre combined a characteristically Augustinian view of the church on earth, in which sinners had their proper place, with down-to-earth common sense about the past. But the drawback to his argument lay in its open-endedness. It could be used to justify any departure from primitive norms, no matter how corrupting.

Having established that churches might hold property Pierre —unlike Jean de Paris—went on to specify what kinds. Tithes (*DPP*, p. 230), first fruits, and oblations (*DPP*, p. 111) supplied the daily wants of the clergy and therefore were essential; in order to fulfil its ministry the church must possess legally enforceable rights over these. The end justified the means. However (with the exception of consecrated objects like chalices) anything else churches possessed had been acquired solely through the gifts of the faithful and was held on the same terms as the previous owner had enjoyed (*DPP*, pp. 112, 116). Therefore there was no case for any kind of superior or overriding ecclesiastical title. Here spoke the canon lawyer anxious for precision. Then Pierre the reformer entered one plea: out of reverence for the practice of the primitive church, it would be

---

[29] Ed. J. Leclerq, *Jean de Paris et l'ecclésiologie du XIIIe siècle* (Paris, 1942), pp. 185-9.

sensible to vest ecclesiastical property as far as possible in corporate hands, in colleges, chapters, or religious communities, which were less prone to greed than individuals (*DPP*, pp. 112–13).

What then of the vexed question of the pope's *dominium* over ecclesiastical temporalities? Pierre initially relied on Jean de Paris to cut this to the minimum: since *dominium* was grounded in natural law, property belonged to laymen; consequently the pope had *dominium* only over what had specifically been given to him (*DPP*, p. 152). But here again, Pierre sought greater precision than Jean. Because St Peter had specifically denied possessing gold or silver, the pope had no claim to the church's treasure; he did not even own the goods in the papal chamber. Should he make grants to his relations from the chamber then his successor was duty-bound to restore them (*DPP*, pp. 160–1) (a piece of advice John XXII would have found it difficult to carry out, granted the state of the chamber on Clement's death[30]). Nor did he own the taxes levied by his chamber; not even the food and drink he rightfully accepted from it was his (*DPP*, pp. 163–4). He must remember that, although the dignity of his see demanded greater disbursement, his personal needs were no greater than those of other bishops (*DPP*, pp. 170–1). Thus trenchantly did Pierre cut the papal monarch down to size. No other contemporary was as crushing.

Yet when Pierre turned from the resources of the curia to the church at large, he apparently contradicted himself by sanctioning very extensive papal intervention in ecclesiastical temporalities. Following Jean, he called the pope *summus dispensator* over the church's property. But while Jean used the term to emphasize the pope's lack of *dominium*, Pierre saw it as a means of describing the full competence conceded to the successor of St Peter in early fourteenth-century canon law. The *summus dispensator* held a position analogous to that of a regent in a kingdom who, though not the actual possessor of the properties he administered, might do what he liked with them, provided he acted in the interests of the heir and had just cause for his more authoritarian actions. The pope might therefore alienate tithes to a layman to assist a crusade or to suppress heresy—though if he did so merely out of fear of a prince he was nothing more than a thief (*DPP*, p. 173) (probably a criticism of Clement V's pliability in the face of pressure from

---

[30] On Clement's policies concerning the chamber and its instability in his reign, see Y. Renouard, *Les Relations des papes d'Avignon et des compagnies commerciales et bancaires de 1316 à 1378* (Paris, 1941), pp. 94–8.

Philip IV and Edward I; John XXII and Benedict XII, on the other hand, did struggle to prevent crusading tithes from being used for other purposes[31]). The pope might give, sell, or buy goods of churches as necessary; and he might alienate or transfer ownership without formality provided he had a just reason for so doing (DPP, pp. 135–6, 139).

Two problems at once arise from Pierre's argument. First, what did the dominium of a church in its property mean when a pope, specifically denied any general dominium, was free to sell or alienate that property without the church's consent? In effect Pierre had separated possession from legal right over property, a division at odds with his earlier contention that dominium was grounded in natural law. Aware of the problem, he attempted backhandedly to preserve the appearance of consistency by postulating hereditary right as the defining characteristic of dominium; lay lords, inheriting their position, were domini; the pope, being elected, was not (DPP, pp. 163, 173). But this distinction, while certainly differentiating the pope from a French baron, only confused even further the position of local property-owning churches.[32]

Secondly, how could the pope exercise unlimited discretion over the property of other churches while he enjoyed only the most restricted rights over revenues and lands traditionally thought to be his own? In terms of logic Pierre's stand could hardly be defended. To make sense of it, we must read what he said in different ways, the first part descriptively, the second prescriptively. On the one hand he condoned early fourteenth-century papal taxation and the extension of papal control over benefices; on the other he warned John XXII not to bring the papacy into disrepute by following the examples of Boniface VIII and Clement V. Thus both the lawyer and the reformer in Pierre had his say. Contemporaries, conversant with the background, probably found the end-product less confusing than it appears at first sight to a twentieth-century reader.

From the secular clergy's point of view, there was little in Pierre's teaching to attract. True, he recognized the validity of their property rights, thereby guaranteeing them safety against lay depredators; and he reiterated the traditional

---

[31] Housley, The Avignon Papacy, pp. 168, 171–2, 177–82.

[32] In De paupertate Pierre was to take a more logical stand on this issue: 'sed dominus papa in bonis ecclesie temporalibus habet plenitudinem potestatis in alienando et faciendo quidquid dominus de suo facere potest . . . videtur habere verum et proprie dictum dominium in bonis ecclesie', Paris, Bibliothèque nationale, MS Latin 4046, fo. 46ʳ.

canonical prohibition on lay taxation of the clergy without papal consent. But he offered no defence against papal taxation, nor against a lay tax which had been properly sanctioned. The combination of the pope's powers as *summus dispensator* and his supreme jurisdiction in spiritualities apparently rendered him an absolute monarch over his clergy. And yet they were not totally without recourse, at least in so far as they were members of the community of the people at large. Not that there was much leeway here. The pope could not be judged, either by a lay (*DPP*, p. 199) or by an ecclesiastical (*DPP*, p. 195) court; nor indeed by a council, since councils derived their authority from him (*DPP*, p. 201). Should he become a heretic, God would depose him from his office, and a council would simply proclaim God's action (*DPP*, p. 195). But any other papal offence would simply have to be tolerated by a Christian people. Having enunciated this apparently clear-cut principle, Pierre immediately went on to undermine it by borrowing from Jean de Paris the idea of legitimate passive resistance to a sinful pope. Just as monks who could not depose their abbot were nevertheless free to disobey such of his orders as violated the law, so the people might resist the pope if he tried to destroy St Peter's to build a palace for his relations or otherwise raided the papal patrimony (*DPP*, p. 196). Pierre did not attempt to reconcile resistance by the people as a whole with the total submission of each individual to the supreme judge of spiritualities. Again he was more concerned to warn John XXII against imitating his predecessors than to work out a consistent political theory. But he seems to have held that although the people had no right to rebel, popes should always beware the potential consequences of driving them to it.

Pierre then turned to the contentious issues associated with papal control of lay temporalities. Here he emphatically denied that salvation for laymen depended on their subjection to the pope in temporalities as well as in spiritualities (*DPP*, p. 202). This noxious doctrine he ascribed to Boniface's letter of admonition to Philip IV, *Ausculta Fili*—which he only knew in the version *Scire te volumus* forged by Guillaume de Nogaret.[33] In returning to the propaganda of 1302–3, he was refighting old battles, battles that both Philip V and John XXII might well have preferred to forget. But he was not the first to dredge up the past. In fact he was probably responding to the arguments of his colleague John of Naples, the second Dominican regent

[33] Ibid.

master during the years 1315–17, who had, in a question apparently disputed in Paris at this time, declared in no uncertain manner the total subjection of all temporal powers to the papacy.[34] It was a point of view demanding immediate refutation; and Pierre was a natural choice to undertake the task.

But if Pierre was responding to John of Naples, he was also warning the new pope against adopting a dangerously assertive position. Employing a favourite story of his, he reminded John of the two Roman lawyers, Bulgarus and Martin, who were interrogated by Frederick Barbarossa on the extent of imperial power. Martin, who flattered the emperor lavishly, was rewarded with a horse; Bulgarus, who told the truth, was punished for it (*DPP*, pp. 152–3).[35] The moral Pierre drew—presumably in criticism of his fellow friar—was that, while it was easy to tell your listener what he wanted to hear, it would not do him any good. He, on the other hand, would be honest. Roman lawyers denied to the pope any jurisdiction in temporalities beyond what he had received by imperial grant (*DPP*, p. 203). Some theologians and canonists took the opposite view, that all earthly jurisdiction derived from the pope, who in practice chose to delegate some aspects to laymen (*DPP*, p. 204). 'I regard the middle way as being truer, saving the past and future judgement of the apostolic see on all matters' (*DPP*, p. 206). Having covered himself against possible future criticism, Pierre went on to enunciate the fundamentally Thomist position that both secular and spiritual jurisdiction derived directly from God; therefore the temporal powers were not subject to the spiritual in temporal matters, although the pope necessarily had enough temporal jurisdiction *casualiter* to protect the spiritualities committed to his care. Pierre bolstered his position with the assertion that Pope Boniface VIII could not really have meant what he apparently said in *Ausculta Fili*, because the canonization of St Louis was incompatible with such a belief (*DPP*, p. 240), and because he would have been far more ferocious to Philip IV had he thought it vital to secure his submission (*DPP*, p. 241). Besides, if the pope really was the fount of temporal jurisdiction, then certain kings, princes, confessors, lawyers, theologians, and canonists must have been wrong; 'Hoc autem videtur inconveniens' (*DPP*, p. 203)—but this seemed implausible. Therefore in the interests of safe-

[34] *Quaestiones variae parisiis disputatae Fr. Johannis Napoli*, ed. D. Gravina (Naples, 1618), pp. 331–4.

[35] *Ottonis Morenae et continuatorum Historia Frederici I*, ed. F. Güterbock, *MGH: Rerum Germanicarum*, n.s. vii. 58–9.

guarding the faith, the letter to Philip should be interpreted as meaning that all laymen were subject to the pope in spiritualities, but in temporalities only so far as was necessary for the maintenance of spiritualities (*DPP*, p. 241).

As always with Pierre, the historical interest of his words lies less in the general principles he enunciated than in the concrete distinctions he made. His train of thought is forgivably messier and more difficult to follow than the elegant arguments of Jean de Paris or of John of Naples because, unlike these men, he aimed to provide positive guidance to a pope in an impossibly difficult situation. Exactly what degree of temporal subordination was meant? All men, including princes, must pay tithes (*DPP*, p. 215). Rulers were obliged to defend the church whether or not they received tribute for so doing (*DPP*, p. 224), to assist in the recovery of the Holy Land, and to help the inquisition (*DPP*, p. 216). Spiritual weapons, including excommunication, could be used to force them to do so. The pope might punish those who attacked ecclesiastics, or even those who failed to avenge their injuries. And, like other ecclesiastical judges, he could inflict secular punishments where necessary. Uniquely, he might act as a judge in temporal matters where no temporal judge existed or where the temporal judge refused to act: 'Since justice is a virtue and therefore a spiritual matter . . . if there were no judges to enforce the law, justice would die and hence also spirituality' (*DPP*, p. 216). As an extension of this principle, the pope might decide disputed successions to kingdoms, both in states subordinated to him and in those free of his lordship where, if he failed to act, war would harm the spiritual life of the people (*DPP*, p. 217); but in such cases, he ought as far as possible to work within the customs of the country. And in a whole range of other political conflicts, princes ought to seek papal mediation rather than resort to arms (*DPP*, p. 218), because it was evil to regard war as the proper arbiter of disputes. On the other hand, the pope ought not to demand homage of princes in return for his mediation.

Pierre had therefore justified the pope's various interventions into the temporal sphere, either by the need to defend the church and the faith, or as vital to the pursuit of peace. Only in the small matter of legitimizing children did he firmly deny papal right (*DPP*, p. 233). But when he came to the chief bone of contention, the pope's right to depose temporal rulers, he discovered that only a complicated answer would solve the problem. According to him the legitimacy of depositions varied partly in accordance with the degree of papal authority over the temporal rulers—on this scale vassal rulers were the most vulnerable (*DPP*, p. 262), infidel rulers the least (*DPP*, p. 264)—and partly with the seriousness of the offence. For a heretical ruler, deposition was automatic; those who refused to assist in suppressing heresy and those who attacked church lands or captured prelates met the same fate (*DPP*, p. 265). Saracen rulers who persecuted Christians should also be deposed. But in the case of a Christian, a serious offence must have been committed and the pope must have the appropriate degree of legal authority to depose; otherwise his judgement was null and he himself had committed a sin (*DPP*, p. 267). This was a far cry from Innocent III's claim to intervene without restriction *ratione peccati*, to combat sin.

Nevertheless, Pierre's spirited defence of the independence of temporal power and his determination to counter hierocratic views in the end left the pope a wide degree of latitude.[36] On his principles Innocent IV's deposition of Frederick II was correct. The pope must have just cause; he must be rational; but he could find some valid ground for almost any course of action he thought necessary against rulers of vassal states. Sovereign kings would obviously be harder to discipline: Boniface VIII's threatened deposition of Philip IV would not have met with Pierre's approval. But since he did not actually deny the pope's ultimate right to depose any gravely offending king, Pope John XXII will have found nothing here seriously to displease him.

The last section of the work was perhaps the part Pierre particularly enjoyed writing. His aim was to demonstrate the different balances between papal and temporal power in the Greek empire, the western empire, and the kingdom of France.[37] Like a good Roman lawyer, he started from the assumption that under the Roman republic and in the first two centuries of the empire, the whole world had been united under Roman dominion, freely accepted by all men (*DPP*, p. 237). Somehow he had to explain why, in the course of history, the Greek emperor had lost his right to rule, and the German emperor and the German

---

[36] I do not accept McCready's description of this as 'moderate anti-papalism', *Theory of Papal Monarchy*, p. 4. But see his fuller treatment of the question in 'Papalists and Anti-papalists: Aspects of the Church-State Controversy in the Later Middle Ages', *Viator*, 6 (1975), 241–74.

[37] His argument is reminiscent of the much shorter one to the same effect in *Rex pacificus*, ed. Barbier (Paris, 1506); but the wording is not sufficiently close to prove that Pierre drew on this text.

princes-elector had become subject to the pope, while the kingdom of France had totally escaped all temporal subjection both
to the empire and to the papacy (except that the pope might
invade temporalities to protect spiritualities). This propaganda
exercise forced him to strain his limited historical talents. It is
not reassuring to find him calling in aid both the Donation of
Constantine[38] which played a central role in his argument, and
Pseudo-Turpin, the twelfth-century Latin chronicle ascribed to
the legendary archbishop of Reims who fought on the Frankish
side at the Battle of Roncevalles. One might almost wonder if
Pierre thought the truthfulness of a source was directly propor-
tionate to its colourfulness. Furthermore, he lacked a sense of
time; centuries melded into one another, the drift of the argument moved forth and back over the timespan, only a vague
chronological framework emerged. Yet granted the oddity of
the propositions he was trying to prove, the whole was not
without merit.

The Greek empire had the simplest history. Created by
Constantine when he moved the capital to Byzantium, it was at
first an elective empire. But its people lost the privilege of
choosing their ruler when they failed to resist Julian and other
heretical emperors (*DPP*, pp. 247–8); then later, when they
themselves became heretical, they forfeited the right to empire.
The pope therefore legitimately transferred it from them to the
Germans, who held it as his vassals. The only problem with this
simple schema was dating the actual moment of transfer.
Charlemagne's coronation in 800 was the obvious moment to
stipulate. But Pierre was slightly uneasy about this, because in
one of his legendary sources he had read that the eastern
emperor in Charlemagne's time was a certain Baldwin, who
bestowed the crown of thorns on his western colleague (*DPP*,
p. 119).[39] Since such a noble figure as Baldwin could not have
been a heretic, either he must be supposed to have died before
800 or alternatively the eastern empire was ceded later. In any
case the Greeks had lost *de iure* right to the empire long before
the *de facto* confiscation of their country (*DPP*, p. 248), presumably in 1204. It followed that the empire of the Paleologi was

---

[38] On the unwillingness of most canon lawyers to employ the Donation see
Muldoon, *Popes, Lawyers and Infidels*, pp. 7, 55–6. Nevertheless, it must be
conceded that Pierre is more scholarly in his handling of the Donation than is
Jean de Paris in *De potestate regia et papali*, ed. Leclerq, pp. 245–6.

[39] Cf. ch. 1, n. 20. There was confusion with the emperor Baldwin II who was
forced to pawn the crown of thorns to St Louis in 1234; but how an event of the
13th cent. got put back into the 9th is unclear.

illegitimate and would remain so until the Greeks abandoned their heresy.

The German empire was more complicated. In handling it, Pierre drew up a series of arguments, often mutually incompatible, which could be essayed against a doubting opponent. The crucial events in need of interpretation were, in his view, the Donation of Constantine which had established papal temporal supremacy over the empire, Pope Sylvester's immediate restoration of most of the empire to Constantine, and the subsequent agreements between Pope Hadrian and Charlemagne and between Pope Leo and Otto I. Each of these redrew the shifting line dividing *dominium* between empire and papacy. In Otto's reign, the church was recognized as having *dominium directum* (superior overlordship) in the empire, while the emperor retained *dominium utile* (effective control) (*DPP*, p. 118). Yet at the same time the emperor had authority within the church, expressed in his rights to approve papal elections and to nominate to various offices. In the course of the eleventh and twelfth centuries the western emperors voluntarily abdicated these infringements on the spiritualities of the church. While *de facto* they retained control of all their own temporalities, the *de iure* position was less clear. When the pope deposed Frederick II, not only from the kingdom of Sicily, where he was a papal vassal, but also from the empire, Innocent IV reasserted the ancient but almost obsolete *dominium directum* over the empire (*DPP*, p. 263). This action undermined imperial hereditary succession; from then on the electors chose the emperor and the pope confirmed him. The new relationship was symbolized by the king of the Romans lying at the pope's feet to receive the imperial crown, an explicit recognition that his temporal power derived from the papacy (*DPP*, p. 260). The pope now ruled over the empire in a vacancy; he could judge and depose the emperor, either for a grave fault, or for his inadequacy to fulfil the role to which he had been called (*DPP*, pp. 265-6) (the ground officially given for the deposition of Adolf of Nassau in 1298).[40] He could take the right of election out of the hands of those bishops to whom he had given it; and though he could not deprive the secular electors in so cavalier a fashion, he could do so as punishment for an offence (*DPP*, p. 268). (Earlier in his work, Pierre had said that they did in fact deserve to lose this right (*DPP*, p. 217).) Alternatively, the

---

[40] E. Peters, *The Shadow King: Rex inutilis in Medieval Law and Literature, 751-1327* (New Haven, Conn. and London, 1970), pp. 232-6.

pope could either restore hereditary succession (*DPP*, p. 268) or, if he had just cause, transfer the empire to another people, the French or the Italians (*DPP*, p. 267). The only thing he might not do was to take the title of emperor himself; for that was incompatible with his office. Thus, in Pierre's opinion, papal-imperial relations had over the centuries gone through a complete cycle; the position was now restored to what it had been immediately after Constantine had handed over the empire to Sylvester. Our author could hardly have developed a theory more appropriate to John XXII's needs in 1317, as he strove to impose his authority on Lewis of Bavaria and Frederick of Austria, the two claimants to the empire elected by rival parties in 1314. Virtually all options were laid invitingly before him.

In total contrast, Pierre denied imperial power any competence in France and tightly restricted papal power there. Although that country had originally been part of the western empire, Pope Innocent III had acknowledged in *Per Venerabilem* that the French king recognized no superior in the temporalities of his kingdom. Pierre traced the origin of French independence to Charlemagne's, or his heirs', division of the imperial lands. It was likely that Charles had exempted France from imperial jurisdiction, either out of particular love for his own part of the world, or from unwillingness to subject one of his sons to another (*DPP*, p. 249); alternatively, the exemption may have been granted later. But what was incontrovertible was that the French had been free of the imperial yoke for quite long enough to have acquired a prescriptive right to freedom (*DPP*, p. 250). More difficult was the problem of French immunity from all but the bare minimum of papal intervention. Pierre strongly rebutted the notion, articulated by Pope Innocent IV in his *Apparatus*, that the pope had *dominium directum* in France as he had in Germany. He regarded this claim as no more than a private legal opinion (*DPP*, pp. 239–40), and pointed out in mitigation of his temerity that Cardinal Jean Le Moine's gloss on *Unam Sanctam* was more extreme in denying the pope's rights in temporalities, and yet the cardinal had not been punished.[41]

[41] Ed. H. Finke, *Aus den Tagen Bonifaz VIII: Funde und Forschungen* (Münster, 1902), pp. c–cxvii. This gloss has usually been dismissed as a forgery (see J. Rivière, *Le Problème de l'Église et de l'État au temps de Philippe le Bel* (Louvain, 1926), pp. 153–55); nevertheless, it is important, as Stella points out, that Pierre, so near a contemporary of the cardinal, ascribed the gloss to him. On the whole Pierre is correct in regarding it as more extreme than his thesis.

But if the French king and the French kingdom enjoyed independence of the papacy as the empire did not, when did they acquire it? Pierre favoured the idea of a specific exemption granted in return for Charlemagne's service to the pope (*DPP*, p. 252); however, he was forced to acknowledge that no trace of such a privilege remained. Though unwilling to ascribe the church's loss of jurisdiction to a fault on her side, he saw a way out of the difficulty: such secular jurisdiction as the church had once enjoyed in France had resulted from the Donation of Constantine, and was therefore man-made, not of divine origin. But purely human jurisdiction could be prescribed against. Since the church had not used that jurisdiction, and had through Innocent III's admission in *Per Venerabilem* specifically denied its existence, it had ceased to possess it (*DPP*, p. 253). Therefore early fourteenth-century Frenchmen could remain faithful to the pope while demanding that he restrict severely any exercise of temporal jurisdiction over them.

Many years later, in a sermon for the feast of St Francis, Pierre pointed out that while it was relatively easy for one servant to housekeep for several scholars who were friends, the job became impossible if they fought each other.[42] The same point might be made for Pierre's attempts to bolster both papal and royal authority. Given goodwill, king and pope might almost have contrived to live according to the guidelines laid down in *De potestate Papae*; but the smallest of tensions would automatically have led them into endless demarcation disputes. Still, to blame Pierre for this would be as unreasonable as to blame ACAS (Arbitration and Conciliation Advisory Service) for the existence of the problems it is designed to ease. Pierre had been accustomed to arbitration in the ecclesiastical courts. He brought to his tract the fruit of that experience: lasting peace could only be achieved by granting to each side the points on which they would in no circumstances yield, and by offering exactness on practices, even at the expense of a certain confusion on principle.

The intellectual originality of *De potestate Papae* lies largely in its rejection of abstraction. Pierre's pragmatism has not endeared him to generations of scholars, because they have correctly diagnosed inconsistencies between what he said in *De potestate Papae* and his stand in later works, particularly

---

[42] 'Pluribus scolaribus sociis et amicis in eadem domo morantibus servit unus famulus, assistens eos emens et parans eis cibos et portans libros. Sed diversis dominis contrariis et inimicis non potest unus similiter et simul servire', Clermont Ferrand, Bibliothèque municipale, MS 46, fo. 229ʳ.

on the ecclesiological issue. Nevertheless the inconsistencies are small in comparison with the broad continuities of outlook. The tract seems to reflect Pierre's abiding convictions. If in the future he was to modify one or another of the opinions he articulated here, it was either because the facts had changed (as in the case of poverty) or because someone else's views would win an argument more effectively (ecclesiology and papal plenitude of power). His basic aim of doing justice to both pope and king never wavered.

His contemporaries judged the work more kindly than twentieth-century critics. No sooner was the tract completed than Pierre was called on to discuss its contents with Guillaume de Pierre Godin, the distinguished Dominican cardinal then resident at Avignon. So impressed was Guillaume by it that he used it as the foundation for his own more influential *De causa immediata ecclesiastice potestatis*.[43] True, he corrected Pierre on one or two points—most significantly, the question of whether the pope might continue to reside elsewhere than in Rome; but the changes were fairly minor. From Pierre and Guillaume John XXII learned that no succeeding pope could afford to refight Boniface VIII's wars;[44] and yet that there were many areas in which he had the ability, even the duty, to resist bullying by the French crown. John's policies on the taxation of the clergy and on crusade taxes demonstrated his willingness to learn.

APPENDIX: PIERRE ON POVERTY

Though only tangentially relevant to the main argument of *De potestate*, Pierre's treatment of poverty (*DPP*, pp. 229–32) is important because it shows his espousal of a definition of poverty close to that soon to be condemned by Pope John XXII in *Ad conditorem canonum* and *Quia quorundam*.[45]

---

[43] Ed. McCready, *Theory of Papal Monarchy*, where McCready makes plain Guillaume's exact indebtedness to Pierre throughout in the *apparatus fontium*. I have accepted McCready's argument. But doubts have been expressed, among others by Miethke, 'Die Traktat *De Potestate Papae*', p. 198 n. 30. For a recent treatment see D. Van den Auweile, 'À propos de la tradition manuscrite du *De causa immediate ecclesiastice potestatis* de Guillaume de Pierre Godin († 1336)', *RTAM* 21 (1984), 183–205.

[44] Though John XXII did argue for the pope's overarching lordship in temporalities everywhere in *Quia vir reprobus* of 1329. But this may be taken within the narrow context of his conflict with Michael of Cesena.

[45] *Corpus iuris canonici*, ed. E. Friedberg (Graz, 1955), ii, Extravagantes Johannis, bk. 22, 14. 3 and 4.

The subject came up in the course of Pierre's defence of tithes. He recorded the objection that God's specific concession of tithes to the priests in the Old Testament was not repeated in the New; rather God limited ecclesiastical ownership to strict necessities in order not to impede the search for perfection. Pierre then asked, since property hindered contemplation, ought not the church to abandon all but essentials? Relying on *Exiit qui seminat*[46] he distinguished between *dominium* (ownership) and *usus* (use). It was obviously possible to renounce the legal ownership of goods, relying only on use of the necessities of life. But was it possible to renounce use? Those who relied on use could either defend their right in the lawcourt and therefore possessed *usus iuris* (legally enforcible right), or they could not, in which case they only had *simplex usus facti* (bare use). In the latter category came serfs who, not being persons before the law, depended totally on their masters' rights. Their example proved that it was not necessary to have *usus iuris* in order to live. It followed that the search for perfection would be enhanced by the abandonment both of ownership and of legally enforcible right.

Pierre denied the relevance of this syllogism to the secular church. Since it existed to supply the needs of the imperfect as well as of those who aspired to perfection, it required property to fulfil its function. But for the religious orders renunciation of private property was essential. The issue of communal property was more difficult. However, since there was a *prima-facie* case that the more an order renounced the more perfect it became, the highest perfection in the religious life should lie in abandoning everything but *simplex usus facti*. [If this was true, then of all the orders in the early fourteenth-century church, only the Franciscans could claim true perfection.]

To this conclusion Pierre raised two objections. First, it must be wrong to identify *simplex usus facti* as the essence of perfection, since the primitive church, more perfect than any present-day religious order, had held property in common. In the future Pierre was to find this a convincing argument (see Ch. 5c); now he contended that although the primitive church had attained perfection in charity and all the graces, it had not achieved all the external signs of perfection, among which was the proper practice of poverty. His second objection was that religious perfection might be assessed by more than one criterion. The claim that orders devoted to contemplation and the salvation of souls were more perfect than those that ran hospitals could be countered by the alternative view that a composite life involving both activity and contemplation was preferable to one consisting exclusively of one or the other. It was characteristic of Pierre's pluralistic approach to the church of his own day that he did not deny this. Each religious order was therefore free to defend its own values.

[46] *Corpus iuris canonici*, ed. E. Friedberg (Graz, 1955) ii, Sexti Decretales, bk. 5, 12. 3.

But for those whose priority was poverty, abandonment of everything that could be abandoned without violating natural law was the correct course. However, circumstances could sometimes alter cases. If the abjuration of property rights led a religious order to beg for its bread, then the impediment to preaching and contemplation thus created could render that order *per accidens* less perfect than one which had not been so drastic. But in general full renunciation enhanced an order's poverty of spirit and gave more meaning to the voluntary character of that poverty.

Here, then, we have a Dominican endorsing what is normally thought of as the Franciscan concept of poverty. Admittedly Pierre's preference for the term *usus iuris* rather than the commoner Franciscan *ius utendi* (which particularly exasperated John XXII in the second version of *Ad conditorem canonum*) toned down the provocative character of his thinking. But his identification of *simplex usus facti* as the essence of religious perfection would, only a few years later, have laid him open to a charge of heresy. The concluding words of his discourse: 'que omnia sine omni assentione dicta esse intelliguntur, solum probabiliter dubitando' (all this should be understood as providing a plausible answer to a problem rather than expressing a conviction) show he knew he was on dangerous ground. Still, as a canon lawyer he continued to accept the authority of *Exiit qui seminat* as it had been traditionally interpreted. His handling of this theme points to an old-fashioned sense of solidarity between the mendicant orders. His analysis at least precludes the view that the intricacies of the poverty dispute, so attractive to modern historians,[47] were common knowledge before they were forced on public attention. Perhaps we should be cautious about the interpretation of John XXII's bulls that sees them as the fruit of Dominican machinations.[48] Though some Dominicans were involved in the discussions at the curia, so also were Carmelites, and the bulk of the Friars Preachers may have been very disconcerted by the bulls.

For the biographer of Pierre, it is important that he was soon to abandon his 1317 definition of religious poverty. Clearly he cannot be praised for consistency; but nor was he to prove totally inconsistent. His *per accidens* argument that preaching and contemplation should not be impeded by the necessity of begging left him room for manœuvre, a means of approaching closer to actual Dominican practice.[49] And if, in compliance with papal pressure, he soon ceased to extol *simplex*

---

[47] Among many recent works see M.-T. d'Alverny, 'Un adversaire de St Thomas: Petrus Johannis Olivi', *St Thomas Aquinas, 1274–1974: Commemorative Studies* (Toronto, 1974), ii. 179–218.

[48] I agree with M. D. Lambert, *Franciscan Poverty: The Doctrine of the Absolute Poverty of Christ and the Apostles in the Franciscan Order, 1210–1323* (London, 1961), p. 241.

[49] S. Tugwell, *The Way of the Preacher* (London, 1979), p. 43: 'The Dominicans, on the whole, do not seem to have followed St. Dominic in his enthusiasm for an extreme and literal poverty . . . But there does seem to have been a fairly strong, persistent tradition of poverty of spirit.'

usus facti, he continued rigidly to adhere to the kernel of his argument, that religious orders should practise poverty of spirit, and that they should refrain from litigating in defence of their sources of revenue; indeed these were points he was to make in his last known academic work.

4. The Testing Time

(a) Pierre and Politics

While performing his tasks as Regent Master in Theology, Pierre also acquired a reputation among the lawyers who worked in the ecclesiastical courts in Paris. They sought his opinion on a variety of problems involving the implementation of sound ecclesiastical principles. For example, one issue, the right of the secular clergy to make wills relating to their own property (though not of course to the property of the church), was often contentious, because a distinction easy to draw in theory proved elusive in practice. Should a certain house built by a bishop be inherited by his heirs or assigned to the diocese? Sorting out knotty problems of this sort clearly gave Pierre a sense of satisfaction. Indeed, his pride in his solutions led him to parade them in his academic writings where they were out of place.[1]

At the same time Pierre was achieving stature within the Dominican order. He extended his acquaintance beyond the Paris circle of Hervé and his friends, who had been his close companions when he was a bachelor, and now appeared as an associate of the master general of the order, Berengar of Landorra, a distinguished figure in Dominican history, who was known as a strong supporter of the Peregrinantes, the missionary arm of the Dominicans, and as a determined upholder of intellectual standards among the friars. Naturally Berengar had no desire to distract Pierre from his role as a teacher—he himself had been responsible for legislating in the general chapter of Carcassonne in 1312 that lectors should not be syphoned off into administration until they had taught for at least two years.[2] But when Pierre had completed this stint, the master general had plans for him. Their noble birth made a bond between them, and the younger friar's legal training was an asset to the other in dealing with the order's business. After their meeting during the inquiry into Durand's writings— which was perhaps their first—greater closeness followed; in

---

[1] e.g. *DPP*, pp. 166-8.   [2] *CUP* ii. 69. 155-6.

Berengar's entourage Pierre began to contend with the affairs of a wider world.

Pierre's introduction to Dominican administration is obscure. But he must already have been a reasonably experienced figure when he was chosen to represent the province of France at the general chapter of Pamplona on 21 and 22 May 1317. A *definitor*—the official title for his office—enjoyed temporarily at least high status in the order: he was permitted to have servants in his retinue, and took his place above the local hierarchy at the head of any convent in which he stayed, not only in the chapter but also at meals and in chapel.[3] In Pierre's case, the eminence he reached was unusually high, for at the crucial time of the general chapter, Berengar of Landorra was called to Avignon (to advise the pope on Flanders before his appointment to the Archbishopric of Compostella) and could not preside over the assembled friars. Pierre was therefore nominated to do so in his place.[4]

The chapter of Pamplona was not a particularly exciting one. Still, one piece of its business must have been very congenial to its president: in the name of the whole order he wrote to King Alfonso of Castille, asking him to assist in procuring the canonization of Raymond of Penafort, the famous canon lawyer, third master general of the order, who had edited the *Corpus iuris canonici*. In praising Raymond's distinction, Pierre will have been conscious of his own suitability to plead the cause. Indeed, since the move was made in response to the pope's expressed willingness to canonize one Dominican,[5] he himself may have been responsible for nominating Raymond. This hypothesis is reinforced by the ultimate failure of the move, presumably because it was later decided, under Hervé de Nédellec's mastership, that the order would prefer the canonization of Thomas Aquinas; canon lawyers normally enjoyed a lower status than theologians among the black friars. But if Pierre's moment of glory was brief it was doubtless pleasurable.

Another piece of business transacted at Pamplona is more difficult to interpret: Pierre was requested to resign from his regent mastership at Paris and allow another friar to take his

---

[3] Reichert, ed., *Acta*, i. 305. On the duties of *diffinitores* at general chapters, see G. R. Galbraith, *Constitution of the Dominican Order* (Manchester, 1925), pp. 99–101.

[4] Baluze–Mollat, *VPA* ii (Paris, 1927), p. 188 cites Bernard Gui's description of the occasion.

[5] Ibid., p. 252.

place. The wording does not make clear at whose initiative this request was made.[6] The chapter had already shown its concern for fairness in academic promotions by legislating that the strict rules of priority for bachelors reading the *Sentences* should be adhered to. Ought the friars' demand to be taken as proof that even their president was not immune from public criticism during the annual meeting? Alternatively, since such a change would normally have been dealt with discreetly by the master general, whose right to organize the teaching at St Jacques was traditionally affirmed at the end of each chapter, was the request an attempt to overcome the embarrassment caused by Berengar's fortuitous absence? On either hypothesis it was time for Pierre to stand down and make way for another man. And since his later career demonstrated tastes somewhat different from those he had pursued during regency in Paris, he may have been glad to be finished with a job not entirely to his satisfaction. In any case the immediate effect of his resignation was to allow him more time for pressing affairs outside the university.

To understand Pierre's first intrusion into national politics, it is necessary to turn the clock back a little. 1316 had been a stirring year in the royal annals. When Louis X died on 5 June 1316, leaving a daughter and a pregnant wife, the succession to the throne of France was in serious doubt for the first time since 987. If Louis's second wife Clemence of Hungary produced a son, then he would be his father's heir; if not, the throne would go either to Louis's daughter Jeanne, on whose legitimacy doubt had been cast by her mother's infidelities, or to his younger brother Philip of Poitiers, who had assumed the regency as the nearest adult male relation. The wardship of Jeanne, still a minor, went to Duke Eudes of Burgundy, the unfortunate Margaret's brother.[7] In fact Clemence gave birth to a son, King John I; but he lived only five days. Philip of Poitiers then sought to set aside Jeanne's claims on the grounds that no woman could succeed to the throne and that Jeanne herself might well be illegitimate. His case was hotly contested,

[6] 'Item ordinamus et volumus quod bacalaurius qui primus incipiet in theologia Parisius, incipiat sub fratre Petro de Palude, magistro in theologia, et illi dictus fr. Petrus in cathedra cedere teneatur', Reichert, ed., *Acta*, ii. 104. *CUP* ii. 203-4, no. 744.

[7] See C. M. Martin, 'The Enforcement of the Rights of the Kings of France in the Duchy and County of Burgundy, 1285-1363', B.Litt. thesis (Oxford, 1965). For the wider problems involved, see A. W. Lewis, *Royal Succession in Capetian France: Studies on Familial Order and the State* (Cambridge, Mass. and London, 1981), pp. 187-90.

both by Eudes and by the nobles of Champagne, which county Jeanne claimed from her grandmother Mahaud of Artois. Their opposition to Philip's accession to the throne of France created a crisis, soon to be exacerbated by support for Eudes from the Count of Flanders and his son the Count of Nevers. Civil war seemed to threaten. But Eudes was not prepared to risk an act that might be counted as treason; when Louis of Nevers began hostilities, the duke disassociated himself from his pugnacious ally. It thus emerged that he was less concerned for his niece's succession than for her—and his—adequate compensation should she abandon her claim. There was room for negotiation.

Between September 1317 and 27 March 1318 chosen arbitrators, the archbishop of Rouen, Henri (lord of Sully), Count Amadeus of Savoy and his son Edward, Guichard de Beaujeu, and Mile de Noyers[8] toiled to reconcile the parties, backed by John XXII who nominated Berengar of Landorra and the archbishop of Bourges to assist them. During the course of the negotiations, Pierre de la Palud was added to their number, and he signed the final treaty.[9] As was so often the case, the arbitrators had difficulty in persuading both Philip and Eudes to appear before them at the same time, but eventually they succeeded, and by 27 March they had worked out an agreement, which included a marriage alliance and a hefty pay-off to the duke. Pierre probably played a minor role in the highly self-interested bargaining that led up to the treaty, though his inclusion among the arbitrators argues for some contribution to the breakthrough. From the perspective of his future career, it was important that he had worked alongside the great men of France, in particular the count of Savoy, with whom his family had traditional links, and that he became known both to the Burgundian Capetians and to the new royal family. The significance of this newly forged link was made apparent on 27 August 1319 when, as the last stage of the pacification process, Queen Jeanne made a will ensuring the eventual inheritance of the county of Burgundy to her new son-in-law, Duke Eudes of Burgundy.[10] In this document she nominated Pierre as one of

[8] P. Lehugeur, *Histoire de Philippe le Long, roi de France 1316–1322* (reissue Geneva, 1975), pp. 101–2 n. 6.

[9] *Registres du Trésor des chartes*, ii. 1. *Règnes de Louis X et de Philippe V le long*, ed. J. Guérout (Paris, 1966), nos. 1491–4. This inclusion suggests that Pierre was at that time acting as Berengar's chosen companion. On the timing, see Inventaire du Trésor des chartes du roy, Reg.JJ. 55, vol. ii, 1501.

[10] S. Guichenon, *Histoire de Bresse et de Bugey* (Lyons, 1650), 2. 2. 287; *Inventaire du Trésor des chartes du roy*, i, Testaments, J. 403, no. 23.

her executors, proof that his connection with the original peace treaty had not been forgotten, and that his later unpopularity with the royal court had proved short-lasting.

This unpopularity arose from Pierre's involvement in the Franco-Flemish question, the grave of many political reputations. Almost immediately after the Burgundian treaty had been signed, he went down to Avignon. There he received a papal letter close, dated 1 April 1318, commanding him to go to Flanders, to persuade the count and the towns of Flanders to accept King Philip's guarantee of good faith, so that the treaty arranged between Philip and Count Robert in September 1317 could be implemented. The long Franco-Flemish war, which had provided the backdrop to the dramatic events of Philip IV's reign, was finally over. But turning the cease-fire into peace was proving very difficult. Although the issues at stake had been at least superficially resolved, the Flemish deeply distrusted the French king's commitment to the terms of the treaty; they feared that, as soon as Philip V had overcome the internal French troubles which they had exploited to their own advantage, he would seek to improve his position. Therefore they wanted to impose on him a guarantee comparable with those the French kings had traditionally exacted from Flemish counts since 1224: the king should take his oath of peace to the pope as well as to the Flemish, so that if he broke it he would incur excommunication; and the leading French nobles should be obliged to enforce the oath on Philip, with the sanction that if he violated it all oaths of fealty taken to him would automatically be dissolved. Naturally the royal procurators recoiled in horror from this demand.[11]

Pope John XXII tried to bridge the gap between the two parties during negotiations at Avignon between 12 and 27 January 1318.[12] But when he failed to convince the Flemish of the efficacy of the guarantee he had himself proposed, he decided to enforce the decision of the cardinals and other learned men he had consulted: the French king's traditional oath should be taken as adequate security. It was the task of Pierre, along with two Franciscans, Étienne de Nérac and William of Ghent,

---

[11] *Lettres secrètes*, ed. Coulon, nos. 538 and 544; for the terms of the treaty see Lehugeur, *Histoire de Philippe le Long*, pp. 56–8. On the traditional oath sworn by the counts of Flanders, see the documents collected by the author of the *Chronique Artésienne (1295–1304)*, ed. F. Funck-Brentano (Paris, 1899), pp. 3–5.

[12] On this see G. Tabacco, *La casa di Francia nell'azione politica di papa Giovanni XXII* (Istituto storico Italiano per il medio evo; Rome, 1953), pp. 114–16.

to induce the Flemish to accept the unacceptable. (He doubtless owed his nomination for this unenviable assignment to Berengar of Landorra, whom John had consulted on the issue.[13]) The mission's chances of success, small in any case, were reduced by the vagueness with which the pope expressed his wishes. Though obviously very anxious for peace, and in that cause willing to threaten the Flemish with the spiritual penalties appropriate to those who hindered a projected crusade (Philip V had taken the cross in 1313, and avowed his intention of crusading as soon as the realm was at peace[14]), John XXII nevertheless had some sympathy for Count Robert and his people. On the issue of security for the treaty, he declared himself in favour of equity rather than a rigid implementation of the law. Therefore when he enjoined his legates to hand over his letters personally to the count and the towns, he also empowered them to do, say, and promote anything else they thought would assist the cause of peace. This was a mistake. In his avid desire to have the treaty implemented, John left too much to the legates' discretion. Perhaps predictably, the result was that they quarrelled amongst themselves.

Papal flexibility towards the Flemish went hand-in-hand with deep anxiety to avoid offending the French king. Therefore John ordered his legates to show their letters to Philip in Paris before they set off for Flanders, and at the same time wrote to the king and to Henri de Sully, the king's chief minister, underlining the support expressed in his council for the French position and his own concern that Flemish obstinacy should not impede the crusade. This proved to be a fatal blunder. As soon as he had read the letters, King Philip convoked an assembly of the bishops from the north and east of his kingdom, whom he persuaded to threaten the Flemish with an interdict if they rejected the pope's advice. He then whipped up public opinion on the issue by encouraging preachers in Paris to declare from the pulpit that if the Flemish did incur excommunication by opposing the pope's wishes, they could be exterminated like Saracens. On his arrival in the city, Pierre de la Palud was

---

[13] On Berengar's advice to Pope John about Flanders see Mortier, 2. 522. Pierre's presence at Avignon at some time between October 1317 and March 1318 is attested by the production of his *iudicium* on Jean de Pouilly, see next section.

[14] C. Tyerman, 'Philip V of France, the Assemblies of 1319–20 and the Crusade', *BIHR* 57 (1984), 17–18; and 'Sed nihil fecit? The Last Capetians and the Recovery of the Holy Land', in J. Gillingham and J. C. Holt, eds., *War and Government in the Middle Ages* (Cambridge, 1984), p. 171 and n. 12.

unwise enough to join in the preaching, though according to himself in more moderate language.[15]

The ill-fated mission then set forth. The journey to Flanders was no doubt fairly comfortable, since the legates enjoyed hospitality from all churches and monasteries on the way.[16] They probably anticipated little trouble; if so, they were swiftly disillusioned. As soon as they had crossed the border into Flanders, Pierre found that he was already notorious as a preacher in Paris of vicious anti-Flemish propaganda. Rumour may have exaggerated; it had not totally misrepresented. And it was reinforced by the party's mere appearance; for, in response to the threatened interdict, all three friars had removed their priests' robes, an action the Flemish interpreted as a pre-judgement against the count and his advisers. The legates, appalled by the hostility they encountered, decided to use the latitude the Pope had granted them and tone down their message. Therefore when they came before Count Robert and his advisers at Kortrijk, Pierre as spokesman employed honeyed tones to set their fears to rest. At the centre of his discourse he placed the canonists' distinction between a papal *monitio* and an *admonitio*. Unlike a monition—the first stage in a legal process which could lead to a judicial sentence—an admonition was a mere act of charity. Since the legates were only empowered to admonish, the Flemish had no ground to fear excommunication; they could listen in comfort to the pope's message.[17] While this probably sounded banal to a canon lawyer's ears, the count's advisers were so struck by it that they asked to set it down in writing as a safeguard against the future ill-will of the French bishops. Pierre's two companions now began to feel uneasy, worried that he had gone too far along the road of conciliation. The French certainly came to agree with their judgement; when Pierre's words were reported in Paris, they were construed as providing the Flemish with an undertaking that the pope was not obliging them to accept Philip's security.[18]

Though reassured by the legates' unequivocal statement, the count's men were still furious at the rumours they had heard of

[15] Baluze-Mansi, *Miscellanea*, ii. 255. For a sermon of similar import delivered earlier, see J. Leclerq, 'Un sermon prononcé pendant la guerre de Flandre sous Philippe le Bel', *Revue du moyen âge latin*, 1 (1945), 168–72.

[16] *Lettres secrètes*, ed. Coulon, no. 552.

[17] Baluze-Mansi, *Miscellanea*, ii. 251–7.

[18] 'Papa nichil nobis precipit, sed tantum consulit. Unde non nos reputamus in aliquo obligatos', Baluze-Mollat, *VPA* i. 122.

Pierre's sermons and at his refusal to wear his priest's robes. When the advocate Baldwin of Zenebeke[19] upbraided him for these, Pierre produced an overly subtle self-justification, replete with canon law niceties, which only increased his two Franciscan companions' distrust of him. Observing his failure to calm Flemish wrath, Pierre nervously over-reacted. Theatrically he begged for pardon, crying out that he had only one life and could suffer death but once. While he later purported to believe these words had moved his audience, Étienne de Nérac and William of Ghent said they had simply irritated the Flemish, who had had no intention whatever of killing the papal envoys.

The preliminaries over, Pierre now tried to persuade the count to accept the pope's advice. He recalled the parable of the father who asked his two sons to go down to work in his vineyard: one refused point blank, but later changed his mind and went; the other agreed very pleasantly, but in fact failed to turn up. The relevance of this parable was at once disputed. The count denied he had committed himself in advance to accepting the pope's judgement on security; he was therefore free to reject it now. Disconcerted, Pierre shifted ground. Since all recent victories had been Flemish, they could afford to be generous; peace would offer them great advantages, whereas continuing in obstinacy might bring excommunication on them. Count Robert ought to hold a council of all his ecclesiastics to discuss the pope's advice; if they told him to accept it he should do so; if not, he could reject it with impunity. At this point Étienne de Nérac's anger was kindled; after the interview he expostulated violently with Pierre in private on the dangers of taking this line. But if Pierre's words infuriated his collaborators, they did nothing to sway his enemies because, having suggested a council, he then declared any cleric who advised the count against accepting papal advice to be unworthy of his tonsure. Count Robert, hearing this, concluded that a council would be futile, and blamed Pierre for the failure to provide sensible guidance.

It swiftly became clear that the mission was getting nowhere. The count was not amenable to persuasion. However, there was still the second part of their duty to perform, the delivery of the Pope's letters to the towns. Robert refused the legates his permission to do this; instead he required them to hand the

[19] He was described as one who 'avoit touz les jours trouvé poins pour le conte tenir en sa rebellion', *Les Grandes Chroniques*, ed. J. Viard, viii (Paris, 1934), p. 350.

letters to the representatives of the towns who were present in Bruges during the negotiations. (This determination that the sealed letters be opened all together in Bruges suggests some suspicion on the count's part that they might after all contain a papal excommunication.) While Pierre was happy to fall in with this suggestion, the two Franciscans regarded it as incompatible with their instructions, and insisted on refusing. There was therefore nothing more for the legates to do in Flanders. Étienne waited behind in case Count Robert wished to communicate with the curia by them; but on being told he would send his own messengers later, he rejoined the others, and together they journeyed south to St Denis.[20]

Pierre's reception in Paris, initially unfavourable, was made downright hostile by a sermon he preached before the court on the text: 'Scandals will arise, but woe to the man through whom they arise', which was interpreted as a deliberate attack on the king. According to the friar's critics, even Amadeus of Savoy, presumably his protector,[21] told him to hold his tongue when he attempted to defend himself against Henri de Sully's anger. Henri freely exploited the differences between Pierre and his Franciscan colleagues, who now openly upbraided the Dominican for making the Flemish more intransigent. Their allegation formed the basis of an accusation which King Philip decided to bring against Pierre before the papal court.

Pierre therefore left Paris for Avignon, and on 1 and 2 July 1318 appeared before the pope to answer the charge. His initial alarm was doubtless somewhat appeased when he saw that John XXII had chosen as his assistants two Dominicans, Cardinal Guillaume Pierre de Godin and Hervé de Nédellec—hardly likely to be totally disinterested parties. Nevertheless, the process was full and formal. Étienne and William made out their case against Pierre, demonstrating (to a modern eye) his incompetence rather than his dishonesty. Two points in his favour emerged as the judges questioned William: first, the Flemish friar had failed to act as interpreter for the party, despite his having been chosen with this role in mind; problems of misunderstanding were therefore predictable. Secondly, the

---

[20] Robert in fact arranged for a meeting between the French and the Flemish at Compiègne in August 1318, but when the time came the Flemish apparently failed to send proper representatives. Baluze-Mollat, *VPA* i. 122, *Grandes Chroniques*, ed. Viard, viii. 342.

[21] This incident confirms Pierre's closeness to the house of Savoy in Paris. It is quite possible that Archbishop Pierre recommended Pierre to his brother in 1310.

judges were inclined to think the legates would have achieved more if they had stayed longer; the Franciscans had unduly hastened their departure. Pierre then spoke in his own defence, accepting most of his accusers' statements of fact but adding his own explanations and different emphases. The process culminated in his swearing an oath that he had said and done nothing in the whole mission which was deliberately designed to impede negotiations or to make the Flemish more obdurate. As far as the pope was concerned, the issue, which was one of intention, not effect, was now resolved. And though King Philip expostulated, both immediately and again in September, John categorically asserted Pierre's good faith.[22] In April or May 1319, he wrote in a more conciliatory tone to Philip, admitting that Pierre might have been at fault, but saying that his undoubted loyalty to the king had brought about his total reinstatement in the pope's favour.[23] Officially the whole affair was now over.

The survival of the papal inquest into the mission has been harmful to Pierre's reputation among historians. Tabacco, for example, has spoken of his 'infelice condotta'.[24] It is, of course, easy to criticize men thrust into a diplomatic hornet's nest, to imagine that a different way of handling affairs might have been more successful. In fact the next two papal legations to Flanders were no more fruitful. The Flemish would only accept King Philip's guarantee when it became clear that it was in their own interests to do so; in other words, not before May 1320. Furthermore, Pope John XXII's wish to offer them some inducement, combined with his fear of offending Philip, had made things very difficult. Nevertheless, it must be admitted that Pierre had added to his problems by indiscreet sermons in Paris both before and after the mission; and by his penchant for fine scholastic distinctions, reinforced by over-dramatic gestures. Understandably in a practised advocate, he was temperamentally prone to throw himself totally into the cause of the moment, with rather little thought for the future consequences of his stand. The Flemish mission was, however, an unfortunate occasion on which to exhibit that trait. John XXII's confidence in Pierre's skills was not shaken as a consequence of this débâcle; as we shall see, he used him again in the succeeding years to investigate ecclesiastical questions. But he seems to have decided either that Pierre was too learned

---

22 *Lettres secrètes*, ed. Coulon, no. 706.
23 Ibid., no. 878.
24 *La casa di Francia*, p. 119.

to be useful among crude laymen, or that his skills did not lie in diplomacy; for he did not send Pierre on another diplomatic mission until 1329, when his target was the Sultan of Egypt, who could be relied on to react unemotionally to canon law distinctions.

As for Pierre, his release from the legation was almost certainly a great relief. He had found to his cost that there was no middle course between the Flemish and the French, since both adamantly held that 'he who is not with me is against me'. Doubtless deeply wounded by the criticism to which he had been exposed, he was glad to spend a couple of years at the papal court in Avignon, while the storm blew over in Paris. It is possible, however, that the impending trial had blighted his prospects of promotion within the Dominican order at a vital moment. At the Lyons general chapter in June 1318, when Hervé de Nédellec was chosen master general in succession to Berengar of Landorra, it had been Jacques de Lausanne, not Pierre, who had stepped into his shoes as prior provincial of France.[25]

(b) Avignon

Before his promotion to the cardinalate and then to the papacy, Jacques Duèse of Cahors had been bishop of Avignon. There he felt at home, as his predecessor Pope Clement V had not. The climate, the language, the food was familiar. The town enjoyed a political calm that Rome had long lacked. It was accessible to the rest of the world down the Rhône valley, yet at the same time less open to unwanted political pressures than Lyons, where Innocent IV had taken refuge. There was, of course, the castle erected by Philip IV on the other side of the river at Villeneuve; but the French presence was too slight to threaten. It would be pleasant to remain there. On the other hand, Pope John XXII was well aware that he had been elected bishop of Rome, and that the prerogatives through which he claimed to reform the church derived from his apostolic succession as heir of St Peter. Could the pope stay permanently outside Rome? It was a thorny question. Pierre de la Palud, whose advice on the point was sought, permitted him to transfer his see to another city, as St Peter had done in moving from

---

[25] 'Frater Jacobus de Lausanna, magister in theologia Parisius, successit in provincialatu fratri Herveo', A. de Guimaraes, 'Hervé Noël († 1323): Étude biographique', *AFP* 8 (1938), 70 and n. 55.

Antioch to Rome; but if John was not willing to take so drastic a step, then Pierre thought he should not remain away from the eternal city for any length of time except for pressing reasons (*DPP*, pp. 188–90). And his advice was strengthened by others.[26]

Therefore in John's pontificate the curia's residence at Avignon was officially regarded as temporary; indeed, it was not until his successor's reign that even the foundation stone for the papal palace was laid there. In the meantime the large papal entourage had to make do in rooms inadequate both in number and in size. Its discomfort was matched by that of the townsfolk; as suppliants and envoys poured in to do business at the court, Avignon became cramped beyond endurance. The Aragonese envoys, writing to King James II in 1316, had complained that 'the streets were full of mud, and the stench unbearable'.[27] While Clement V had compensated his followers for their poor quarters by giving them a high standard of feasting and service,[28] Pope John's determination to cut back on expenditure put an end to this. Austerity was the order of the day.

The large Dominican house between the city wall and the Rhône, which had offered intermittent hospitality to Clement, was presumably Pierre's home from 1318 to 1320. There he will have taken pleasure in the excellence of the company; for Masters of Theology and other learned Dominicans flocked to Avignon, drawn to the city in part by the reputation of the papal school, which in 1318 was under the mastership of Guillaume de Laudun, an old acquaintance of Pierre's from St Jacques; and also by the presence of the Dominican cardinals, among them Guillaume de Pierre Godin, with whom Pierre became intimate.[29] This group felt a sense of excitement, of being at the centre of power, as they took advantage of their opportunity to press the new pope for ecclesiastical reforms of their own devising. Now that the corruption of Clement V's pontificate had been cleansed, particularly by the bull *Execrabilis* of 19 November 1317 (which reinforced existing legislation

---

[26] For Guillaume de Pierre Godin's tough line on the question see W. D. McCready, *The Theory of Papal Monarchy in the Fourteenth Century: Guillaume de Pierre Godin, 'Tractatus de causa immediata ecclesiastice potestatis'* (Toronto, 1982), p. 18.

[27] H. Finke, ed., *Acta Aragonensia*, i. 224, no. 147, quoted in K. M. Setton, *The Papacy and the Levant, 1204–1571*, i (Philadelphia, 1976), p. 175 and n. 57.

[28] See B. Guillemain, *La Cour pontificale d'Avignon (1309–1376): Étude d'une société* (BEFAR; Paris, 1962), pp. 44–6, on Clement V's expenditure for his entourage.

[29] See McCready, *Theory of Papal Monarchy*, pp. 9–33.

against pluralism), it was time to turn to wider issues. The serious doctrinal problems of the church awaited resolution, and Pope John was known to be willing to tackle them.

Arriving in Avignon at a time of ferment, Pierre at once found himself at its heart. His own escape from the dock forgotten by everyone with amazing rapidity, he was almost immediately appointed to one of the first papal commissions authorized to examine potentially deviant doctrines. These commissions have recently been described as 'a large-scale take-over by the papal court of functions hitherto widely distributed among universities, diocesan and provincial councils and the general chapters of religious orders'.[30] Both in his quodlibet and in the *De potestate Papae* Pierre had in fact urged the pope to take the initiative and put an end to doctrinal disputes as only he had the authority to do. Therefore he was in total sympathy with John's centralizing step. And since the commissions, though they investigated propositions not people, were similar to trials, his legal experience naturally recommended him for membership. He was in the right place at the right time.

One of the most urgent problems Pope John XXII faced on his accession was the rift within the Franciscan order between the Conventuals, under the master of the order Michael of Cesena, and the various groups of dissidents, many Italian and South French, who claimed that they alone were the true heirs of their founder. For these Spirituals, the imitation of St Francis's apostolic poverty involved a rigid regime of austerity at odds with the learning and clericality of the late thirteenth- and early fourteenth-century order. They denied themselves all but the minimum necessities of life, wore short cloaks as an outward sign of their commitment to poverty, and railed against the corruption of their brethren. Under pressure to conform with Conventual ways, they had in the course of the thirteenth century developed a defiant prophetic interpretation of history, tinged with the teaching of Joachim of Fiore, according to which the conversion of St Francis had inaugurated the sixth age of the church, an era of persecution for those of the true faith, which would end in the appearance of Antichrist, according to some in the person of a pope; the seventh age would then see the triumph of those once persecuted and the final victory of Christ. John XXII's reaction was summed up in

---

[30] R. W. Southern, 'The Changing Role of Universities in Medieval Europe', *BIHR* 60 (1987), 140. See also W. J. Courtenay 'Inquiry and Inquisition: Academic Freedom in Medieval Universities', *Church History*, 58 (1989), 168–81.

his letter *Quorumdam exigit* of 7 October 1317, in which he declared firmly that in the religious life, the duty of obedience came before poverty and chastity. The Spirituals must conform, both in their outward clothing and in their inner thoughts, to the orders of their master general and of the pope.

Direct command was supplemented by indirect pressure. Pierre Jean Olieu (henceforth referred to as Olivi), a distinguished Franciscan author who had died in 1298, was regarded by many Spirituals both as a saint and as the academic proponent of views essentially in accord with theirs. The complicated and controversial question of whether this was really so need not concern us here.[31] But their belief had spurred the Conventuals to constant attacks on Olivi's writings. Despite Clement V's initial reluctance to become involved, he had felt obliged to do something to still the storm within the order; under his guidance the Council of Vienne on 6 May 1312 had rejected four of what were understood to be Olivi's theses.[32] But this insult to their hero's memory failed to diminish recruitment to the Spiritual cause in Southern France, Italy, and Catalonia, or to halt the spread of their ideas to the beguins (lay followers). In 1317 Provençal Dominicans were so worried about the veneration in which Olivi was held that they destroyed his shrine at Narbonne and scattered his remains, to prevent the celebration of his feast day. But the recording of miracles went on and by 1318 the situation was critical. In response to an appeal for help from Michael of Cesena, John XXII judged that the time was now ripe for a close examination of Olivi's great prophetic work, the *Postill on the Apocalypse of St. John the Divine*, in which many readers had detected criticism of the Roman church, and which the Conventuals had condemned at the general chapter of Marseilles.

The initiative in prosecuting the case lay with Nicholas, cardinal bishop of Ostia, who extracted from the *Postill* a large number of passages he thought either heretical or 'temerarius' —ill considered. These he submitted to a panel of eight masters

---

[31] See R. Manselli, *La 'Lectura super Apocalipsim' di Pietro di Giovanni Olivi* (Rome, 1955); M. Reeves, *Joachim of Fiore and the Prophetic Tradition* (Oxford, 1969), pp. 194–201; D. Flood, *Peter Olivi's Rule Commentary* (Wiesbaden, 1972); M. D. Lambert, 'The Franciscan Crisis under John XXII', *Franciscan Studies*, 32 (1972), 123–43; D. Burr, *The Persecution of Olivi* (Transactions of the American Philosophical Society, n.s. 66. 5; Philadelphia, 1976.) On the whole question of Olivi and papal authority, see B. Tierney, *The Origins of Papal Infallibility, 1150–1350* (Leiden, 1972), ch. 3.

[32] Burr, *The Persecution of Olivi*, pp. 79–80.

of theology, presided over by Gui de Terreni, master general of the Carmelites, and including both Pierre and Guillaume de Pierre Godin. The masters, who received a copy of the commentary, had first to satisfy themselves that each passage did indeed come from it, and then to record under their own seals their judgement on each.[33] This procedure somewhat distanced them from the work as a whole and limited their opportunities to assess Olivi's intentions, since they could interpret the individual excerpts as they chose. Furthermore, they were free to condemn an article not for what it explicitly said, but for what they thought it might imply, and to brand it ill considered if the unlearned might understand it in a heretical sense. As a trial of Olivi's orthodoxy, the examination was at best inadequate; as a means of protecting the early fourteenth-century church from Spiritualist teaching it was more effective.

The suspect doctrines the masters found in Olivi's *Postills* concerned, first, the person of St Francis: he was portrayed as a figure second to Christ alone in the history of Christianity. This they condemned as unjust to all the saints of the New Testament. The claim that the rule of St Francis was the true evangelical rule of Christ undervalued the exemplary achievement of the primitive church under St Peter; it was ridiculous if read as meaning that the two were identical (here the masters prepared the ground for John XXII's bull *Cum inter nonnullos* of 1323) and heretical if understood as placing the rule beyond the authority of the pope and the Roman church.[34] Secondly, the masters condemned as 'temeraria et figmenta irrationabilia' a central prophecy: that the sixth age of the church, inaugurated by St Francis, and its successor the seventh, would be as much holier than the first five ages as the church was holier than the synagogue. This went hand in hand with the belief that the Roman church's primacy in the first five ages was being justifiably superseded in the sixth. Here lay the most dangerous aspect of the book: Olivi's apparent identification of the Roman church with the *ecclesia carnalis* which in the sixth age would be subordinated to the true *ecclesia spiritualis*. (Some Spirituals went beyond this to allege that the *ecclesia carnalis* had commited adultery against Christ her lord.[35]) Like the Waldensians before them, Olivi's followers had been led by their own reforming zeal to heap criticism on a church that did not follow

[33] *CUP* ii. 238–9, no. 790.

[34] On the 15th-cent. allegation that this clause was added later, see below, ch. 5, n. 86.

[35] Baluze–Mansi, *Miscellanea*, ii. 258–70.

their own rule. They would have to pay the penalty for their presumption.[36]

Having completed their examination of the propositions put to them, the masters each sealed the lengthy scroll on which their views were inscribed. It now became a semi-legal document, an official statement of unacceptable opinions.[37] The pope's immediate aim in ordering its compilation was to dissuade intellectual sympathizers of the South French and Italian Spirituals from throwing in their lot with them. Those whose minds were not completely closed might hesitate before committing themselves to views which had been explicitly condemned by the church. In conformity with this aim, Pierre and his colleagues on the panel defined faith for the present and established censorship for the future; they did not seriously sit in judgement on the past. They assumed that had Olivi been alive to recant the theses he would have done so, and therefore his reputation remained intact. The reluctance of the curia to condemn so well known a scholar delayed the final judgement against him until February 1326 when, at the climax of the struggle over Franciscan poverty, Pope John finally pronounced him a heretic. But even while the masters were deliberating, four Spirituals who had refused to bow to *Quorumdam exigit* were burned for heresy at Marseilles, thus illustrating the difference in the treatment habitually enjoyed by the learned and that meted out to poor dissidents.

Pierre probably contributed more in presence than in substance to the Olivi proceedings, the bulk of the work being done by Cardinal Nicholas and Guillaume de Laudun, master of the papal school.[38] While they were busy, Pierre and Gui de Terreni were engaged on another task: at the request of the pope, they read and criticized a small book entitled *De statibus ecclesie secundum expositionem Apocalypsis*, written in Catalan by an unknown Franciscan, setting forth in a slightly different context many of the propositions declared heretical in Olivi's work. Since Gui de Terreni came from Catalonia, he can have had no problem in reading the text; but the choice of Pierre de

---

[36] Burr, *The Persecution of Olivi*, p. 85.

[37] It may have influenced Bernard Gui in his *Manuel de l'Inquisiteur*, ed. and tr. G. Mollat (Paris, 1964), i. 113; the tenets he ascribes to the beguins are very close to those found in the masters' propositions; see M. Reeves, *The Influence of Prophecy in the Later Middle Ages: A Study of Joachimism* (Oxford, 1969), pp. 221-2.

[38] J. Koch, 'Der Prozess gegen die Postille Olivis zur Apokalypse', *RTAM* 5 (1933), 302-13.

la Palud as his coadjutor should perhaps be taken as a tribute to his linguistic skills. There were, after all, many men from the Midi at the curia; Pierre was far from the most obvious candidate for the job.

The book they examined has not survived. But thanks to Pierre's insistence on quoting extensively from any work on which he commented, its main lines of argument can be reconstructed.[39] The author postulated three ages in the history of the world, those of the Father, described in the Old Testament and concluded with the birth of Christ, of the Son, described in the New Testament and coming towards its end in the author's lifetime, and of the Holy Spirit, which would be inaugurated by the judgement of Babylon and end with the Second Coming. Gui and Pierre agreed that there might be some truth in parts of this schema, but affirmed that it was dangerous to preach it to the common people—'periculosum est vulgaribus sic loqui' (an instance of the clergy objecting to statements in the vernacular which would have concerned them less if expressed in Latin). But—as with the Postill—the real trouble arose when the author linked the church as he knew it in his own day with the Babylon to be judged, contending that its sins would bring about its destruction, and that only a small group of the elect, the Friars Minor who lived according to true poverty, would survive to form the church in the third age. St Francis, as the angel who opened the sixth seal, had heralded the end of the second age and the coming of Antichrist. Disasters and wretchedness would follow; the elect would be persecuted. But in the end Antichrist would be vanquished. The Rule of St Francis, which was Christ's rule, would ultimately prove to be the vehicle for salvation—'St. Francis is, after Christ, the first and principal founder, teacher and observer of the evangelical rule' ('beatus Franciscus post Christum est primus et principalis fundator et inceptor ac contemplator regule evangelice'). Following his example the elect would then convert the whole world.

Predictably Gui and Pierre were incensed by the allegation that the church of Rome was a carnal church, corrupted by property-holding and unworthy to survive. As they said, 'The faith of the church, under the special guidance of the Roman church, remains, has remained and shall remain without either

[39] Ed. J. M. Pou y Marti, OFM, *Visionarios, beguinos y fraticelos catalanes (siglos XIII-XV)* (Vich, 1930), pp. 483-512. See G. Leff, *Heresy in the Later Middle Ages: The Relation of Heterodoxy to Dissent, c.1250-c.1450* (Manchester and New York, 1967), i. 211.

stain or wrinkle' ('Fides ecclesie ad regimen precipue Romane ecclesie manet, mansit et manebit absque macula et ruga').[40] They interpreted Christ's words 'I shall be with you to the end of the world' as proof that the church as they knew it would last until the second coming. To assert that only those religious who rigidly observed poverty constituted the true church was wicked, poisonous, and heretical—'pessimum, venenosum et hereticalem'; common ownership of goods as practised by most religious orders was entirely justified. Furthermore, the tract betrayed excessive reverence for St Francis and exaggerated his part in the history of the world. The saint himself would have been dismayed by the role his disciples had accorded him, since he was a humble man. Besides, St Francis was not mentioned in the Apocalypse; Bonaventura's identification of him as the angel of the sixth seal was not binding on Christians; and those who accepted it should interpret it spiritually not literally. As the doctrine was vulgarly understood it was heretical. Furthermore, the whole idea of an age of the Holy Spirit undermined the significance of Pentecost and limited the importance of the Day of Judgement. To believe that the small group of elect in the third age would be of greater dignity and authority than the apostles had been was to attach more significance to prophecy than to Scripture. In their final peroration against the Catalan work, Gui and Pierre characterized it as above all an attack on the fourteenth-century church; it must be totally misguided, since the alternative hypothesis, that all the doctors of the church had erred, was incredible.

The Avignon period thus opened Pierre's eyes to dangers within the cult of poverty that he had not hitherto suspected. In condemning Olivi and the unknown Catalan author, he believed himself to be upholding not only the Roman church but also the true Franciscan order. As he said, the whole church knew that the Conventuals kept the rule in the sense in which it had been intended; only the Spirituals preferred their own interpretation, and through their arrogance had incurred the wrath first of their own order and now of the pope. The persecutions they were enduring were the fruit of their own obstinacy, not a sign of the coming of Antichrist. At the root of the Spirituals' heresy lay their identification of Franciscan poverty with the life lived by Christ and his apostles, despite the Scriptural statements

---

[40] I interpret the emphasis on 'Roman' here as necessitated by the Catalan pamphlet's vocabulary. I do not agree with T. Turley, 'Infallibilists at the curia of Pope John XXII', *Journal of Medieval History*, 1 (1975), 78, that it demonstrates Pierre's continued adherence to a doctrine of papal infallibility.

that Christ had had four tunics, and that Judas had carried money in his bag to succour the apostles. The Spirituals compounded this error by alleging that the life of the elect in the age of the Holy Spirit would be purer and finer than that of the early Christians. They were as wrong about the past as they were subject to delusions about the future. And the small element of their creed that went back to genuine Franciscan sources, above all to Bonaventura, they twisted in such a way as to make it a snare for the unlearned. Granted the danger their ideas posed for Christianity, Pierre and Gui thought it fair to equate the Catalan tract with the *Eternal Evangel* (Gerard of Borgo San Donnino's pamphlet condemned in 1256), and to regard the proceedings against that notorious work as a precedent for their judgement.[41] In their eyes all apocalyptical thinkers were tarred with the same brush.

It is relevant to the uncompromising nature of Pierre's criticism that he thought he was dealing with a tiny minority of fanatics. The Conventuals had attacked their own brethren with such violence that the Spirituals had in recent years shunned the curia, and Pierre had presumably never met one. He judged them only by what they had written, or what they were alleged to have written. It was their arrogance, their claim to monopoly of perfection, that particularly upset him, trained as he was in a pluralistic tradition. This explains why, as they piled up their criticisms, he and Gui went further than they probably realized in attacking beliefs held also by Conventuals. By disputing the thesis that Christ and his apostles had observed Franciscan poverty, and by casting doubt on the role of St Francis as the angel of the sixth seal, they in fact struck at the heart of widely accepted Franciscan tradition. Their work may have been responsible in some small measure at least for encouraging Pope John XXII to follow his own convictions in 1322-3, when he challenged the orthodoxy of the doctrine of apostolic poverty.

The bulk of Pierre's stay at Avignon was taken up not with the Spirituals, but with the trial of Jean de Pouilly. Much of this was shadow boxing. Although a friend of the Dominicans and initially of the Conventual Franciscans, Pope John XXII had

[41] H. Lee, M. Reeves, and G. Silano, *Western Mediterranean Prophecy: The School of Joachim of Fiore and the Fourteenth-Century 'Breviloquium'* (Toronto, 1989), pp. 67-70. For Gui de Terreni's later treatment of the theme of apostolic poverty, see M.-T. d'Alverny, 'Un adversaire de St Thomas: Petrus Johannis Olivi', *St Thomas Aquinas, 1274-1974: Commemorative Studies* (Toronto, 1974), ii. 189.

begun his pontificate with one firm resolution: he was not prepared to reopen the question of mendicant privileges to preach and hear confessions. The Council of Vienne's decree *Dudum*, which had revoked *Inter cunctas* and reaffirmed the validity of *Super cathedram*, was to be promulgated, despite the intense pressure of the friars brought to secure its modification. On 25 October 1317, the decrees of the Council of Vienne, *Dudum* among them, became part of canon law. The friars had no alternative but to obey. The Dominican chapter general sadly, perhaps even bitterly, ordered its members to adhere strictly to the new law.[42] But no man refuses his friends' dearest wish without trying to soften the blow. Pope John's way of achieving this was to allow a lengthy show trial of Jean de Pouilly in Avignon. If the mendicants were to be denied their privileges, they should at least have the satisfaction of seeing their most tireless opponent condemned for his temerity. Despite the interest the incident has aroused among intellectual historians—Koch, Sikes, Tierney, Zuckerman[43]—the trial's true significance lay not in the realm of thought but of consolation prizes. The noise and agitation boiled down to nothing more than the removal of a very small piece of grit from the ecclesiastical machine.

The arguments on both sides had not changed since 1314–15, when Pierre had dealt with them in his quodlibet and—in more abstract form—in the *De potestate Papae*. But after the provincial synod at Senlis, the adversaries had taken them from the relative calm of the schools out to the pulpits of the Paris area. Some Franciscans alleged that Jean, in his speech in the vernacular at Senlis, had not only waxed indignant about the appalling nonsense friars preached—a charge Jean admitted—but also thundered that by hearing confessions the friars were poisoning a large part of the world and would take it to hell with them—which Jean denied. He, on the other hand, accused some of his opponents of preaching that it was more efficacious to visit a tavern or a brothel than to take sacraments from sinful priests. He further upbraided the master of the Franciscan house in Paris for ascribing to him in a disputation opinions exactly the opposite of those he actually held,

[42] Mortier, ii. 536, iii. 19 n. 2.

[43] J. Koch, 'Der Prozess gegen den Magister Johannes de Polliaco und seine Vorgeschichte (1312–1321)', *RTAM* 5 (1933), 394–7; J. G. Sikes, 'John de Pouilli and Peter de la Palu', *EHR* 49 (1943), 219–40; Tierney, *The Origins of Papal Infallibility*; C. A. Zuckerman, 'Dominican Theories of the Papal Primacy, 1250–1320, Ph.D. thesis (Cornell University, 1971).

thereby provoking a riot in the school.[44] If this slanging-match was unedifying, it was also parochial, and could in normal circumstances have been ended fairly rapidly. But the papal interregnum from April 1314 to August 1316 had entailed the absence of a mutually acceptable arbitrator to calm the atmosphere.

John's election was the signal for a group of Franciscans, presumably those of Paris, to send the new pope an indictment accusing Jean de Pouilly of thirteen serious errors. This document John submitted to a number of intellectuals at Avignon,[45] including Pierre de la Palud, who was there with Berengar of Landorra. Already familiar with the background to the whole controversy, Pierre produced, between October 1317 and March 1318, a lengthy and one-sided *Iudicium* on the indictment, taking all the charges as proved (thereby showing himself less fair to Jean than he had been to Durand, Olivi, or the Catalan author), and putting new emphasis on the danger to the Roman church he descried in Jean's ideas. (It is true that Jean, educated in Paris during the days when Nogaret and Plaisians pursued their vendetta against Boniface VIII, had been less than tactful in his criticism of Pope Benedict XI.) In particular Pierre pointed out that many current practices of the curia, restricting or extending the jurisdiction of particular bishops or curates, were incompatible with Jean's claim that priests' and bishops' jurisdiction was bestowed on them by Christ (Vienna, Österreichische Nationalbibliotek, MS 2168, fo. 12ʳ); Jean was by implication casting doubt on their validity.

Pierre's defence of *Inter cunctas* remained the one he had enunciated in his quodlibet; but his ecclesiology now owed more to Hervé de Nédellec's *De ecclesiastica potestate et papali*[46] than to his own *De potestate Papae*. He interpreted the Petrine commission and Christ's last words to Peter before the Ascension as suggesting that whatever the situation for the apostles and disciples, their successors the bishops and parish

---

[44] *Responsio Johannis*, Vienna, Österreichische Nationalbibliothek, MS 2168, fo. 12ᵛ.

[45] Y. Congar, 'Aspects ecclésiologiques de la querelle entre mendiants et séculiers dans la seconde moitié de xiiiᵉ siècle et le début du xivᵉ', *ADHLMA* 28 (1961), 68; A. Maier, *Ausgehendes Mittelalter: Gesammelte Aufsätze zur Geistesgeschichte des 14 Jahrhunderts* (Rome, 1964–77), ii. 511–16. On the chronology see Koch, 'Der Prozess gegen den Magister Johannes de Polliaco', pp. 394–7.

[46] Ed. Barbier (Paris, 1506), under the title 'Durandus de Sancto Porciano, *De iurisdictione*'.

priests owed their powers in individual dioceses and parishes to the pope.[47] The *Iudicium* has aroused modern historians of ecclesiology to complain of Pierre's inconsistency.[48] But, acting on this occasion in the role of a semi-official advocate for the mendicant cause, he felt free to state the case in terms more extreme and more persuasive than those he had earlier employed to express his own opinion. (However, his choice does indicate the relative insignificance of ecclesiological principles in contemporaries' views of the affair.) His advocacy achieved its immediate purpose: it moved John XXII on 27 June 1318 to cite Jean to appear at Avignon. And he arrived in the town at almost the same time as Pierre returned from Flanders. The stage was now set for three years of tiresome wrangling, at the beginning of which Pierre played the part of prosecuting counsel.

The consistory was summoned. Jean introduced his defence by protesting his reverence and obedience to the pope and cardinals. He then replied to Pierre's elaboration of the *Iudicium* that many of the charges grossly misrepresented what he had said; that his accusers took literally some comments he had made ironically; and that he had intended no disrespect to the Holy See in trying to confound the friars. However, he still adhered to his main points: parishioners who had confessed to friars ought to confess the same sins to their parish priests; *Inter cunctas* was not an interpretation but a subversion of *Omnis utriusque sexus*; and since bishops and priests had received their power to bind and loose directly from Christ it could not be justly taken from them. He concluded by boldly challenging his opponent to deny this last contention, based as it was on the Gospels.[49] In response, Pierre argued that Jean's claim to have been misrepresented was belied by his words in other parts of his *Responsio*; that the charges to which he admitted demonstrated his denigration of the Holy See; that double confession was unacceptable because it undermined

---

[47] 'Probabile est quod successoribus apostolorum episcopis et successoribus discipulorum curatis per seipsum immediate nullos populos subiecit, sed vicario suo Petro et eius successoribus subiciendos dimisit', Vienna, Österreichische Nationalbibiothek, MS 2168, fo. 11ᵛ.

[48] See McCready, *Theory of Papal Monarchy*, pp. 26–8; Zuckerman, *Dominican Theories*, p. 169, Appendix 1.

[49] 'Quia intelligo et intellexi curatos immediate potestatem recepisse a Christo et eis esse collatam in suis predecessoribus DXXII discipulis, quod . . . non potest quis negare nisi velit dicere evangelistam discere falsum et per consequens dicere heresim', Vienna, Österreichische Nationalbibliothek, MS 2168, fo. 16ᵛ.

the sacraments; and that Jean's claim to have Gospel authority for his ecclesiological views was highly debatable. He ended, 'De ore tuo te judico' (from your own mouth I condemn you: Vienna, Österreichische Nationalbibliothek, MS 2168, fo. 35ʳ). But if Pierre had made up his mind on the issue, the consistory had not. Even an important mendicant supporter, Pierre Roger, soon to be archbishop of Reims and subsequently Pope Clement VI, would not accept the indictment as an accurate account of Jean's words.[50] It had to be shortened and redrafted to reflect the admissions Jean had actually made. And in the second stage of the trial, which opened before a new consistory in October 1319, Pierre played an insignificant part, only appearing when Jean attempted to turn the tables by making accusations based on a dim memory of what the Dominican had said in his 1314 Advent quodlibet. Pierre's *Responsiones ad ea que sibi imposuit magister Johannes de Polhiaco* (Vienna, Österreichische Nationalbibliothek, MS 2168, fos. 101ʳ-111ᵛ) effectively argued his own defence by quoting from a written report of his quodlibet and by repeating what he had already said against Jean. He was in no serious danger from charges backed only by spite; but nor on the other hand had he anything new to say.

His withdrawal from the limelight provided him with an opportunity to repackage his arguments in pamphlet form. His *Articulum circa materiam confessionum* took the issue of double confession out of the law court into the study; it was intended to be pondered over at leisure by all interested parties. Pierre reluctantly made one new concession: he agreed that the pope could, if he wished, legislate by virtue of his *potentia absoluta* to make double confession necessary. But if he did so, the new law would be purely human, not divine.[51] Otherwise his arguments were the familiar ones. However, his dry sense of humour did once emerge. Jean de Pouilly had asserted that, while there was doubt about the practice of confessing to friars, everyone agreed that confessing to parish priests was efficacious; therefore it made sense to avoid what was in doubt. Pierre replied that all sorts of things were doubted by some people. Many Paris masters regarded it as a mortal sin for a secular cleric to retain more than one fat benefice, or for any ecclesiastic to engage in money-changing. All money-changers ought, on Jean's line of argument, to be

---

50 Maier, *Ausgenhendes Mittelalter*, ii. 513-14.
51 *Articulum*, ed. Barbier (Paris, 1506), ratio 3.

condemned as mad and blind for not abandoning conduct about which at least some people felt doubts. 'But it would be hard to take this line, especially since the Roman curia publicly uses money-changers.'[52] Diplomatically he did not spell out the implications of his remark on pluralism; but his aim in introducing both Paris criticisms was clearly to jolt the cardinals into an awareness of their own vulnerability.

In the end Pierre and his fellow mendicants carried the day on the practical side of the dispute. By the bull *Vas electionis* of July 1321, Jean de Pouilly recanted his contentions that those who confessed to a friar were obliged to confess the same sins to their parish priests, that while *Omnis utriusque sexus* remained canon law even the pope could not exempt parishioners from their obligation to confess to their parish priests, and that the pope could not grant general, as opposed to special, licences to hear confessions. He undertook to declare his change of heart publicly in the schools.[53] Since he had always expressed his willingness to bow to the judgement of the Holy See there was no ground for punishing him further; and his career does not seem to have suffered. He continued to teach at the Sorbonne, where he was venerated for the rest of his life.[54]

From Pierre's point of view, what mattered was that he had won on the issue of double confession. His conclusion on *Inter cunctas*, that although it was totally annulled in so far as it was an act of legislation, in so far as it was a true declaration of faith it was irrevocable (*Articulum*, ratio 4), had been accepted as the official doctrine of the church. In practice, therefore, laymen were no longer inhibited from confessing to friars by the fear of having to repeat the process to their parish priests. On the academic plane, the consequence of the friars' victory was that canon lawyers and theologians continued to subject papal bulls to intense scrutiny in order to distinguish eternal truth from mutable command. The implications of this were to echo throughout the polemical literature of the fourteenth century.

In the short term, the gainer from the trial was the pope. John wanted to preserve both the friars' right to hear confessions and his own power to grant general privileges, while at the

---

[52] *Articulum*, ed. Barbier (Paris, 1506), ratio 4. Cf. what he said on Book 4 of the *Sentences*, 37. 2, which is discussed by P. Michaud-Quantin, 'Aspects de la vie social chez les moralistes', *Miscellanea Mediaevalia*, 3 (1964), 40; he sees no irony here.

[53] *CUP* ii. 243–5, no. 789 and 245–6, no. 799.   [54] Mortier, ii. 538.

same time insisting on the enforcement of *Super cathedram*. From this perspective the trial of Jean de Pouilly was a means to an end; all arguments irrelevant to the attainment of that end should, once it was over, be forgotten as quickly as possible. The curia was careful not to decide on the contentious ecclesiological issue that had lain behind some of the debate: whether, as Jean de Pouilly asserted, bishops and priests derived their authority directly from Christ, or whether, as Hervé de Nédellec and, echoing him, Pierre contended, all jurisdictional authority was delegated to lesser ecclesiastics by the pope. The substantial intellectual effort expended by both sides on twisting Scriptures, ransacking canons for support, and undermining the opposition's interpretations of their sources, therefore came to nought. These labours were only contributions to a ritual rugger scrum before John XXII blew the final whistle. The good of the church was the pope's one concern, and that demanded the swift end to a paltry and unedifying squabble.[55]

---

[55] During his Avignon period Pierre was also engaged in attempting, with others, to end a quarrel between Master Raoul de Perceaus and Jean de Arrebleyo, knight, and his sons, which was finally settled on 14 June 1320. The affair had aroused the interest of Jeanne, Queen of France, of Mahaud d'Artois, and of Charles de Valois. It therefore offered Pierre the opportunity to renew his links with the queen's circle and to see curial arbitration processes at first hand (*Lettres secrètes*, ed. Coulon, nos. 1089, 1090, 1096).

5. Teacher and Preacher

(a) Compilation and Exegesis

Pierre left Avignon at some time in 1320, well before the final conclusion of Jean de Pouilly's trial. On his return to Paris and St Jacques, he advised the bishop of Beauvais on what to do with a cleric who had confessed to murder.[1] The following year he was chosen as *definitor* for the French province to the general chapter of Florence, where he put his Avignon experience to good use. As one of a team of masters, headed by Hervé de Nédellec, now master general, he investigated a group of Dominicans guilty of minor asceticisms that had brought them under suspicion of Spiritualist links. In fact the panel found them innocent of any offence; but to prevent subsequent trouble, it commanded that there should in future be neither sects nor eccentric behaviour among the Preachers.[2]

This was the last occasion on which Pierre played any notable role in the central administration of his order. There is no obvious explanation for so abrupt a change in his daily occupation. Since 1314 he had been pursuing a path that led other men to greater responsibility in provincial or general chapters, to more inquests and more involvement in the outside world. During Hervé's master generalship, his patronage should have been sufficient to ensure for Pierre any promotion he might wish. Prior provincial of France would have been the next step on the ladder; but when Jacques de Lausanne died at the end of 1321 his successor was Hugues de Vaucemain.[3] Nothing more came Pierre's way. On the other hand there is no sign that he was out of favour after 1321. If he did not participate in the great Dominican enterprise of securing Thomas Aquinas's canonization in September 1323, it was because others were much closer to the saint in temperament and understanding. In fact he was probably overlooked within the order because he chose not to be remarked. He had several very important enterprises to occupy him over the next eight years, and he could not afford to be diverted from them.

---

[1] *Registres du Trésor des chartes*, ii. 1. *Règnes de Louis X et de Philippe V le long*, ed. J. Guérout (Paris, 1966), no. 3033.

[2] Reichert, ed., *Acta*, ii. 137–8.

[3] Mortier, iii. 88.

Pierre's disappearance from the public eye between 1321 and his return to Avignon in 1328 prior to his election as Patriarch of Jerusalem on 27 March 1329 makes it hard to establish what he was doing during these years. In accordance with the conventional Dominican career structure, a man of his intellectual achievement who had not been promoted to a high administrative role would have expected nomination as lector to some important provincial *studium*, to share the benefits of his theological learning with those not privileged to be educated at St Jacques.[4] In fact he seems to have been sent to Orléans, but probably as prior, since in one of his later sermons he spoke of receiving a scholar into the Orléans convent: 'Once, when I was inducting a young scholar into the order in Orléans, it happened that . . .' ('Michi accidit in Aureliensi, cum induxissem unum scolarem iuvenem ad ingressum ordinis . . .'; Clermont Ferrand, Bibliothèque municipale MS 46, fo. 171^r). The only time in Pierre's career when he was both free to reside at Orléans and sufficiently responsible to be involved in recruiting scholars was after his return from Avignon in the early 1320s. That he was there then is substantiated by several references in his sermons to events occurring in or near Orléans, including a story of a corrupt *prévot* in a small village just outside the city (Clermont Ferrand, Bibliothèque municipale, MS 46, fo. 106^r), and one about a doctor there who refused to treat patients until they had been to confession (fo. 25^r). Furthermore, he knew legends about Henry the Liberal's pilgrimage to Jerusalem (fo. 160^v) which are more likely to have been current on the Loire than in Paris. And his residence there, close to the count of Blois's lands, would explain Charles IV's choice of Pierre as negotiator with the count in 1325.

It must be assumed that Pierre found Orléans congenial; despite the lavish and noisy life-style of some of its students, it remained the ideal environment for a French canon lawyer. But the atmosphere among the scholars was still rather tense because as recently as 1320 the university had come back from a brief and unhappy exile in Nevers, following a major conflict between the masters and the inhabitants of the town.[5] The return had been the product of an uneasy compromise between the parties worked out by Pope John XXII (an old scholar of Orléans), which was reluctantly accepted both by a bare

---

[4] See the legislation of the General Chapter of Florence in 1321, in Reichert, ed., *Acta*, ii. 133–4; *CUP* ii. 241–2, no. 795.

[5] Rashdall, ii. 145–8.

majority of the townsmen and by King Philip V, who had supported them.[6] For the first few years of the new regime, both sides had to tread carefully. The masters' problems were compounded when it gradually transpired that the exile had seriously disrupted the university's academic tradition. The great reputation it had enjoyed throughout Europe during the days of Jacques de Révigny and Pierre de Belleperche was in jeopardy, new talent difficult to attract.[7] In fact it proved impossible completely to restore the university to its previous state. With the eye of hindsight the early 1320s, when Pierre was in the city, emerge as years of decline for the famous law school.

Nevertheless, Pierre probably felt relieved to be once again in the familiar atmosphere generated by lawyers. Indeed, he may even have echoed William of Mâcon's earlier praise for the intelligence of Orléans lawyers over that of Paris students, 'peritiores in jure quam Parisienses et melius intelligentes'.[8] As an inmate of the Dominican convent, he was not formally a member of the teaching staff of the university, which consisted of two doctors in Decrees, three in Decretals, and five in Civil Law.[9] But before the move to Nevers, the university congregation had met in the convent of the Friars Preachers in the city; it probably continued to do so while Pierre was there.[10] And in other ways the connection between the masters and the Dominicans had always been very close. At this time Pierre apparently gave the legal opinion later quoted and approved by the Bologna doctor Frederic de Senis,[11] which concerned the residue of a testator's estate after his specific bequests had

---

[6] For the large number of formal agreements, see M.-H. Jullien de Pommerol, ed., Sources de l'histoire de l'Université d'Orléans, i. Le Chartrier au début du XVIe siècle (Paris, 1974), particularly the inquest into the townsmen's opinions on pp. 48–9, no. 117.

[7] E. M. Meijers, Études d'histoire de droit, iii. Le Droit roman au moyen âge (Leiden, 1959), pp. 59–90, 95–105, 108. On complaints about the fewness of pupils, see M. Fournier, Statuts et privilèges des Universités françaises depuis leur fondation jusqu'en 1789 (Paris, 1890), i, no. 78.

[8] BN MS cod. reg. 3120, fo. 33, quoted by B. Hauréau, 'Guillaume de Macôn, canoniste', HLF 25 (1869), 380.

[9] Rashdall, ii. 145.

[10] De Pommerol, ed., Sources, p. vi and p. 17, no. 49; pp. 57–9, no. 135. The university was given a chapel for its meetings in 1345; Fournier, Statuts et privilèges, i, no. 29.

[11] Naples, Biblioteca Nazionale, MS I. A. 4, fo. 59^v. Although the bulk of Frederic's opinion is dated to 1324, see C. Cenci, Manoscritti Francescani della Biblioteca Nazionale di Napoli (Florence, 1971), p. 107, his endorsement of Pierre's point on the testator's state of mind must have been entered in the manuscript after 1329, since he refers to Pierre as 'Dominus frater Petrus de

been met, an appropriate problem for a canon lawyer. Frederick's attribution to Pierre of the title *doctor utriusque iuris* is the likely consequence of his being connected in men's minds with the law school at Orléans. But apart from this one opinion and a few sermons, none of Pierre's other surviving works can be assigned to his Orléans residence rather than to the period in Paris which followed it.

By 1325, Pierre had returned to St Jacques. His first-known task there was a dramatic one—to preach a sermon in the vernacular denouncing the Visconti of Milan and publicizing the indulgences available to those who would fight them.[12] This was to be his only direct involvement in John XXII's head-on clash with the Visconti, of which he presumably approved since he had endorsed in the *De potestate Papae* the claims to papal supremacy in the empire and in Italy that justified John's actions. Pierre's contribution to papal propaganda was small— his was only one of several sermons preached simultaneously in France that day. But together those sermons marked an important turning-point in Franco-Papal relations. Up till that time first Philip V and then Charles IV had exhibited some sympathy with the Visconti position, finding the root-and-branch policy of John XXII distasteful.[13] But after the Sachsenhausen appeal of 1324, in which Lewis of Bavaria had indicted John as a heretic, compromise was impossible. The king of France could no longer tolerate Lewis or his Visconti allies. Pierre's sermon was a public symbol of the pope's victory.

In terms of Pierre's career the occasion was significant as his first Paris appearance in his new job. The large body of extant sermons contained in Clermont Ferrand, Bibliothèque municipale, MS 46 supports the view that he had by now become preacher general of the Dominican French province, a position to which he must have been elected by a provincial chapter.[14] (All lesser preachers were limited as to the areas in

Palude ordinis Fratrum Praedicatorum utriusque iuris doctor et sacre pagine magister Patriarcha Jherosolimitanus'.

[12] *CUP* ii. 278, no. 835.

[13] N. Housley, *The Italian Crusades: The Papal-Angevin Alliance and the Crusades against Christian Lay Powers, 1254-1343* (Oxford, 1982), pp. 84-6.

[14] F. Stegmüller, *Repertorium Biblicum Medii Aevi*, iv (Madrid, 1954), p. 356 describes him as *concionator Parisiensis* from 1319 to 1329, but this seems too early. On the laws concerning preachers general see G. R. Galbraith, *Constitution of the Dominican Order* (Manchester, 1925), pp. 163, 169, and 172; and H. C. Scheeben, 'Prediger und Generalprediger im Dominikaner Orden des 13. Jahrhunderts', *AFP* 31 (1961), 112-41.

which they might preach; but a preacher general enjoyed the privilege of access anywhere within his province.) While still a Bachelor of Theology Pierre's sermons had earned him a reputation as an up-and-coming young man. Now in his maturity this office proved ideal for him, and he flung himself into the task with zest. Although he was once again based on St Jacques, his way of life was different from what it had previously been; for now he had turned his back on the schools. Perhaps, like the friar described by his near-contemporary Dominican historian Galuagno de la Flamma, he had grown disenchanted with the philosophical approach to Christianity, and feared that he too might be told on the Day of Judgement, *Tu non es frater sed philosophus* (you are not a friar but a philosopher).[15] He certainly lambasted his former colleagues; in a sermon preached in honour of the recently canonized Thomas Aquinas, he accused scholars of all four Parisian faculties of aiming to satisfy their vanity, not to discover the truth, in their arguments, lectures, disputations, and determinations (Clermont Ferrand, Bibliothèque municipale, MS 46, fo. 63^r). But since he was equally, if not more, critical of other professions, too much should not be made of this. More plausibly, his change of attitude represented a conscious return to the way of life he had been taught to admire at Lyons, where the influence of Humbert de Romans's writings continued to be strong, and where preaching was held in the highest regard.

Throughout the period 1321–8, whether in Orléans or in Paris, that part of Pierre's days which was not taken up with preaching was devoted to commenting on the Bible and to collecting sources for a history of the crusades. These activities could not be undertaken without helpers. By the time he returned to Paris he had a team of scribes working for him in his own chamber.[16] His enjoyment of a chamber instead of a simple cell represented a substantial modification of the original standard of Dominican austerity; but it must have been commonplace by this time, since the general chapter of Paris in 1326 prohibited private chambers to all friars except those of such standing that their requests could not be refused without 'inconvenience'.[17] Pierre was surely one of these. As an addi-

---

[15] *Gualvagno de la Flamma, Cronica Ordinis Praedicatorum ab anno 1170 usque ad 1333*, ed. B. M. Reichert (Rome and Stuttgart, 1897), p. 83.

[16] For his chamber, see *Cartulaire de l'église de Notre Dame de Paris*, ed. B. Guérard (Paris, 1850), iii. 226, no. 303, 'acta sunt hec in camera dicti magistri Petri, apud fratres Praedicatores'.

[17] Mortier, iii. 9.

tional relaxation of earlier ways he received sums of money specifically for his own use; for example, the king's cousin Alphonse of Spain rewarded him as executor of his will with a sum of 50 Paris pounds.[18] Again, this was not uncommon. The 1321 chapter of Florence, which Pierre had attended, had unblushingly legislated that 'If provincials find convents in such distress that they cannot provide friars with the necessities of life, they must of necessity avoid this wretchedness by taking gifts or loans from the more opulent friars.'[19] Despite his lengthy defence of the principle of common property, Pierre was accustomed to live at least to some extent on an independent income. His existence was in consequence not uncomfortable.

Pierre's apparent detachment from the general run of conventual life at this period was due in part to his office as confessor to several important men, which took him from his peaceful chamber into the busy worlds of Orléans and Paris society. Dominicans were the confessors *par excellence* of the period. Habituated as they were to public criticism of their own failures in the regular chapters of faults within their priories, they had developed a very professional and quite sympathetic approach to the role. Because confidentiality obtained, no indisputable evidence survives of Pierre's actual conduct; nevertheless he was remembered as a fairly flexible spiritual adviser, who held that a man might impose on himself a suitable penance for an offence he had forgotten to confess, without having to return to his confessor—an unfashionable opinion in which he agreed with Hostiensis.[20] But if relatively relaxed on details, he was urgent on the necessity for the sacrament, and not above touting in his sermons his own suitability for the role of confessor:

Papal privileges given to the Preachers allow them after their sermons to hear the confessions of any members of their audience who, having heard the word of God, wish to confess to them. The Pope in granting this privilege supposed that many sinners would be goaded into this. (Clermont Ferrand, Bibliothèque municipale, MS 46, fo. 13ʳ)

---

[18] H. M. Delaborde, 'Un arrière petit-fils de St. Louis: Alfonse d'Espagne', *Mélanges Julien Havet* (Paris, 1895), p. 425.

[19] Mortier, ii. 550. On money in the order see W. A. Hinnebusch, *The History of the Dominican Order, i. Origins and Growth to 1500* (New York, 1966), pp. 159-60.

[20] R. Creytens, 'Santi Schiattesi O.P., disciple de S. Antonin de Florence', *AFP* 27 (1957), 265.

Pierre's nomination as executor for the will of Alphonse of Spain and his presence when a codicil was added to the will suggest strongly that he administered the last rites to this great-grandson of St Louis, the ex-canon of Notre Dame who had become a knight at the command of King Charles IV.[21] And he was certainly confessor both to at least one successful lawyer and to Jean Haudry, a rich burgher of Paris (whose wishes in respect of presentations to two family chapels the Dominican tried to press with an unsympathetic bishop of Paris).[22] Both these incidents occurred in 1327. Somewhat earlier he may have been spiritual adviser to Blanche, duchess of Brittany, who chose him to persuade her son Robert of the soundness of retaining Berengar de Laudun, brother of Pierre's old friend Guillaume de Laudun, now archbishop of Vienne. 'Beau fils, nous croyons que beau pere maistre Pierre de la Palu vous en escrit.' Berengar had left the king's service for Robert's, and Blanche feared her son was unappreciative of the honour done him.[23] To write a letter for a great lady on so personal a matter points to an intimacy easily explained by the shared confessional.

In *De potestate Papae*, Pierre had demonstrated his awareness that a priest could not exercise spiritual authority without being led into the temporal sphere. He can therefore have been little surprised to find himself similarly involved. In December 1325 he was sent by King Charles IV to the count of Blois, on secret business affecting royal interests—'pro certis et secretis negotiis ipsum Regem tangentibus'.[24] Judging by the next two entries in the *Trésor*, he took with him a hefty bribe in the form of some household furnishings. It has been tentatively suggested[25] that the affair related to the count's failure to hand over his wife's dowry; if it was indeed connected with marriage law, Pierre was an appropriate envoy. Any discredit he had

[21] See Jean Dunbabin, 'From Clerk to Knight: Changing Orders', in C. Harper-Bill and R. Harvey, eds., *The Ideals and Practice of Medieval Knighthood* (Bury St Edmunds, 1988), pp. 36–7; on the historical background, Jerry R. Craddock, 'Dynasty in Dispute: Alfonso X el Sabio and the Succession to the Throne of Castille and Leon in History and in Legend', *Viator*, 17 (1986), 197–219.

[22] See B. Smalley, English Friars and Antiquity in the Early Fourteenth Century (Oxford, 1960), pp. 251 and 345, and ed. Guérard, *Cartulaire de l'église de Notre Dame*, iii. 226. On Haudry, see *Registres du Trésor des chartes*, ii. 1. *Règnes de Louis X et de Philippe V le long*, ed. J. Guérout (Paris, 1966), no. 382.

[23] Ed. C.-V. Langlois, HLF 36 (1927), 555.

[24] *Les Journaux de Trésor des chartes de Charles IV le Bel*, ed. J. Viard (Paris, 1917), p. 1497, no. 9344.

[25] Fournier, *HLF*, p. 47 n. 2.

incurred at the royal court as a result of the Flanders mission must by this time have been forgotten. More conclusive proof of this occurred the following year, when Henri de Sully, who had been particularly incensed against Pierre in 1318, used him on a mission to Pope John XXII at Avignon. The occasion was a delicate one. The pope had pronounced a delayed sentence of excommunication on Hélie, bishop of Tournai, for his failure to pay dues to the apostolic chamber. Henri de Sully, now governor of Navarre and hence involved with the Ventadour family to which Hélie belonged, was anxious to parry the blow. At the same time Charles IV had an obvious interest in the question, since Tournai was a royal bishopric and excommunicated bishops were a local hazard. But the king had no desire for a show-down with the pope. Somehow Hélie was persuaded to resign in return for the lifting of the sentence, and a Cahorsin was provided to the see. Pierre and Bertrand, canon of Clermont, acted as go-betweens in bringing the negotiation to a satisfactory conclusion; in a letter to Henri de Sully, John XXII specially commended their diligence.[26]

The odd excursion into the corridors of power excepted, Pierre's day-to-day activities were inconspicuous to the world at large. Much of his time was devoted to the compilation of a book of excerpts from chronicles on the crusades, entitled *Liber bellorum Domini pro tempore Nove Legis* (an updating for the Christian era of what was described in Numbers 21: 14 as 'the book of the wars of the Lord'). The enterprise, no doubt satisfying to his Joinville family pride, allowed him to indulge his natural taste for reproducing the words of others. The result has been criticized by one modern commentator[27] as peculiarly lacking in the interpretations and judgements usually found in historical productions. But it is false to assume that Pierre was trying to write history; except for his preface to the second part, he was content to be an anthologist. Though he never stated his reason for compiling the *Liber*, it is possible that he was asked by John XXII for a reference book on the crusades to be lodged in the papal archives; Petrarch recorded of John that because he was too busy to read all the books he knew he should, he was very grateful to those who would

---

[26] *Lettres communes*, ed. Mollat, nos. 23491, 24127, 25240, 27035. The possibility arises that Pierre spent some time in 1326 at the Dominican house in Tournai.

[27] J. F. Benton, 'Theocratic History in Fourteenth-Century France: The *Liber bellorum Domini* by Pierre de la Palu', *University of Pennsylvania Library Chronicles*, 40 (1974), 43.

summarize them for him.[28] But whether or not John requested the *Liber*, its completion probably encouraged him to promote Pierre to the Patriarchate of Jerusalem in 1329.

The work survives in two important fragments, one in Vatican MS Regina Christiana 547, covering all the Palestine crusades except the second and that of Frederick II, the other in Paris, Bibliothèque Ste Geneviève, MS 865 and University of Pennsylvania, MS Lea 45, devoted to the Albigensian crusade. Clearly a large part of the original is still missing. Count Riant, in his important discussion of the Vatican manuscript (at that time the only one known), speculated that the *Liber* was originally a tripartite work, attacking first the Jews, then the Saracens, and thirdly the heretics.[29] The subsequent discovery of the other two manuscripts partially vindicated his suggestion, since they did indeed tackle the problem of heretics. But the Albigensian war comprised the first, not the third, part of the whole; and a description of the book at the beginning of the Ste Geneviève MS, fo. 1^r, suggests that Pierre only ever intended to cover Saracens and Cathars: 'Centesimus quintus articulus primae partis *De bello Domini* contra quosdam Sarracenos et contra Albygenses hereticos tam gladio spirituali quam visibili . . .' (The hundred and fifth article of the first part of *De bello Domini* against certain Saracens and the Albigensian heretics, employing both the spiritual and the visible sword . . .). It would, in any case, have been hard to find appropriate sources for wars against the Jews; and, granted his Roman law training, Pierre might have shirked establishing a legal justification for attacking them.[30] I do not therefore think that he ever intended to follow the tripartite plan so popular among twelfth-century writers.

The chief criteria for judging a compilation are ease of use by the reader and the quality of the sources cited. Although structuring his work was always difficult for Pierre, the laborious indexes at the beginning of the second part[31] and the headings and *conclusiones* appearing throughout were proof of his desire to be helpful. 'User-friendly' devices of this kind,

[28] B. Guillemain, *La Cour pontificale d'Avignon (1309-1376): Étude d'une société* (BEFAR; Paris, 1962), p. 132.

[29] 'Description du *Liber bellorum Domini*', *Archives de l'Orient latin*, i (1881), 289–322; the second part of this article contains the list of headings for the main part of the book and then those for the addition, edited by I. Giorgi; therefore the article will henceforth be referred to as Riant and Giorgi.

[30] Cf. *DPP*, pp. 120, 121.

[31] Riant and Giorgi, pp. 295–322.

many pioneered by the Dominicans,[32] were commonplace by
the early fourteenth century. Even so, Pierre's exploitation of
them should earn him some credit with modern critics. More
perplexing is the logic behind the arrangement of the various
excerpts in the first part. Why did Pierre intrude a full text
of the *Vita sancti Amici et Amelii* between two sections of
Albigensian history, the first taken from later compilations by
Vincent de Beauvais and Bernard Gui, the second from the
contemporary account of Pierre des Vaux-de-Cernay?[33] The
fragmentary nature of the manuscript at this juncture prevents
a conclusive answer. But if Pierre, like most of his contemporaries, thought of heresy as spiritual leprosy, then the story of a
king who was prepared to cut off his sons' heads to cure a
friend of that fatal disease may have had an allegorical, if no
literal, relevance to the war against the Cathars. Its presence
also attested to his own fascination with legend.

The second part of the *Liber*, covering the Palestine crusades,
is a more successful compilation. Pierre found some interesting
sources, a good text of Walter the Chancellor, many of Jacques
de Vitry's letters, Oliver of Paderborn, the *Excidium Acconis*,
and a unique piece of Charles of Anjou's sworn deposition in
the canonization process of St Louis.[34] Elsewhere he relied on
later but reputable compilers, on Jacques de Vitry's *Historia
Orientalis*, on Vincent of Beauvais, and on the recently completed histories of Guillaume de Nangis and Bernard Gui;[35] less
excusably he also drew on Jacopo da Varazze's *Legenda aurea*.
One can imagine him returning with these sources to his chamber and distributing them to his scribes,[36] with instructions to

[32] See R. H. and M. A. Rouse, *Preachers, Florilegia and Sermons: Studies on
the 'Manipulus Florum' of Thomas of Ireland* (Toronto, 1979), pp. 3–42.

[33] Benton, 'Theocratic History', pp. 42–3 and n. 12.

[34] Count Riant, 'Déposition de Charles d'Anjou pour la canonisation de Saint
Louis', *Notices et documents publiés pour la Société de l'histoire de France*, 335
(1884), 155–76.

[35] Fournier, *HLF*, p. 82 n. 3, points out that Pierre's reference to Gui's
chronicle as *Chronicon Lodovense* means that the *Liber* cannot date from before
1324, the year in which Gui became bishop of Lodève.

[36] I suggest that Fr. Alfonso Buenhombre was one of these. Pierre in a
sermon recounted two stories Fr. Alfonso had told him about miracles occurring
at Vivier while he was there (Clermont Ferrand, Bibliothèque municipale,
MS 46, fo. 156ᵛ); this suggests Alfonso's presence in Pierre's household at the
time this sermon was preached. When in 1336 Alfonso was imprisoned by the
Sultan, he whiled away the time translating the history of the Patriarch Joseph
out of Arabic into Latin for Pierre de la Palud, showing that he knew exactly the
kind of material that appealed to Pierre. See G. Meersseman, 'La Chronologie

cut the narrative systematically into isolatable incidents and to
provide each of these with a heading and a reference. He then
had these mini-chapters inscribed on the manuscript, in an
order that sometimes allowed the reader to compare different
versions of the same incident (e.g. the taking of Jerusalem
described by Robert the Monk, Fulcher de Chartres, Raymund
d'Aguilers, and Baudry de Dol: Vatican MS Regina Christiana
547, arts. 120–4), but otherwise had little overall coherence.
For example, after writing a brief account of the first crusade
drawn from later compilations, Pierre then produced a lengthy
appendix, 'Secunda particula addita secunde parti' (Vatican
MS Regina Christiana 547, fos. 132–261), devoted to another
version based on first-hand sources. Despite the oddities of the
Liber, it is perhaps too easy for the modern scholar, spoiled
by easily accessible critical editions of the chief crusading
sources, both to discount the amount of work involved in it
and to underestimate its usefulness to contemporaries. As
late as the sixteenth century it was valued by historians; and
even Guichenon had heard that it contained much omitted by
William of Tyre.[37]

In addition to the mosaic of sources, the second part of the
Liber contains one hitherto unnoticed original piece of writing,
Pierre's interpolation into Jacques de Vitry's prologue to the
Historia Orientalis. Jacques began his history by recalling that
God had transferred the ownership of the Holy Land from
people to people as a punishment for sin or as a reward for
contrition.[38] Pierre took up this theme, speaking of the gains
and losses of Palestine for Christian rule during the course of
history. The gains he attributed to Philip the Arabian, Charlemagne, and Godfrey de Bouillon (Vatican MS Regina Christiana
547, fos. 38ʳ–39ʳ). Of these the first particularly interested him
because, as he said, Christians of his day should not talk
loosely of being deprived of the Holy Land without establishing
which Christian ruler had first acquired a right to it.[39] *De facto*
Roman possession of Palestine dated back to the conquest of
the first century BC; but *de iure* ownership came only with the

des voyages et des œuvres de frère Alphonse Buenhombre O.P.', *AFP* 10 (1940),
77–108.

[37] Benton, 'Theocratic History', p. 38. S. Guichenon, *Histoire de Bresse et de
Bugey* (Lyons, 1650), 2. 2. 287.

[38] For Jacques, see *Gesta Dei per Francos*, ed. J. Bongars 2 vols. (Hanover,
1611), particularly pp. 1051–3. I have not yet managed to find C. Buridant, ed.,
La Traduction de l'"Histoire Orientalis' de Jacques de Vitry (Paris, 1986).

[39] Riant and Giorgi, p. 295.

conversion of Philip the Arabian to Christianity.[40] Pierre apparently believed that since Philip's reign God had intended perpetual Christian possession of the Holy Land, though He had been obliged briefly to intermit this three times in response to Christian sins. It was a comforting doctrine to adhere to in the years after 1291.

Nevertheless, Pierre saw three small problems blocking his path to convincing others. In the first place, he had to prove that *de iure* possession of the holy places did not belong to the restored Greek emperors. This he found relatively simple. A swift run through Byzantine history convinced him, as it had done in the *De potestate Papae*, that their heresy had deprived the Greeks of the right to rule, in Palestine as elsewhere: 'Omnes ... heretici et schimatici a Christi corpore separati non possunt inter Christianos de iure officio regis fungi' (fo. 39[r]). Then he had to explain how it was that the heir of Philip the Arabian should be the pope rather than the German emperor. In the short term this too was easy: since John XXII had refused to recognize Lewis of Bavaria there had been a vacancy in the empire, during which the pope legitimately exercised imperial power, just as Matthew and Judas Maccabaeus had reigned in Israel when there was no king.[41] For a longer-term solution, Pierre revived an argument he had dismissed in the *De potestate*: that since the time of Pope Sylvester I the empire had been held in fief of the pope (fo. 38[r]), a premiss permitting papal resumption of lordship when necessary.[42]

Pierre's third difficulty led him away from contemplation of history into a more original and strongly topical problem: though God certainly meant the Christians to regain possession of Jerusalem, did He mean them to use force to that end? The

[40] 'Et sic patet prima acquisitio et acceptio regni Israel et dominium terre sancte de iure et de facto simul in persona imperatoris Philippi huius nominis primi, quia ille primus fuit ex imperatoribus Christianis; nec aliquis alius Christianus ante eum dominatus est de iure et de facto simul in Jerusalem nec in parte terre sancte' (fo. 38[v]). Though the source for Philip's conversion is Eusebius's *Ecclesiastical History*, bk. 6, ch. 34, Pierre embroidered on it; according to a marginal note in the MS, he was drawing on the Miracles of St Poncius the Martyr.

[41] 'Sacerdos enim supplet vicem regis, et deficiente rege Juda temporibus Machabeorum sacerdos Mathias et filii eius gubernavit [sic] terram sanctam. Et sic papa vacante imperio gerit vicem imperatoris, immo administrat imperium duplice iure suo' (fo. 38[r]).

[42] This demonstrates Pierre's dependence on the teaching of Pope Innocent IV for his defence of crusade; see J. Muldoon, *Popes, Lawyers and Infidels: The Church and the Non-Christian World, 1250-1550* (Liverpool, 1979), pp. 6-7.

lawyer Pierre was naturally cautious about advocating war as
the instrument for the recovery of the Holy Land. But he saw no
alternative. As he observed, there was no hope of any Christian
succeeding the Mameluk Sultan by hereditary right; nor was
there a chance that the Sultan's subjects would elect a Christian as his successor. Therefore war was the only possibility
open to the faithful—'Solum per viam belli nobis relinquitur
acquirenda' (fo. 39^r). This final sentence of the interpolation is
surely a call to crusade. It sheds new meaning on the prayer
with which Pierre opened his interpolation: 'May the Lord
grant that I may bring this little book to a perfect conclusion in
the recovery of the holy land, the conversion or destruction of
the Saracens, and the restoration of the eastern churches'
('Concedet michi dominus quod in recuperatione terre sancte,
sarracenorum conversione vel destructione et in reperatione
orientalem ecclesiam libellum valeam consumare', fo. 37^v).
These were not simply pious words. By the time Pierre decided
to put some of his own opinions into the mass of excerpted texts
and indices which make up the *Liber*, he had probably already
been appointed Patriarch of Jerusalem (March 1329) and was
anticipating the journey he made to Cairo in 1330. Here,
characteristically but more pointedly than in any of his other
writings, what he had said was intended to be a guide to action,
in this case his own.

Like his Lyons predecessor Hugues de St Cher, Pierre is
reputed to have commented on the whole of the Bible during the
course of his life, though he may in practice have confined his
observations on certain books to their prefaces.[43] Around the
time he was writing, Jacques de Lausanne and Dominic Grima
were similarly engaged, which suggests (despite the conservative nature of their work) that early fourteenth-century friars
felt some new impulsion to the task. In 1308 the Dominican
general chapter had drawn attention to the recent neglect of
Scriptural exegesis; Berengar of Landorra had specifically
appointed Dominic Grima to the task; and in 1321 it was said
of Pope John XXII that he had conceived a new and special
affection for Biblical experts.[44] Thus in some circles there was

---

[43] 'Scripsit copiosissime iuxta omnes sensus Scripture Sacre super totam
Bibliam', H. B. Scheeben, 'Die Tabulae Ludwigs von Valladolid im Chor der
Prediger Brüder von St. Jakob in Paris', *AFP* 1 (1930), 254; Peter of Nimeguen,
Prologus ad III Sententiarum Fr. Petri de Palude (Paris, 1517), 'Verum illa super
singulos divine scripture libros commentaria (ut Parisiensis nostra biblioteca
prefert) . . .'. On the prefaces, see Fournier, *HLF*, p. 60.

[44] Reichert, ed., *Acta*, ii. 34. J. Verger, 'L'Exégèse de l'Université', in P. Riché
and R. Lobrichon, eds., *Le Moyen Âge et la Bible* (Paris, 1984), p. 225. Stephen of

certainly a sense of the need to return to Christianity's Scriptural foundations for greater understanding of the truth. But if Jacques, Dominic, and Pierre were consciously trying to supply that need, then their success was on a small scale, as the paucity of manuscripts shows. The wider public waited for their Franciscan contemporary Nicolas de Lyre to finish his *Postillae perpetuae super totam Bibliam* in 1332 before demonstrating enthusiasm.

The unpopularity of Pierre's commentaries should be ascribed to their plagiarism and their characteristic voluminousness. Dating those still extant—Leviticus, 1 and 2 Kings, Judith, and the Psalms, with fragments on Genesis and Exodus[45]—is not easy. Some should perhaps be allocated to Pierre's bachelor days; indeed, the absence of *quaestiones* in any might argue for their common origin in bachelor courses,[46] were it not that no bachelor could have lectured on so many books. But in their final forms at least the huge sprawling works on the Psalms and on Leviticus smack of compilation by a team of friars, and must therefore have been written in Pierre's chamber during the 1320s. Pierre here followed the example of Hugues de St Cher, on whose orders a group of clerks had produced the great bulk of commentaries which circulated under his name. And the results were similar—fuzzy, verbose products, lacking in consistency or clear direction.[47] Sometimes they simply regurgitated other works: the short commentary on Psalms 1–17 in Paris, Bibliothèque nationale, MS nouvelle acquisition 1759 was little more than an abbreviation of St Thomas Aquinas. But the fuller version covering Psalms 1–51 in Paris, Bibliothèque Mazarine, MS 223 added to the Aquinas foundation quotations from Cassiodorus, Jerome, Augustine, and Gregory the Great, along with Walafrid Strabo, Hugh and Richard of St Victor and St Bernard. For Leviticus (Paris, Bibliothèque de l'Université, MS 168) Pierre drew on Dominic Grima for the literal sense and Origen and Richard of St Victor for the mystical.[48] There was

---

Kettleburgh's letter on John XXII is translated by R. W. Southern in 'The Changing Role of Universities in Medieval Europe', *BIHR* 60 (1987), 134.

[45] Stegmüller, *Repertorium*, iv. 356–61, who notes the extensive copying from Dominic Grima in the Genesis commentary. For Dominic's career see B. Guillemain, *Le Cour pontifical*, p. 387.

[46] B. Smalley, *The Gospels in the Schools* (Oxford, 1985), p. 205.

[47] B. Smalley, *The Study of the Bible in the Middle Ages*, 3rd edn. (Oxford, 1983), pp. 270–3; R. E. Lerner, 'Poverty, Preaching and Eschatology in the Revelation Commentaries of "Hugh of St. Cher"', in K. Walsh and D. Wood, eds., *The Bible in the Medieval World* (Oxford, 1985), pp. 181–9.

[48] Fournier, *HLF*, pp. 60–1.

little that reflected his own views or the needs of his own world.

The commentary on Judith (Paris, Bibliothèque Mazarine, MS 199) was, however, rather different, in that it offered more evidence of his personal involvement. The scribe of the only extant manuscript named its author as Patriarch of Jerusalem, thereby dating its transcription to after 1329; and he described the work as a compilation, a judgement borne out by the most cursory glance at the contents. It began with quotations from the prefaces to commentaries on Judith by Hugues de St Cher, Pseudo-Nicolas de Gorran, Dominic Grima, and Rhabanus Maurus—whom Pierre apparently thought a contemporary of Judith! It then cited in toto the preface of St Jerome. This motley collection introduced a detailed and very lengthy pastiche, notable for its reliance on the works of Gregory the Great, on miracle collections and on saints' lives, and on twelfth-century learning, rather than on more recent authorities. Both in substance and in structure the commentary was deeply conservative. Each chapter of the text was expounded first in the literal, then in the allegorical, and finally in the moral sense. As Pierre apparently understood it, the literal sense was less concerned with grammar, logic, or philology than with history, with what really happened and how it could be explained. The allegorical sense started with the literal sense but interpreted it in a way that reinforced lessons found elsewhere within the Bible; in particular it prefigured New Testament happenings. The moral sense offered precise advice to the audience, very occasionally to that of Pierre's own time. Effectively, then, Pierre had turned his back on the Thomist method of exposition, with its firm emphasis on the literal sense, its concern with increasing knowledge,[49] in favour of a form of commentary the Carolingians would not have found avant-garde. He addressed himself less to the learned than to ordinary (though necessarily literate) clerks, for whose convenience he employed strong imagery and even a few *exempla* of the type found in preacher's manuals. In short, he was providing sermon fodder, not forwarding scholarship.

The allegorical interpretation of Judith Pierre offered was entirely traditional. The story of the cities besieged by their enemies was a description of the struggle between Christendom and the devil. The walls of the devil's city were made up of

---

[49] See B. Smalley, 'Use of the "Spiritual" Senses of Scripture in Persuasion and Argument by Scholars in the Middle Ages', *RTAM* 52 (1985), 44–63; cf. Verger, 'L'Exégèse de l'Université', pp. 204, 206.

stones hewn from the sins of those who attacked the faith or who undermined it by asserting that usury or fornication were not moral offences. The walls of the heavenly Jerusalem, on the other hand, were built from the four cardinal virtues and their resulting gifts (commentary on Judith, ch. 1, allegorical interpretation, part 1). Holofernes signified any servant of the devil, or even Antichrist himself, ably supported by the Jews (ch. 3, allegorical interpretation, part 1). The people of Israel fearing the attacks of Holofernes represented the church in its time of trial, imploring God's help against her enemies (ch. 4, allegorical interpretation, part 1). And Judith cutting off Holofernes' head prefigured Christ slaying the devil (ch. 13, allegorical interpretation, part 1). The moral interpretation was equally conventional. For example, the rise and fall of Nebuchadnezzar signified the mutability of fortune among kings, and introduced a discussion of the transfer of empire from the Romans to the Greeks and then to the Franks (ch. 1, moral interpretation, part 1). Kings who aspired to dominate the world should remember that their fate was in God's hands.

Yet interspersed like raisins in the heavy pudding of well-worn sentiments, there were occasional remarks that appear to have come from Pierre's own pen.[50] For example, in chapter 16, moral interpretation, part 3, there is an extended simile between vassals attacked by enemies and Christians seduced by temptation, which incorporates Pierre's favourite distinction between *dominium directum* and *dominium utile*. The author describes two different vassals, one who has been given a fief from his lord's own land, making him dependent on his lord; if he is attacked, his lord will automatically help him because he himself stands to lose; the other a nobleman holding land allodially, who voluntarily does homage to a lord and surrenders to him *dominium directum*—overlordship—over a part of his land, while retaining *dominium utile*—ownership—over it; should he be attacked, his lord is not bound to help him because he does not derive anything more than a limited amount of military service from the relationship. The Christian is like the first kind of vassal; everything he has he receives from God, on whom he is completely dependent. When therefore he is

---

[50] In order to be certain what is original in the commentary it would be necessary to trace all the scraps Pierre's scribes brought together and eliminate anything known to have been written by another hand. I have not been able to do this. In particular I have not checked it against Dominic Grima's commentary in Toulouse, Bibliothèque municipale, MS 30, fos. 28^r-51^v. I have therefore relied on my own instinct to identify his additions; the method is obviously fallible.

besieged by the devil, he can call upon God in full confidence of obtaining His assistance.

Commenting on the trumpet blast with which the Israelites rejoiced after Judith had slain Holofernes, Pierre was reminded of that other famous battle noise, Roland's horn at Roncevalles. According to the *Gesta Karoli Magni*, Roland, seeing that his troops were being slaughtered, finally decided to blow his ivory horn, which burst as he blew; angels then carried the sound to Charlemagne whose army was three days' march away. In the same way the early apostles went forth to all lands preaching the gospel, they suffered martyrdom and poured forth their blood, in order to spread the Word across the world.[51] In his sermons Pierre demonstrated his belief that worthwhile allegories could be derived from secular literature (see next section); here, making the same point, he strained after a parallel between a much-loved scene from epic and the Christian gospel.

Equally typical was Pierre's penchant for introducing historical material wherever possible. Holofernes bestowing gifts on Judith from his treasury reminded him of the conduct of one of his favourite heroes, the emperor Philip the Arabian, who had bestowed riches on Pope Sixtus and on St Lawrence (ch. 12, allegorical interpretation, part 1). When speaking of the spiritual state of the kings of this earth before their conversion to Christianity, he alleged that the Roman emperors before Philip and Constantine, the kings of the Franks until the time of Clovis, and the kings of the Britons until Arthur (or perhaps his father) had all alike been subjected to the devil.[52] Since Geoffrey of Monmouth, a favourite fount of inspiration, did not mention Arthur's conversion, Pierre must have supplied the idea that Arthur was the first Christian British king either from his own imagination, or from some other source. But at least he had a rough idea of when the conversion of Britain took place.

It struck Pierre as interesting that the devil chose great princes and philosophers to do his fighting for him, whereas God preferred fishermen and women as his soldiers (ch. 3, moral sense, part I). This led him to contemplate the downfall of the proud. He told a story also to be found in one of his

---

[51] 'Sic enim in omnem terram exivit sonus predicationis apostolorum, et confracta sunt corpora eorum et fusus sanguis venarum per martirum' (ch. 15, allegorical interpretation, part 2).

[52] 'Omnes monarchie fuerunt per ydolatriam diabolo subiecti, et Romani imperatores usque ad Philippum et Constantinum Magnum, reges Francorum usque ad Clodoneum, et reges Brettonum usque ad Arturum vel forsitan patrem suum' (ch. 2, allegorical interpretation, part 4).

sermons (Clermont Ferrand, Bibliothèque municipale, MS 46, fo. 241ᵛ), about the emperor who although pious and merciful became so arrogant that he asked his chaplains to omit from their chant: 'He hath put down the mighty from their seats.' As a consequence he woke up one morning to find himself wandering around his court unrecognized by anyone; and when he was taken before the emperor who asked who he was, his answer resulted in his receiving a beating. Only after total repentance was he reinstated (ch. 3, moral sense, part 5). Pride comes before a fall was the lesson all Christians should learn from the fate of Holofernes.

Litigiousness and aggression among the clergy was a very real danger. They should fear the devil fanning anger in communities and between clerics by upholding invidious laws and inciting trouble, for through strife and appeals churches are destroyed.[53] (Might the invidious laws referred to perhaps be the constitutions *Dudum* and *Multorum* of the Council of Vienne, to both of which Pierre objected?) Confessors also were subject to a particular weakness: they must try not to display idle curiosity about the sins that were recounted to them.[54] But if these were relatively recent arrivals on the scene of clerical temptation, the oldest one of them all, idolatry, was still a live issue. Commenting on Judith showing Holofernes reverence, Pierre was reminded not only of Daniel, who refused to worship idols, but also of St Louis's messengers to the Mongol Khagan, tempted to venerate that ruler—'Similiter nuncii regis Francie missi ad regem Tartarorum voluerint eum adorare ut ipse petebat' (ch. 10, allegorical interpretation, part 5).

The traditional lesson that Christians should not imitate pagans in fighting one another left Pierre saddened by the bellicosity of his own contemporaries. Not only in Lombardy where Guelf fought against Guibelline, father against brother, but throughout all Christendom there were wars and kingdoms were set against kingdoms.[55] Nevertheless, he sought to en-

---

[53] 'Similiter etiam timendum est clericis ne diabolus in eis faciat ... in collegiis et personis iras et invidias leges suscitando zizania seminando quod est in multis, et per lites et per appellationes ecclesie destruuntur' (ch. 10, allegorical interpretation, part 5).

[54] 'Non debemus ex curiositate quedam actus alienos scrutari; nec sacerdos debet indiscrete peccata scrutari in confessione ne scandalum faciat confitentibus ei peccata' (ch. 8, allegorical interpretation, part 2).

[55] 'Nec solum in Lombardia ubi pugnant contra se Guelfi et Jeboloni, pater adversus fratrem, sed per totam Christianitatem sunt guerre et regnum adversus regnum' (ch. 4, moral sense, part 1).

courage bellicosity in one direction at least. Commenting on
Ozias sending troops from all parts, he said: 'If each Christian
region and city would send an armed force to aid those Christians who have been besieged, oppressed and thrust into
captivity by the Turks and Saracens, they would swiftly eject
the invaders and usurpers from the ancient confines.'[56] It was
an appropriate thought for a man just about to be appointed
Patriarch of Jerusalem. Thus, into the fabric of a very old-
fashioned commentary, Pierre wove a few strands of his own
thread, strands which illustrate his chief preoccupations in the
years 1321–8.

So Pierre had plenty to occupy him in his chamber and
beyond its limits as he preached and confessed around Orléans
and Paris.[57] But his last major endeavour before returning to
Avignon brought him back to the sphere of high politics. In
1328 Thierry d'Hireçon, bishop of Arras and Mahaud of
Artois's unpopular minister, died after a career of systematic
self-enrichment. Recognizing that a good part of his wealth had
been diverted from his lady's purse, in his last will he left a
sizeable share to Mahaud. But when she attempted to lay
hands on this, she met with violence from the other heirs. She
therefore appealed to the law. Because the case involved
ecclesiastical as well as secular sources of revenue, it was
unusually complicated. The king nominated a commission
consisting of two masters of theology, Pierre and Pierre de
Beaumes, bishop of Paris, and three, later five, professors in
both laws. On 5 February 1329 the commissioners entered a
judgement (Bibliothèque de Tours, MS 1164, no. 10, pièce
originale)[58] in Mahaud's favour. The case was significant for
Pierre's future; it created a bond of sympathy between himself
and Mahaud; and it gave him an insight into Thierry d'Hireçon's
affairs which was to prove important in 1330.

[56] 'Si sic omnis regio et civitas Christianorum mittent armatam iuventutem
in auxilium aliorum Christianorum a Turcis et Sarracenis obsessorum, op-
pressorum, captivatorum, cito fungerentur de finibus antiquis quos invaserunt
et sibi usurpaverunt' (ch. 15, literal sense, part 3).

[57] I do not believe that Pierre was responsible for the index to Jacopo da
Varazze's *Legenda aurea*, ascribed to him in the redaction in Amiens, MS 462,
fo. 212^r, 'Explicit tabula super legendas sanctorum edita a quodam fratre ordinis
Praedicatorum, et creditur fuisse fr. Petrus de Palude, patr. Ierosolimitanus'
(see *Catalogue général des manuscrits des bibliothèques publiques de France*
19 Amiens (Paris, 1893), p. 224). My examination of the index in Naples,
Biblioteca Nazionale, MS VII. F. 29, fos. 29–53 has led me to conclude that it
was drawn up by someone of sharper analytical mind than Pierre. But if it was
Pierre's, then it presumably belonged to this period.

[58] Fournier, *HLF*, p. 47 and n. 6.

(b) Sermons

Pierre's sermons are probably his greatest achievement; further-more, they are indubitably his own. Perhaps surprisingly, he relied little on standard *exempla*, and hardly at all on preacher's manuals (though he did occasionally echo Guillaume Peyraut's *Summa de vitiis et virtutibus*[59]). Shouldering the responsibility of fishing for men's souls, he felt obliged to do his own thinking in order to frame lessons appropriate to each of his audiences. The effort involved revealed his talents as a communicator. In the pulpit his visual imagination ran riot, his stream-of-consciousness connections clicked into place, his exploration of the byways always brought him back to the main points. The diffuseness that can irritate in his copious schol-astic works was under tighter control. He provided his listeners with a magic lantern of colourful images flashing past, each one pregnant with meaning.

But as a counterweight to their vividness, the central mess-age of his sermons was almost unrelievedly gloomy: there were innumerable ways for even a well-meaning man to incur hell-fire; only one in a thousand could hope to escape the pains of purgatory; the road to heaven was steep, stony, and very narrow, and those who thought they were on it were very often deceived. As Pierre saw it, the point of preaching was to prick his listeners' consciences, to remind them ceaselessly of the need for confession and contrition, to point out the sinfulness in actions they had never thought of confessing. 'Acknowledge, listener, how grievous are your sins for which the son of God had to suffer' ('Agnosce, o homo, qualia sunt vulnera tua pro quibus necesse fuit dei filium vulnerari', (Clermont Ferrand, Bibliothèque municipale, MS 46, fo. 8^r). Given this view of his function, he did not expect to be popular. In a Christmas sermon sharply critical of princes and magnates, he remarked that the miller who grinds the flour for the bread of salvation is often hated by the great men whom he serves, and is some-times put to flight or even hanged by them.[60] The note of self-

---

[59] Neither Étienne de Bourbon's *Tractatus de diversis materiis praedicabilibus* nor Humbert de Romans's *De modo prompte cudendi sermones* seems to have had much effect on the substance of Pierre's sermons. The few *exempla* he used do not appear in F. C. Tubach, *Index exemplorum: A Handbook of Medieval Religious Tales* (Helsinki, 1969). Pierre's Clermont Ferrand sermons are not mentioned in J. B. Schneyer, *Repertorium der lateinischen Sermones des Mittelalters für die Zeit von 1150–1330* (7 vols.; Münster, 1969–80); see iv. 718.

[60] 'Ille qui servit de veritate et iusticia dicenda consulenda iudicanda et facienda est pistor, serviens ut de pane vite et intellectus et aqua sapientie

dramatization was a pale reflection of the one he had struck during the Flemish mission of 1318.

The flavour of Pierre's preaching, with its up-to-date imagery, its sharp criticism of contemporary mores, and its reliance on models to promote good behaviour, is well conveyed by a sermon on the feast of St Nicholas, the patron saint of students, which is found in Clermont Ferrand, Bibliothèque municipale, MS 46, fos. 7ʳ–14ʳ. It begins, as Pierre's sermons habitually do, with an arresting image: in this case of a traveller setting out for a distant place and remembering, while still engaged on his outward journey, to plan for his return. By analogy, those who celebrate Christ's first coming at the beginning of Advent should think also of his second coming on the Day of Judgement. During His time on earth Christ appeared in the guise of a perfect doctor; not only did He cure men of their ills, but He did it without charge. Like the physician who pays his own expenses and gives healing medicines free to the poor, He paid a heavy price for our salvation: since original sin could not be rooted out either by natural law or by the sacraments of the Old Testament, He suffered for us. The ultimate self-sacrifice in a doctor would be to make himself ill, or even to die, in order to cure a patient. Christ did that for men. But at the second coming, Christ will appear not as a doctor, but as a judge. The occasion will be like a *Parlement*, at which the king inquires into the conduct and administration of his justices, *baillis*, and seneschals; those who are judged to have performed well are rewarded, sometimes by being made masters in *Parlement* and judges of the realm; but those who have failed are severely punished.[61] So Christ will judge his princes, prelates, and judges.

After this striking beginning, Pierre turns to the main subject of the sermon, St Nicholas, whose life he presents as an example of Christian excellence. For Nicholas followed the path of righteousness both in healing and in judging; compassionate and helpful to the afflicted, he understood the need to

---

salutaris, qui quamvis fuit summe necessarius magnatibus tamen fit eis odiosus, repellitur et fugatur, proscribitur, quandoque trahitur et suspenditur' (Clermont Ferrand, Bibliothèque municipale, MS 46, fo. 34ʳ).

61 'Ad modum quo bonus rex facit tempore parliamenti in quo omnibus et de omnibus facit iustitiam, et specialiter de justiciariis suis, ballivis et seneschallis . . . quia si inquesta facta inveniuntur bene administrasse, amplius exultantur et fiunt magistri parliamenti et cum rege iudices toti regni, quia virtutum premia merentibus tribui convenit et gratiosi ascendendum ad honores. Si autem inveniuntur male administrasse puniuntur gravius quam ceteri' (fo. 8ʳ).

repent of his own sins. He was like a palm tree in that, rooted in the sensual things of this world, he nevertheless stood erect, stretching his spiritual faculties like branches towards heaven. King Alexander, though lord of all the world, still needed Aristotle to teach him how to avoid vice. Nicholas by contrast was preserved from sin by his own pure innocence, which he had received in response to prayer, and which he kept intact throughout his life.

The gentle south wind brings prosperity in its train, but breeds pestilence in the air. The harsh north wind, on the other hand, kills the pestilence. Prosperous men only bother to confess once a year, if that; but when ill-fortune strikes, they rush to confess and communicate. Adversity makes a man's soul clear as crystal. St Nicholas kept an even keel between the two winds; when prosperous he gave abundantly to the poor, and when penury hit, he suffered it with patience. He never consorted with women, unlike many contemporary priests who scandalize others by their incontinent lives. These men should remember the story related in the *Historia Tripartita*[62] of a certain priest in Alexandria who slept with prostitutes; his behaviour so shocked his parishioners that they avoided the confessional. From his day to this, the Greeks have been reluctant to go to confession. Because the sins of one man can ruin a whole people, everyone should vigorously upbraid a priest who keeps a concubine. St Nicholas was severe in judging the sinners in his parish.

In his chastity, St Nicholas was like the flower of the palm tree: it is pretty and sweet-smelling, and has a fruit with a hard, incorruptible kernel. (Had Pierre actually seen a palm tree, or was he merely drawing on a stock metaphor?) Other clerics are more like the elderflower, which is attractive on the outside, but smells putrid. They are chaste in body because they would be ashamed not to be, but their minds are prurient, their eyes shamelessly in search of women. Yet others resemble the rose, which is beautiful but has no fruit. These are scholars, for example Plato and his disciples, who preserve chastity not for the love of God but for the sake of their studies. Because their motive is wrong, their action is valueless, for virginity is praiseworthy not in itself, but as a sacrifice to God: 'Virginitas laudatur non quia virginitas sed quia deo sacrificia.'

---

[62] Because the detail is vague and Pierre puts his own gloss on the story, it is difficult to identify. But it may be that in *Cassiodori-Epiphanii Historia ecclesiastica tripartita*, ed. W. Jacob and R. Hanslik (Corpus scriptorum ecclesiasticorum latinorum, lxxi; Vienna, 1952), bk. 4, ch. 37.

Virtue is acquired in three stages: first there must be good soil, *fundamentum*, then food, *nutrimentum*, and finally growth, *augmentum virtutis*. As the *fundamentum virtutis*, Nicholas learned from his parents how to suppress sensuality, thereby permitting spirituality to flower. Good parents may do this by commending their sons to poverty, which is an escape route from sin and an aid to the salvation of others; the protection they thus offer is like the rush basket in which Moses' parents hid their baby. But some wicked parents make their children oblates or clerics, not for religious reasons, but to be rid of them and reduce the number of claimants on their goods; or alternatively, to assist their clerical relations in the acquisition of prebends, priories, or dignities. The *nutrimentum virtutis* is acquired from the mother's milk, as St Augustine acquired his moral education from St Monica. Bad parents, however, provide the milk of pigs; as a result their children become like basilisks, which imbibe so much poison in their infancy that when full-grown they can slay a man who merely looks at them. The *augmentum virtutis* demands equal growth in all parts of a child's soul; otherwise he will turn into a spiritual monster. He must learn true values, must feel remorse for his past sins, and must continue in the path of righteousness until his life's end. St Nicholas is the perfect example for men. When a duel ends, the vanquished man is dragged off to the gibbet; the victor, surrounded by his rejoicing friends and relations, is taken to the palace, to receive his crown. St Nicholas was crowned in triumph for the purity of his life. So may others be when they die.

One can imagine Pierre in his chamber at St Jacques, preparing this for a large festival mass on 5 December in the Franciscan house in Paris (the traditional place for feast-day sermons). In his mind's eye he envisaged the congregation—an important group of people, including doctors, judges, and some royal servants; there would also be clerics of all stations, and a large number of students at the university. Somehow the life of St Nicholas must be made relevant for all of them; each individual must leave the sermon with a clearer notion of his duty before God. Because the human attention span was so short, people's personal concerns so all-embracing, Pierre had constantly to engage their interest, express each main point briefly, force his message home with unexpected metaphors, and make his hearers examine their own motives, whether for preserving virginity or for putting their sons into a monastery. Preaching of this calibre was an immensely arduous task.

Most of Pierre's sermons cannot be dated satisfactorily.[63] But those contained in Clermont Ferrand, Bibliothèque municipale, MS 46, though organized in accordance with the feasts of the church year, do appear to be preserved roughly in the order in which they were preached. (Since the collection was written for Nicholas of Saint Saturnin, Master of the Sacred Palace at Avignon, who was created a cardinal in 1378, it is possible that unusual care was devoted to its compilation.) Some of the early sermons may date to his Orléans days—the one given on the feast of St Thomas the Apostle (fos. 24ᵛ–32ᵛ), primarily concerned with the habits of advocates, is a likely candidate. That for St Thomas Aquinas's feast day (fos. 60ᵛ–70ʳ) was probably produced shortly after his canonization in 1323.[64] Some of those at the end of the collection, including the one devoted to the crusade (see Ch. 6b), were certainly delivered as late as 1330 or 1331, after Pierre's elevation to the patriarchate of Jerusalem.

The Clermont Ferrand corpus contains a substantial minority of sermons which, though preserved in Latin, were clearly meant to be delivered in French, since from time to time the French for a key phrase is given after the Latin.[65] For example, in a sermon on St John and St Paul, Pierre says:

Primum quod sustinuerint dolorem et laborem temporaliter *per multas tribulationes*, secundum quod videlicet ceperint et acquiserint vigorem et colorem spiritualiter *oportet nos intrare*, tertium quod per hoc venerint ad honorem et dulcedinem eternaliter in regnum Dei. Gallice: il soustiendrent labeur et douleur temporel et de ce prennent et acquirent vigour et kaleur espirituel et per ce vinrent a honeur et douceur perpetuel. (Clermont Ferrand, MS 46, fo. 142ᵛ)

Neither the numbering of points nor the Biblical quotations are found in the French version, which is spare, clear, and fluent, with a rhythm of its own. This suggests that the sermon was originally composed in the vernacular and only acquired its more complex Latin form when being written down for a future

---

[63] The collection called *Thesaurus novus enarrationis evangeliorum* attributed to Pierre in 15th- and 16th-cent. printed editions was shown by Fournier to be misascribed in 'Notes tirées des sermons inédits du frère prêcheur Pierre de la Palu', *Mélanges Albert Dufourcq* (Paris, 1932), p. 109. But A. Duval, *Dictionnaire de spiritualité*, xii. 2 (Paris, 1986), col. 1632, says that those on Easter and on the Sanctoral are genuine.

[64] Fournier, *HLF*, p. 76.

[65] For the most recent treatment of similar sermons see D. d'Avray, *The Preaching of the Friars: Sermons Diffused from Paris before 1300* (Oxford, 1985), pp. 90–5.

readership. That Pierre should concern himself with French style is proof, if proof were needed, of his intention to appeal to less learned laymen. In his own words, 'simplex et humilis sermo non curiosus nec subtilis est utilis populo' (a simple, humble sermon without eccentricities or subtleties is useful to the people: fo. 203^r). But by no means all his lay audiences were unlearned. As he also remarked, many of the advocates in the secular law courts were as competent in Latin as they were in French (fo. 32^r); and the king's *prévots* and *baillis*, who were often his targets from the pulpit, were a literate group. There was no automatic need to condescend to his audience merely because he was using the vernacular.

As one might expect with Pierre, his sermons were on the one hand lengthy, on the other loosely and unsystematically organized. The relationship between the text chosen and the content of the sermon was usually somewhat hazy, though individual words within the text might inspire images and a moral lesson. In the body of the discourse, quotations from the Scriptures and the Fathers were regularly interspersed, as if to lend authority; but, as can be seen from the excerpt above, these could be omitted with no loss of sense. Drawn from a concordance—possibly the third St Jacques concordance[66]— sometimes they were piled relentlessly one upon the other, to the point where they obscured the main line of argument. Pierre may have chosen them himself; but their omission from the French version perhaps suggests their subsequent insertion by a scribe.

Once launched into his main theme, the story-teller in Pierre often got out of hand. On one occasion, to underline the significance of Easter, he was reminded of an episode in Geoffrey of Monmouth's *Vita Merlini*—a work according to him commonly ascribed to Bede! (fo. 91^v). It related how Vortigern, whom he refers to only as *quidam dives*, tried to build a castle which repeatedly fell down. The British chieftain was advised by his wise men that his enterprise would not be successful until he had sprinkled on the site the blood of a boy born of a mother but no father. Merlin, who knew this description fitted himself, took issue with the counsellors and correctly diagnosed the problem: there was beneath the site a lake occupied by two dragons, one red, one white, engaged in mortal combat. The

---

66 R. H. and M. A. Rouse, 'The Verbal Concordance to the Scriptures', *AFP* 44 (1974), 5–30; and 'La Concordance verbale des Écritures', in Riché and Lobrichon, eds., *Le Moyen Âge et la Bible*, pp. 115–22. If Pierre did indeed use this, he did so earlier than any of the examples quoted by the Rouses, p. 121.

castle could not be built until the dragons had been killed.[67] Pierre could not resist telling the whole story through to the successful erection of the castle, though for the purposes of his sermon what concerned him was only the wise men's analysis of the situation. Having slain the dragons, he returned to what the royal advisers had said. According to him, the Holy Spirit had talked through their unconscious words, foretelling Christ, born of a mother with no father, whose blood would be the foundation of the church—'Spiritus qui locutus est per os asine, [Num. 22], per illorum ora locutus est, aperiens quod sanguine Christi qui natus et in terris de matre sine patre fundata est ecclesia' (fo. 91ᵛ). It must have been easier for the audience to enjoy the narrative than to anticipate its alleged point. But his treatment of the theme illustrates Pierre's conviction that sound Christian allegories could legitimately be drawn from all sorts of non-Scriptural literature; and on a less high-minded plane it provided an excuse to indulge his love of romance.

Historians have long recognized the anti-Establishment bias of some Mendicant preaching.[68] Though a figure on the fringes of the court, a friend of Amadeus V of Savoy till his death in 1323, and known to Mahaud of Artois and her daughters, Pierre pulled no punches in condemning the aristocracy for their worldliness, or the court for its greed. The high standards of the past had long been forgotten. Whereas palaces had once been places of prayer and devotion, they had become robbers' dens, in which the ruination of merchants was regularly canvassed.[69] This kind of criticism was perhaps too vague to cut much ice. But he was often more specific. He indicted the magnates of inequity in judicial affairs, in that they were willing to punish the poor and weak much more harshly than those—no matter how grave their offences—who had influence

---

[67] The outline of the story is also to be found in Geoffrey of Monmouth, *Historia Regum Brettonum*, vi. 18. Pierre's recital has affinities with Robert de Boron's *Merlin*; see F. Bogdanov, *The Romance of the Grail: A Study of the Structure and Genesis of a Thirteenth-Century Arthurian Prose Romance* (Manchester and New York, 1966), p. 4.

[68] G. R. Owst, *Literature and Pulpit in Medieval England* (Cambridge, 1933), pp. 287–374.

[69] 'Domus enim principum solebat esse domus orationis propter fidem et devotionem quem habebant de die et nocte ad divinum officium audiendum; et quia qui non cessat orare non cessat benefacere, semper erant in oratione quia semper per bona opera querebant domino placere et servire. Sed nunc facta est spelunca latronum in qua omnes tractatus et consilia sunt de spoliando mercatores' (fo. 59ʳ).

or money to assist their cause.[70] Both magnates and king held huge birthday feasts at which they demanded gifts, and expected their tenants and poor men to cover the costs by special aids and grants. In this they imitated Herod, who paid for the delights of his feast by giving John the Baptist's head on a charger to Herodias's daughter (fo. 34[r]). Magnates not only took everything their poor tenants possessed but also the things they ought to possess—the debts owed to them by their masters but never repaid. To oppress and beggar the peasants was as foolish and as self-destructive as eating the flesh of dolphins, an act which deprived sailors of their guidance at sea (fo. 58[r]).

Turning from the general moral failings of the privileged class, Pierre attacked specific officials. The Master of the Requests must have been chastened by the beginning of the sermon on Corpus Christi, in which he was accused of refusing to delay his meals to hear cases brought by poor men.[71] Equally, the most successful advocates in the royal court cannot have enjoyed being told that they ought not to charge more than other men on account of their expertise. Though they, like others, might exact a modest sum for their labour, to sell their superior knowledge was a form of simony (fo. 31[v]).

Criticism of the king himself was normally slightly more oblique. Nevertheless it was to be found, even in a sermon for the feast of St Louis delivered at the Sainte Chapelle in the royal presence (fos. 192[v]–197[v]). Pierre's main theme was that while Louis, whose name he derived from *lucis doctor vel lucis dator*, had spread light throughout France during his reign, that light had now been eclipsed, the spiritual benefits he had bestowed were now being wasted. 'Sed heu hodie . . . qui debent in lampadibus Christi oleum ponere eas extingunt, oleum debitum subtrahendo' (fo. 197[r]). The money St Louis had given to the churches was being stolen, the respect he had accorded to clerical opinion was now withheld, the justice he had taught men was now perverted. As a consequence darkness and gloom pervaded the country. There was no trace in this sad summary

[70] 'In curiis magnatum quidam forte minus quam alii delinquentes sunt pauperes et ignobili et ideo a nullo sustentantur nec defenduntur et propter hoc suspenduntur. Alii amplius delinquentes non solum merentur ab officiis suis deponi sed etiam suspendi; sed quia sunt divites, nobiles sive potentes, habent fautores, sustentatores, defensores . . . et ideo tales non suspenduntur vel deponuntur sed depositi reponuntur et ulterius promoventur' (fo. 34[r]).

[71] 'Dicit lex imperatoris: sedebunt iudices a mane usque ad vesperam causas populi audiendi. Quod non servant Magistri Requestarum qui nec dimitterent nec tardarent prandium suum propter querelas pauperis curiam sequi' (fo. 137[v]); see also the attack on fos. 229[v]–230[r].

of the flattery other preachers often bestowed on the descendants of the canonized king.

But this was vague in comparison with the Dominican's repeated and virulent attacks on royal monetary policies, particularly changes in the value of coins, which were damaging to the population at large.[72] His indictment was aimed against the coinage fluctuations of 1326–7, which had brought large profits to Charles IV's treasury at the expense of his subjects. It took courage to condemn both devaluation and revaluation, especially since the church had pressed hard for the return to sound money in 1306 and did so again in 1329–30. But Pierre was correct in thinking that revaluation could have harsh effects on the poorer classes.[73] Perhaps more interestingly, he obstinately refused to identify the royal interest, a mere private concern, with that of the public. He expatiated on the adverse effects *mutatio monete* could have on merchants, even those who spent very little time in the realm (fo. 131ᵛ). And he dared to make a passing reference to the tyranny of those who did not prefer the public good of stable coinage to personal enrichment (fo. 35ʳ)—in which he anticipated Nicole Oresme in *De moneta*.[74] Those who promoted the policies of which Pierre disapproved, the royal counsellors, came in for harsh words; he even compared some of them to demons. Nevertheless, he knew it was inadequate to blame counsellors, since good kings automatically had good counsellors.[75] The king could not be totally shielded from responsibility.

The sermon Pierre preached on the Feast of Corpus Christi, apparently in the presence of Philip VI and his court, reached what must have been the only just permissible maximum in scathing criticism of royal behaviour. His violent opposition to

[72] 'Huiusmodi sunt falsi monetarii qui bulliuntur in mundo quibus peiores sunt qui fabricant novam monetam bonam vel malam, fortem vel debilem, quando talis monete mutatio cedit in generale dampnum toti populo, licet videtur prodesse fisco regio, quia utilitas publica est preferenda private' (fo. 34ᵛ).

[73] J. Favier, *Philippe le Bel* (Paris, 1978), pp. 165–6.

[74] *De moneta*, ed. C. Johnson (London, 1956), p. 47. It is perhaps worth remembering that the king may have received a *quid pro quo* for listening to insults of this kind. Charles IV had won from Pope John XXII the right to a year's indulgence each time he listened to a sermon in public; ed. B. Barbiche, *Les Actes pontificaux originaux des Archives nationales de Paris*, iii. 1305–1415 (Vatican, 1982), p. 160, no. 2624.

[75] 'Accidit autem duobus colloquentibus de rege suo, et unus diceret "Magnum dampnum est de rege nostro quod non habet bonos consiliarios, quia in se est bonus, et si haberet bonos consiliarios esset optimus." Alius vero dixit quod si rex esset bonus in se bonos haberet consiliarios' (fo. 36ʳ).

royal monetary and ecclesiastical policies (along with a reference to the Sultan's views on the legal ownership of the Holy
Land) suggests that the tirade dates to shortly after Pierre's
return from Egypt in 1330, when he had been informed about
the sharp controversy over ecclesiastical jurisdiction that had
raged during his absence in 1329–30. As Patriarch of Jerusalem
and a man in the news, he could afford to take the risk of blunt-
ness. His target was those who counselled the king to break his
coronation oath and attack the churches. They should remember that God takes the right to rule away from nations who
incur His wrath through their injustices. Even the king of
France is not immune from deposition.[76] The message was a
tough and unwelcome one. Pierre's proof was characteristically
discursive, taking in vast sweeps of ecclesiastical and imperial
history, tracing through the centuries the transfer of imperial
power from people to people, as he had done in the *De
potestate Papae*; this led to the equally familiar conclusion that
while the empire was held in fee of the papacy, the kingdom of
France was held allodially. But then came a novelty: since God
is the overlord of allods, then through an offence against God
the king might justly forfeit his kingdom. Those who counselled
a king to commit such a crime might justly incur the penalty of
Pietro della Vignea, Frederick II's legal adviser, who was
blinded by his master for instigating the imperial attack on the
church. Behind these ominous words, delivered in the presence
of the men they were designed to threaten, lay an acute ap-
preciation that the king's and his ministers' interests did not
necessarily totally coincide. Both must be made to fear for the

[76] 'Unde cum rex Francie iuret in sua coronatione iustitiam facere et
ecclesias conservare, false lingue [tongues, i.e. counsellors] sunt qui ei
contrarium consulunt, quia consulunt ei perdere honorem suum terrenum
scilicet et divinum, Ecclesiasticus 10 *Regnum a gente in gente transfertur
propter iniustitias*, sicut translata est monarchia a Caldeis ad Persas, ab illis ad
Grecos, ab istis ad Romanos . . . Unde consulere regi utilitatem propriam vel
divitiam contra utilitatem communem et pauperum est ei falso consulere . . .
sive hoc sit de facienda moneta forti qui dicitur obesse communitati et prodesse
sibi et divitibus; sive hoc sit de moneta debili quando hec mutatio est . . . Dicunt
Chronice quod ecclesia Romana transtulit imperium Romanum et occidentale a
Grecis ad Germanos in persona magnifici Karoli, quia Greci non defendebant
illam oppressam . . . Et adhuc residet apud eos, quia imperium Romanum
occidentale datum a Constantino Magno Romane ecclesie in persona Beati
Sylvestri ex tunc a quandoque teneatur ab ecclesia Romana in feudum . . . Rex
Francie tenet regnum suum a Deo sicut vassallus feodum a domino per feloniam
in dominum commissam amittendum . . . Si igitur ecclesias non defendit nec
custodit sed ledit et opprimit, non solum in ecclesiam [crimen] committit sed
Deum offendit et contra Deum suum feloniam committit, ut fidem et iuramentum
frangit. Ideo iusto Dei iudicio regnum perdat' (fos. 140ᵛ–141ʳ).

future. Plain speaking of this kind was a rarity at the courts of the last Capetian and first Valois kings of France. Pierre was still the man of courage he had shown himself to be at the Templar inquest in 1311. (Though it is, of course, possible that the sermon as recorded later was more direct in its criticism than the one actually preached.)

Ironically, Pierre's moral disapproval of all forms of devaluation did not prevent him from exploiting it as a metaphor to make a didactic point: it was useless for men to attach importance to worldly goods, since they could not last. The man who thought the florin in his purse was a prize worth having had woken up one day recently to find that, by royal edict, it had lost half its value.[77] Given the times, it was not sensible to lay up treasures on earth, which in any circumstance distracted a man from his proper occupations. In fact, riches were like the bait on a fish-hook; though the occasional fish might see the hook, avoid it, and yet take some of the bait, most who approached it were caught (fo. 288ᵛ). The jaws of hell gaped for the rich. Therefore those who possessed wealth enough to live should not try to accumulate more; rather they should be charitable. To a congregation of doctors, Pierre held up as an example a doctor known to him who never charged the poor for his services and who, though he asked a modest sum of those who could afford it, gave away what he did not need in bursaries for poor scholars (fo. 25ᵛ).

Worse than avaricious laymen were luxury-loving clerics, ambitious for promotion. They should remember that to have one's name inscribed on a roll for future royal or papal promotion (an early reference to these *matriculae*) meant little. Those thus privileged often died before they actually acquired the promised benefice; and even if they did acquire it it might prove worthless. Besides, on the Day of Judgement all such rolls would be burned.[78] Men who were in a position to disburse

---

[77] 'Sicut nuper edicto regis floreni ceciderunt a medietate sui valoris in quo uno verbo homines spoliati sunt medietate suarum divitiarum' (fo. 226ᵛ). See also fos. 131ʳ and 131ᵛ. Pierre is referring to the edict of December 1330, described in the Continuation of *Chronique latine de Guillaume de Nangis*, ed. H. Géraud (Paris, 1843), ii. 131. The term 'florin' was popularly used for any gold coin. For an explanation of royal monetary policy on relative gold and silver values, see H. A. Miskimin, *Money, Prices and Foreign Exchange in Fourteenth-Century France* (New York, 1970), p. 92 and J. B. Hennemann, *Royal Taxation in Fourteenth-Century France: The Development of War Financing, 1322–1356* (Princeton, NJ, 1971), Appendix 1, pp. 321–5.

[78] 'Multi sunt scripti ad beneficia et dignitatus in matricula regis vel bulla apostolica qui antequam assequentur moriuntur, et cum adepte fuerunt postea

the goods of the church should regard themselves as the vicars, not the owners, of church revenues, which were intended for the poor (fo. 106^r). To give church goods to relations was dangerous; many clerics would burn in hell for their practice of nepotism—'Multi enim clerici et prelati comburuntur in inferno qui suos consanguineos nimis dilexerunt in mundo' (fo. 41^r). But the secular clergy had no monopoly of failings. The besetting sins of the religious were gluttony and self-admiration; the worst monks were nothing more than whited sepulchres (fo. 57^v). Any Preacher or Minor or other religious who boasted that he was more perfect than the others by this very boast demonstrated his own inferiority (fo. 80^r)—a comment surely intended as a blow against the Spirituals.

Nevertheless, Pierre's sermons concentrated less on the occasional failings of the friars than on their great potential for good. He summed up their function in a singularly tasteless metaphor: the Preachers act first as the teeth of the church in reducing sinners to pulp (fo. 41^r); they then drag the pap down into the stomach of the church, where it is forcibly fed on the milk of Holy Scripture and turned into Christ's body (fo. 42^r). Pierre painted his *confrères* as remorseless in their energy, violent in their war against sin. His sermon on the Feast of St Dominic (fos. 168^r–179^r) contained a small history of the inquisition, based on Bernard Gui's account, which provided the opportunity not only to praise the order's commitment to the extirpation of heresy, but also to condemn the Council of Vienne's decree *Multorum*, by which control of the inquisition was shared between the friars and the bishops, to the detriment of its efficiency (fo. 171^r).

Pierre's criticisms of his contemporaries are fairly standard in content, if more specific and nearer to the bone than the common run. He angled what he had to say very exactly to his audience: a sermon to an assembly containing doctors enjoined them to avoid all forms of sorcery (fo. 25^r); one to advocates implored them not to plead unjust cases (fo. 32^r); one on St Andrew to a largely lay audience used vivid military metaphors in driving home his points (fo. 1^v–7^r). Sometimes he would cite topical illustrations: equating the devil's temptations with poison in the human body, he referred to a treasurer of Sens who had recently died after having been bitten by a puppy (fo. 88^r). To illustrate the deprivations suffered by those who

in pulverem et cinerem rediguntur. Et in illa die omnia ad nichilum revertentur, bulla eorum comburentur, scripta eorum delentur' (fo. 123^r).

rebelled against God, he called in evidence the losses now inflicted on the count of Flanders who had revolted against the king (fo. 240^r).[79] Elsewhere he made his point by a verbal snapshot, for example of young men diving for gold, silver, and precious jewels in the river (fo. 109^r), symbolizing the search after God's wisdom; or others choosing to wash their tunics and chemises directly in the spring rather than in the stream that flowed from it (fo. 144^r), symbolizing the desire to reach the very fount of wisdom. Birds—particularly falcons, vultures, and eagles—flowers, and trees offered material for more standard metaphors, edifying and educational at the same time. For Pierre never forgot that sermons, as well as opening the path to heaven, provided some laymen with their only form of secondary schooling.[80] And though he preferred to instruct in biology, he was quite happy to explain eclipses (fos. 98^r and 98^v) or the causes of drought (fo. 83^v), to expound canon law (fo. 87^v), and to remind his audience of elementary rules of legal procedure (fo. 226^v).

The sermons echo the personal idiosyncrasies with which we are familiar from Pierre's other works: first, his tendency to express complicated relationships in terms of feudal bonds of one sort or another. Just as a *stipendiarius*, a mercenary soldier, may hold his money fee of the king at will, for life, or hereditarily, so may a man hold goods in this world from God (fo. 122^v). Christians enter the kingdom of God as apanage-holders, in virtue of their status as God's second-born children; thus they owe total loyalty to Christ, the first-born son of God, through whose generosity they enjoy what they have (fo. 44^v). And Pierre uses again the metaphor already familiar from his commentary on the *Sentences*: the effect of original sin is like the consequence of forfeiture on the heirs of the man who originally incurred the penalty (fo. 154^r). The second familiar trait is the constant use of military vocabulary to express man's struggle against the forces of evil. Sometimes Pierre

[79] This dates the sermon to after 17 September 1330 when Louis of Nevers, who had gained substantially from royal help at the Battle of Cassel in 1328, to which Pierre apparently makes reference, then turned against Philip VI on account of his support of Robert of Artois, and allied with Edward III of England.

[80] See S. Tugwell, ed., *Early Dominicans: Selected Writings* (New York, Romsey, and Toronto, 1982), p. 251 on Humbert de Romans's list of the requirements for a good performance at preaching: 'Another factor is a good collection of items of secular knowledge which are useful for edifying people and building them up. Anyone who is engaged in building collects things from all over the place which may be useful for him to build with.'

seems merely bloodthirsty. One simile he drew on frequently was that of the duel, in which the loser was hauled off to be hanged, while the winner was crowned and fêted. Considering the regularity with which he exhorted his audience to fight duels against the devil and all his helpers, it is odd to find him, in the sermon on St Louis, sharply attacking those secular courts that still employed duels to conclude quarrels where other methods had failed (fo. 197^r).[81] Even if Charlemagne had permitted duel as a means of dealing with Ganelon, other men should avoid it. This comment introduces the more literary form of Pierre's hunger for battle and bloodshed—his fascination with Charlemagne, his references to the *Visio Turpini* (fo. 161^r) and the *Gesta Karoli in Hyspania* (fo. 198^r), and also the citations from Geoffrey of Monmouth. The third notable characteristic is the serious attempt to provide a historical framework for the church's development from the end of the apostolic period. Since writing the *De potestate Papae*, Pierre had learned that there were two Italian emperors before the coronation of Otto I; his brief history of the Roman imperial power in the sermon on Corpus Christi therefore now included a Lombard tenure before the German (fo. 140^v). Uncritical though he was in many ways, he cared about historical truth in so far as he knew it. If he was a poor historian, it was not for the want of trying.

There is one central theme in Pierre's sermons which probably had an important effect on his future career: his commitment to the recovery of the Holy Land. He interrupted his minatory Corpus Christi sermon to recount the Sultan's alleged response to the Christian claim that Muslim domination over the holy places was illegal; the Sultan pointed out that since the Christians had earlier taken Palestine by force from the Muslims they had no right to it. In the face of what appeared to the Dominican to be such intransigent obtuseness, it was the duty of the French king and his counsellors to mount a crusade, rather than spending their time on the disreputable plans he feared they were hatching (fo. 140^v)—a tantalizing allusion. More surprisingly, he concluded the sermon on St Gregory (fos. 71^r–77^r), chiefly devoted to doctrine, with a prophetic call to take arms in Palestine. According to him, Muhammad's provision in the Koran that his law should be defended by

---

[81] Although Philip IV attempted to suppress the judicial duel, Louis X was pressured by the aristocracy into restoring it. R. W. Kaeuper, *War, Justice and Public Order: England and France in the Later Middle Ages* (Oxford, 1988), p. 247.

the sword proved he knew it was not founded on wisdom and justice and therefore could not survive except by force. Christians should understand that since Islam was born of the sword it would perish by the sword. The story of Sampson prefigured Christ's judgement on Islam: as Sampson won victories against the Philistines in his youth and vigour, so did Charlemagne and Godfrey de Bouillon; as he slipped from the path of the Lord and allowed himself to be captured, so did the Christians of Outremer. But all hope is not lost.[82] As Sampson brought down the columns of the temple on the heads of the Philistines, so shall the Christians recover the Holy Land. As Sampson died in the struggle, so shall some crusaders, and their names will be entered in the catalogue of martyrs (fo. 77[r]). Thus did Pierre prophesy in his attempt to reverse the events of 1291.

(c) *The Poverty Controversy*

The split between the Franciscan Conventuals under Michael of Cesena and Pope John XXII was the most painful rift the medieval Roman church ever suffered, separating the pope from that section of religious which, more than any other, had traditionally bolstered his authority.[83] The storm clouds gathered rapidly after the condemnation of Olivi's *Postill* in 1318 had broadened the basis of disagreement; whereas the earlier Avignon inquests had been directed only against Spiritual historicism, the conflict now spread to apostolic poverty and its implications. Pope John, long bothered by the problem of reconciling the order's understanding of *dominium* with his own legal preconceptions, started to worry about its claim to uniqueness in imitation of Christ. In order to air his concern, in March 1322 he revoked the prohibition on debate contained in *Exiit qui seminat* (the 1279 bull of Nicholas III which had ratified Bonaventura's teaching on poverty). Michael of

---

[82] 'Sampson iste est populus Christianus, qui prius per Karolum Magnum et per Godfredum recuperaverunt [sic] ab eis terram cum multa strage Sarrecenorum, humiliaverunt eos, quorum fortitudo fuit a deo non ab homine. Postmodum per culpam deserente deo captus est, per omnia privatus, captivatus. Sed si revertatus ad dominum redditur sibi pristina fortitudo' (fo. 76[v]).

[83] The best study remains M. D. Lambert, *Franciscan Poverty: The Doctrine of the Absolute Poverty of Christ and the Apostles in the Franciscan Order, 1210-1323* (London, 1961). For a more recent treatment of the controversy, see B. Tierney, *The Origins of Papal Infallibility, 1150-1350* (Leiden, 1972), pp. 171-204.

Cesena, fearing that the rest of *Exiit* was also in jeopardy, at once produced at the general chapter of Perugia an encyclical stating the traditional Franciscan position in unequivocal terms, backed by the assertion that 'What the apostolic see has approved as sound dogma is always to be adhered to and may not in any way be abandoned.' If his intention was to halt the pope in his tracks, he failed miserably. John promulgated *Ad conditorem* in December 1322, *Cum inter nonnullos* in November 1323, and *Quia quorundam* in November 1324. These bulls, by renouncing papal ownership of Franciscan goods, necessitated change in the practices of the order. But this was minor compared with their doctrinal impact. They condemned the proposition that religious perfection lay in abandoning ownership (*dominium*) and the right of use (*ius utendi*), retaining only the use itself (*simplex usus facti*); and they categorized it as rebellion against the Roman church to hold either that Christ and His apostles had held no property individually or in common, or that they had enjoyed no right of using, giving, selling, or exchanging their goods. Thus John denounced Franciscan convictions deriving in large part from Bonaventura himself. The Conventuals were stunned.

John's authoritative pronouncements galvanized his enemies. The Spirituals received support from new quarters. Marsilius of Padua, who determinedly challenged the pope's power of excommunicating rulers, reinforced his position in his *Defensor pacis*[84] by citing *Cum inter nonnullos* as proof of the need for radical reform in the church. Lewis of Bavaria in the Sachsenhausen appeal of May 1324 was emboldened to accuse John of heresy. The various opposition groups, motivated by very different political or religious sentiments, rallied in united protest. But the reaction of John's friends was muted, that of his hitherto most stalwart supporter Michael of Cesena confused. For three whole years Michael wrestled to reconcile the new bulls with *Exiit qui seminat* and with *Exivi de paradiso* of the Council of Vienne, which he interpreted as an endorsement of *Exiit*. But by December 1327 when he was summoned to Avignon he had seen the futility of his obfuscations. In April 1328 he was publicly upbraided by the pope for the stand he and the order had taken in 1322 at Perpignan; realizing that he was going to be forced to recant, he slipped quietly out of

---

[84] Ed. C. W. Previté-Orton (Cambridge, 1928). For an English translation (which offers the translator's view of Marsilius's meaning) see A. Gewirth, *Marsilius of Padua: The Defender of the Peace*, ii (New York, 1956).

Avignon on 28 May 1328, and fled, with William of Ockham, to Lewis of Bavaria. Under the emperor's protection, he launched at Pisa an intemperate tirade on the 'so-called Pope',[85] which circulated Europe in the form of a longer and a shorter appeal against John XXII.

There had been six years of tough debate between March 1322 and Michael's flight. Throughout this period Pierre de la Palud's pen lay still. His opinion had almost certainly been sought;[86] he had doubtless participated in the formal debates at all schools on which Pope John had insisted before the promulgation of *Ad conditorem* and *Cum inter nonnullos*. But unlike his contemporaries John of Naples or Gui de Terreni he did not choose to write on the matter until the point of no return. Then, after Michael's rebellion against papal authority had created a public scandal, Pierre was summoned to Avignon[87] and asked by the pope to respond to the shorter appeal. By this time compromise was impossible. The Franciscans faced a stark choice: either they accepted papal authority and reformed their order on a basis of property held in common; or they identified John XXII as the pseudo-pope of Olivi's prophecies, and escaped with their minister-general to the court of Lewis of Bavaria. Pierre's tract *De paupertate Christi et apostolorum contra Michelem de Cezena* (Paris, Bibliothèque nationale, MS Latin 4046, fos. 36ᵛ–60ʳ) was designed to persuade them of the merits of the former course. However, its survival in only one manuscript suggests that it did not circulate far in Franciscan circles.

The restraint Pierre exhibited in this tract was explicable in terms of the suffering the whole affair apparently caused him. Though he (with Gui de Terreni) had helped in 1318–19 to prepare the way for John XXII's bulls, he had not then been fully aware of the ramifications of the controversy. His own adherence in 1317 to a definition of poverty now condemned

---

[85] Edited in Baluze–Mansi, *Miscellanea*, iii. 303–10.

[86] *CUP* ii. 274, no. 828. According to the 15th-cent. chronicler Nicholas Glassberger, Pierre, with other members of the 1318 commission, was summoned to Avignon in 1323 to add another clause to the earlier condemnation (*Analecta Franciscana*, 2 (Florence, 1887), 149). But the clause Nicholas quoted, on the identity of Franciscan poverty with that of Christ, is usually held to have been part of the original condemnation. Alvarus Pelagius (*De statu et planctu ecclesie* (Venice, 1560), fo. 144ᵛ) said that in 1323 recourse was had to the *consilium magistrorum*, which I interpret as meaning that the masters' sealed letter of 1318 was consulted.

[87] Continuation of *Chronique latine de Guillaume de Nangis*, ed. Géraud, ii. 108.

created awkwardness for him, as did his regular support of Michael in his fight against the Spirituals. A major change of heart was not easy. Therefore he framed *De paupertate* solely to refute Michael's allegation that Pope John XXII was a heretic, without embroiling himself in irrelevant aspects of the issue. He began by citing Michael's nine charges in full, so that his readers could refer back to them as they considered his arguments for the defence; and he reckoned his task completed when he had demonstrated all nine to be untenable. Pierre spoke less to theologians, either at the papal court or in Paris, than to the rump of the order, the friars left masterless after Michael's flight; his concluding message was: those who had thought as Michael did before the pope defined otherwise had committed no sin; only those who now insisted on adhering to old opinions were heretics (fo. 60ᵛ). By 1328 this was a common-sense approach. If the Franciscan order was to survive at all, it could not afford to refight the issues. It must bury the past and accept that John's bulls, far from subverting the Franciscan way of life, had simply corrected a misapprehension about what was central to it. The Friars Minor must now rise, shake themselves, and get on with living.

A clue as to how Pierre thought this might be done is to be found in his fine sermon on St Francis (Clermont Ferrand, Bibliothèque municipale, MS 46, fos. 228ᵛ–235ʳ), which seems to have been preached rather late in his career, probably after 1328, certainly well after 1324. Here he carefully avoided all reference to the most controversial aspects of the Franciscan prophetic tradition, whether Conventual or Joachite. By allowing that Francis may have been a herald of the second coming as John the Baptist was of the first (fo. 234ᵛ), he made a small concession to Bonaventuran thinking; in addition he accepted Francis's unique status as the only saint in Christian history to bear the stigmata (fo. 230ᵛ). Nevertheless he insisted that the real significance of Francis's life for Christians in this world was simple: he had set an example of how to live by overcoming all the temptations of this world; by minimizing the impact of original sin, he had gone on to inherit true freedom in heaven— his very name, Francis, meant freedom (fo. 230ʳ). To drive his lesson home, Pierre drew a complicated parallel between the degrees of freedom allowed to different categories of freedmen in Roman law and the different degrees of emancipation from sin that could be achieved by Christians. Francis, by his excellent life and ample penance, had achieved the highest degree of emancipation open to men: on his death he had escaped the pains of purgatory.[88] Those who followed him should concentrate as he did on preaching, hearing confessions, and providing living examples of Christian perfection, not just to secure their own salvation but also to save others (fo. 234ᵛ).

The words of the sermon were passionate and committed. Pierre was convinced that the Franciscan way of life remained crucial to the survival of the church in the world. Yet had a Friar Minor heard this sermon about a decade before it was delivered, he would have thought it a distinctly eccentric variation on the usual theme because, while the virtues extolled were genuinely Franciscan, they were not presented in the standard way. Pierre advocated poverty as a means of preventing distraction, not as an end in itself; he said nothing of the need to avoid litigiousness; nor did he mention Christ's example, so dear to Francis's heart. In portraying the saint as triumphing over sin he was offering advice to his disciples: the Friars Minor, rather than brooding on their own distinctive character, should concentrate on those aspects of life they shared with all other Christians.

The sermon shows Pierre at his most constructive. As advocate for John against Michael of Cesena he was, understandably, less so; he had, after all, been asked to demonstrate the folly of Michael's charges, not to submit a consistent alternative viewpoint. Still, he did try to be fair. As a lawyer he was intrigued by the disputes over *dominium* and *usus*, appreciated some of Michael's points, but emphasized that, in employing these words in their commonly accepted legal meanings, John's bulls were perfectly rational. To use or consume a thing without either possessing it or having the right to do so was an unlawful act and therefore sinful.[89] Since perfection could not lie in theft, Michael of Cesena was obviously wrong in condemning John for his refusal to accept the Franciscan definition of perfection.

With his fellow Dominicans, Pierre interpreted the Scriptural passages the Franciscans used to prove the apostles' absolute poverty as actually demonstrating common ownership in the primitive church. On this reading of the texts the Franciscans

[88] Here Pierre drew on his teaching about the way in which penitence can change eternal punishment into temporal punishment and even, in the case of perfect contrition, abolish punishment altogether. Commentary on Book 4 of the *Sentences*, 19. 7.

[89] 'In constitutione in medietate ubi probandum quod non possit esse usus rei licitus sine jure utendi, intendit talem rationem quia nullus potest uti licite re aliena nisi ex concessione domini sibi facta' (fo. 51ᵛ).

were wrong to claim that the apostles had rejected *dominium*. Not only did they have full proprietorship of their goods as a community, but each individual apostle was given *dominium utile*—ownership—in what he needed (fo. 42ʳ). Pierre compared this with a communally owned meadow, on which each villager might graze his animals, but none might alienate or sell the whole (fo. 41ʳ). On this analogy, the church had always followed the example of Christ by vesting its goods in colleges and religious foundations. While the Franciscans claim that Christ's poverty had been perfect was certainly true, its perfection had lain not in abjuration of ownership but in lack of desire to own (fo. 46ʳ). As to the manifestation of such perfection in the contemporary church, though the contemplative orders ought indeed to renounce litigiousness as the Franciscans taught, there was no reason why the secular church, following the example of St Peter, should do so when its public property was at stake (fo. 50ʳ); indeed, St Thomas of Canterbury was held in high esteem precisely because he had been willing to fight for the church's rights (fo. 46ᵛ).[90] Sanctity and litigiousness could go together, as indeed could sanctity and wealth.

This conservative and fairly conventional argument was the prelude to Pierre's main preoccupation, the refutation of Michael of Cesena's attack on papal legislative power. In the bull *Ad conditorem*, John XXII had declared 'There is no doubt that it pertains to the founder of the canons, when he perceives that statutes put forward by himself or his predecessors are disadvantageous rather than advantageous, to provide that they be no longer disadvantageous.' In the pope's opinion *Cum inter nonnullos* had simply remedied a defect in *Exiit qui seminat*. For Michael of Cesena, however, *Cum inter nonnullos* had undermined the Catholic faith by contradicting a statement the church had earlier accepted as orthodox. The fundamental question was the one that had been raised in the Jean de Pouilly controversy: if on the one hand canon lawyers contended that no pope was bound by the disciplinary bulls of his predecessors, and on the other all Catholics knew that no pope could alter divine law, how could any papal bull be satisfactorily assigned to one or other category? But while there was no novelty in the underlying issue, the tone adopted during the discussion was quite new. For Jean de Pouilly had limited his attack to criticism

---

[90] St Thomas of Canterbury was a familiar figure in the La Palud household, since the family had long connections with the collegiate church of Fourvière in Lyons, dedicated to the Virgin and St Thomas; J. Beyssac, *Les Prévots de Fourvière* (Lyons, 1908).

of *Inter cunctas* after Benedict XI's death, but Michael was publicly denouncing John XXII as a heretic across Italy and Germany and calling on all who heard him to fight against the pope in defence of the Catholic faith. The argument had changed from a bad-tempered squabble among Paris schoolmen into a major international row, in which virtually no ecclesiastic could afford to be neutral.

Granted the tension of the years 1328-9 and the impassioned violence of Michael's Pisa shorter appeal, Pierre's response was surprisingly temperate. He began by accepting that certain popes of the early Middle Ages had erred; repetition of error by a pope was therefore a possibility. None the less, it was not up to individuals like Michael to accuse John of such error—he must await the judgement of a general council: 'Si summus pontifex errat non est cuilibet eum corrigere nec ei errores imponere sed tantum concilii generalis [sic]' (fo. 55ʳ). Pierre agreed that a papal pronouncement which contravened the true faith or Christian morality should be rescinded (fo. 54ʳ). Equally he agreed that no pope could legitimately revoke a statement made by one of his predecessors which was clearly consistent with Christ's words and which had been explicitly accepted by the church. But he emphatically denied that any pope who had consulted with his cardinals and bishops before pronouncing had ever erred in the faith; furthermore, he denied that this could happen (fo. 55ʳ).[91]

Using this statement of faith—similar to the one in his Quodlibet of 1314—as his premiss, Pierre set out to offer possible explanations for the discrepancies between Pope Nicholas III's *Exiit* and Pope John XXII's three bulls. The first and obvious way of accounting for head-on contradiction was to deny its existence, to argue that the two points of view were only apparently in conflict; deeper understanding of their meaning would allow them to be harmonized. John XXII had pointed in this direction in *Cum inter nonnullos* and in *Quia quorundam*, Michael had long entertained hopes of reconcilia-

---

[91] 'Romanus pontifex non potest revocare nec destruere illa que in fide et moribus sunt a suis predecessoribus diffinita que aperte sunt dictis Christi et apostolorum consona et a sanctis patris in conciliis ex certa scientia et ab universali ecclesia specialiter et explicite recepta ... Christus est veritas dicens Dico ego vobiscum sum omnibus diebus. Item hoc est verum fatum de ecclesia romana que dispositione deo omnium ecclesiarum caput est, regula et magister, non quin successor Petri in sede romana possit ad horam errare sicut Petrus, sed romana ecclesia cum et capite et membris cardinalibus et prelatis creditur numquam errare ... Impugnantes istam constitutionem universalis ecclesie impugnant universalem ecclesiem que errare non potest' (fo. 55ʳ).

tion, and Pierre deliberately left this door open to the Franciscans (who eventually took it). But he introduced the possibility tentatively—'posset dici'; he offered no new arguments to support it; and he passed over the issue fast (fo. 54^r). He was, it seems, as little convinced by it as were his Dominican and Michaelist contemporaries.[92] That, however, was not the point of raising it. His main task was to demonstrate the logical holes in Michael's contention that the pope was destroying the faith by contradicting it. The burden of proof lay firmly on the shoulders of the man who dared to launch such criticism.

The second alternative offered a possible constitutional explanation: for a papal statement to bind in perpetuity it had to be properly promulgated. There could, in Pierre's view, be no doubt that John's recent bulls had been, since they had been discussed in the schools and approved by cardinals and prelates.[93] But the status of *Exiit* was more doubtful. He knew of no evidence that Nicholas III had consulted before producing it (fo. 56^v). If it had in fact been improperly promulgated, then error might well have crept in. On this assumption, the church had patiently tolerated that error until such time as a better understanding of the question had emerged (fo. 54^r), and Pope John had then done his duty in giving legislative form to the improved version. The Roman church, far from vacillating in matters of faith, as Michael accused it of doing, was establishing the truth step by step with increasing clarity.

This hypothesis arose out of Pierre's conviction of the church's inerrancy, combined with his need to know when it had truly spoken. In 1314 he had stipulated consultation with the cardinals as necessary for a properly promulgated bull. Now he defined the Roman and universal church, 'ecclesia Romana et universalis', as including not only the cardinals but also the prelates—'Romana ecclesia cum et capite et membris cardinalibus et prelatis' (fo. 54^v); furthermore, he now regarded consultation with the schools as a relevant, if not a necessary, criterion for a valid statement of faith.[94] The change in ter-

---

[92] Here I disagree with R. Chabanne in his entry on Pierre in *Dictionnaire de droit canonique*, vi (Paris, 1957), cols. 1481-4, who thinks Pierre was seriously interested in this solution.

[93] On John's order that the bulls should be read in the schools, see *CUP* ii. 276, no. 833; ii. 279, no. 836.

[94] 'Iste constitutiones nove sequentes de dominio Christi et apostolorum in communi et in speciali et quod non est usus facti licitus sine iure utendi et similia . . . sunt facte de consilio fratrum et prelatorum in romana curia . . . et in istis concordat et consentit universitas magistrorum in theologia et in decretis in generalibus studiis' (fo. 55^v).

minology, the addition of 'universal' to 'Roman', was a small one, perhaps so small that he was not conscious of it. Yet by broadening his definition and incorporating the prelates within the inerrant church, he clearly demonstrated his position as lying within the mainstream of theological opinion. If he had ever deserved the label 'infallibilist', he clearly no longer did so.

Did this second hypothesis in fact represent Pierre's own opinion? It was certainly consistent with much that he had maintained throughout his scholarly career. Yet it would be uncharacteristic of him to stipulate that the supreme test of a papal bull's truth lay not in its contents but in the way in which it was promulgated. Unlike Marsilius of Padua, he did not elsewhere conceive of religious truth as the automatic outcome of proper constitutional procedures—though these were always a useful curb on error. That the Roman or universal church had never erred was his deep-rooted conviction; but Christ's promise to Peter was its true buttress. In his mind consultation was apparently the catalyst rather than a reactive agent of truth. Nevertheless, his thesis was seductive and induced in John's supporters a sense of confidence.

The third hypothesis Pierre offered questioned Michael's assumption that the issue was a matter of faith.[95] If there was doubt whether *Exiit* was concerned with faith, or if it expressed an opinion that was no more probable than its contrary, then any succeeding pope was free to revoke it without untoward consequence for the church's beliefs. It was simply a law like any other law, and could not bind future legislators.[96] Pierre was notably detached in his handling of this tricky point. And his fourteenth-century readers may have been quick to detect within his argument an implied source of comfort for the defeated party. Although the Franciscans had no immediate alternatives between blind obedience to the papal diktat and

---

[95] For the view that John XXII had always believed the matter to be purely one of discipline, see J. Heft, *John XXII and Papal Teaching Authority* (Lewiston and Queenston, 1986), p. 166.

[96] 'Dicendum quod diffinitio summi pontificis omnes sibi subditos ligat sed non potest ligare successorem qui nichil habet ab eo quia par in parem non habet imperium. Ideo quod unus summus pontifex diffinit potest alius renuntiare prout dictum est. In tali condicione evidenter constat alterum illorum aliud diffinire contra fidem vel bonos mores alterum econtra, standum esset illi cuius dicta evidenter fidei consonant et non alteri sive prior sive posterior diffinit. Sed in dubio et ubi equalis probabilitas est utrique, posterioris diffinitioni standum est potius quam prioris quia prior non potuit ut dictum est successori legem imponat' (fo. 54^r).

rebellion, in the longer term they might profit by a case made out in these terms; for if *Exiit* was not a statement of faith, then John XXII's canons probably were not either; therefore a future pope might be prevailed upon to annul them. Pierre even mentioned the possibility: 'successor potest legem precessorum totaliter revocare et contrariam ordinare et tunc prima habetur pro non facta, secunda tenet donec fuerit revocata' (a succeeding pope can totally revoke the law of his predecessors and ordain the opposite; in this situation the earlier law is treated as if it had never existed and the present one obliges until revoked; fo. 54^r). There were, therefore, covert grounds for hope. But naturally the Franciscans were denied freedom of speech to agitate for this change of policy.[97]

Pierre was in the fortunate position of only having to demonstrate the futility of his opponent's indictment; he did not need to build up a case of his own on poverty. Which of the three hypotheses he propounded convinced him he did not say— probably he alternated between the second and the third. And on all issues other than the pope's heresy, he was in the game of damage limitation, as can be seen in his conciliatory tone on the Scriptural part of Michael's appeal. Michael's opinions on poverty had in the past been held by many Catholic people (fo. 43^r);[98] if it was now wrong to say that the apostles possessed nothing after Christ had sent them off to preach, it was equally perilous to hold that Judas, in taking charge of the purse on Christ's orders, was demonstrating his true apostleship.[99] The safe middle way postulated that the apostles always adhered to Christ's command in taking nothing for their journey when they preached, but that for all other occasions they had modest possessions in common (fo. 58^v). They thus avoided not ownership, but any superfluity (fo. 57^v). Such austerity was compatible with Franciscan practice, if not theory, and must have offered some consolation to the Franciscans who remained in France after Michael's flight. Again, in keeping with his desire to cause the minimum offence, Pierre was careful to make no new accusations of his own. (He did condemn Olivi's writings,

[97] Heft, *John XXII and Papal Teaching Authority*, pp. 179–80, argues that John would not have thought a subsequent revocation of his bulls possible, because the theses they condemned were condemned on Scriptural grounds. But Pierre did not necessarily share this view.

[98] Was he thinking of his own position in 1317?

[99] This may have been a caricature of Pope John XXII's argument, later incorporated in *Quia vir reprobus*, that propriety was of the essence of perfection; see G. Leff, *Heresy in the Later Middle Ages: The Relation of Heterodoxy to Dissent, c. 1250–1450* (Manchester and New York, 1967), i. 248–9.

but for a proposition that had already been declared heretical; fo. 43ᵛ.) Only at the end of the tract did he call Michael a heretic, and that less for his heterodox opinions than for his contumacious refusal of obedience to his spiritual lord.[100] Nevertheless *De paupertate* does prove that on one central point Pierre had changed his mind: though while writing the *De potestate Papae* he had considered *simplex usus facti* to be the expression of perfect poverty, by now he had been converted to John's view that it was 'vana, fictiva atque simulata'. Most of the arguments he produced to back up this contention were the standard ammunition of the papal party. One, however, was all his own: he declared the Franciscan connection between the renunciation of *dominium* and poverty to be misleading; the rich man is not the noble who owns *dominium* and high justice but has nothing to live on; rather he is the merchant who has no *dominium* but enjoys an abundance of grain, wine, and oil (fo. 53ʳ). The reference to comparative noble and mercantile standards of living in early fourteenth-century France is revealing and characteristic. But it was a debater's point that did not clarify the major issue at all.

De paupertate was but one in an endless stream of polemical tracts for or against the Franciscan case, dealing with such rarefied questions as whether a servant who is given bread by his master has a usufruct or any other right to that bread; or the logical relation between use and abuse. Apart from the relative moderation of its tone, there is little of high intellectual worth in Pierre's tract. Yet at one point it exhibited a concern with the fundamentals of the faith that was usually lacking in such polemics: in arguing that it was not in fact *dominium* but original sin that lay at the heart of the world's disorientation (fo. 57ʳ), Pierre showed both the soundness of his basic theological training and a well-grounded sense of proportion. Had these characteristics been commoner, the fourteenth-century church would have been less troubled.

---

[100] There is much in common between *De paupertate* and the tract of Cardinal Jacques Fournier (the future pope Benedict XII), as reconstructed by P. C. Schmitt in *Un Pape réformateur et un défenseur de l'unité de l'Eglise: Benôit XII et l'ordre des Frères Mineurs, 1334–1342* (Florence, 1959), pp. 158–67.

6. Patriarch

(a) Egyptian Mission

While he was at Avignon, on 27 March 1329, Pierre was appointed Patriarch of Jerusalem,[1] a venerable title of high prestige. On one level it was not a particularly surprising promotion; his predecessor in the office, Raymond Béguin, had been a fellow student at St Jacques.[2] Dominicans were sound appointees to a post which often required of its incumbent that he should preach the crusade,[3] and Pierre's rhetorical skills were well known. On the other hand, since the fall of Acre in 1291 and the loss of almost all the churches and lands subordinated to it, the patriarchate had usually been relatively insignificant among Latin bishoprics. Only Pierre de Pleine Chassagne had achieved standing in the church, and that chiefly through his office as papal legate during the 1316 Hospitaller crusade.[4] Raymond Béguin had lived inconspicuously in Cyprus on the surviving revenues of his office, supplemented by what he could get from the bishopric of Limassol which he had held in commendam.[5] A man of Pierre's aristocratic standing might well, despite his Joinville connection, have resisted the promotion to so uninviting a see, pleading in his defence the Dominican order's disapproval of friars becoming bishops.

But on this occasion there was the possibility of better things. The deciding factor in Pierre's acceptance was the hope, current in the second half of the 1320s, that the Mameluk sultan of Egypt, al-Nazir Muhammed, might negotiate a settlement with the Latins permitting them to return to Palestine. Al-Nazir's kindness towards Christians in the East, his restoration of a church in Cairo to the Latin rite, and his reputation for

---

[1] Lettres communes, ed. Mollat, no. 44849.

[2] A. de Guimaraes, 'Hérvé Noël († 1323): Étude biographique', AFP 8 (1938), 66 n. 42.

[3] J. Delaville le Roulx, La France en Orient au XIVᵉ siècle (Paris, 1886), i. 78.

[4] See N. Housley, The Avignon Papacy and the Crusades, 1307-1378 (Oxford, 1986), pp. 111, 245.

[5] Lettres communes, ed. Vidal, no. 21; on the revenues of the patriarchate, swelled by the gift of the church of the Holy Sepulchre in Aquapendente, see L. de Mas Latrie, 'Les Patriarches latins de Jérusalem', Revue de l'Orient latin, i (1893), 16–17.

justice had been interpreted in Europe as indicators of political flexibility. The sultan was in regular communication with King James II of Aragon—to the considerable annoyance of the pope, because the Aragonese in pursuit of Egyptian goodwill frequently breached the blockade on trade in the Mediterranean which had been a central plank of papal policy since 1291.[6] But the connection allowed rumours of the sultan's goodwill to circulate. In 1327, in response to a vague suggestion that al-Nazir might surrender Jerusalem to the king of France, both Charles IV and John XXII attempted to open talks with him. Charles through his envoy Guillaume de Bonnesmenil,[7] John through two apostolic nuncios. Though both efforts failed, they were sabotaged by Christians, not Muslims, which kept hopes for the future alive. And in 1328 the sultan sent courteous letters to Philip VI and John,[8] thus confirming their optimism on Palestine.

When Pierre became patriarch, the prospect was entertained in Avignon of his restoration to the see in Jerusalem and his consequent government of the Latin church throughout Outremer. In June 1329 the pope gave Pierre, his household, and six literate Dominicans permission to visit the Holy Land, committing to his care the Holy Sepulchre, the Dominican enclosure, and all other churches in Outremer. This grant was accompanied by an indult to celebrate mass everywhere, to consecrate and reconsecrate churches and chapels, and to dispense in cases of secret baptisms or other sacraments conducted without due ceremony[9]—proof that John expected Pierre to find an underground Christian community surviving in Palestine.[10] Together these papal letters outlined a coherent

---

[6] G. Meersseman, 'La Chronologie des voyages et des œuvres de frère Alphonse Buenhombre O.P.', *AFP* 10 (1940), 79; A. S. Atiya, *Egypt and Aragon. Embassies and Diplomatic Correspondence between 1300 and 1330* (Leipzig, 1938), pp. 11–12.

[7] M. H. Lot, 'Essai d'intervention de Charles le Bel en faveur des chrétiens d'Orient, tenté avec le concours de Pape Jean XXII', *BEC* 36 (1875), 588–600.

[8] Recorded by Sanudo, see P. Viollet, *HLF* 35. 59 and n. 3; see also Raynaldus, *Annales ecclesiastici*, v. 411.

[9] *Lettres communes*, ed. Mollat, no. 45363.

[10] Pierre certainly thought that there were large numbers of Latin Christians in the East who dared not openly confess their beliefs through fear of the death penalty. Clermont Ferrand, Bibliothèque municipale, MS 46, fo. 29ᵛ: 'Multi enim negaverunt Christum pro timore qui tamen credebant cum corde; et adhuc usque hodie sunt multi apostate inter Sarracenos qui fidem Christi tenent corde et confiterentur ore coram Christianis occulte sanctis, et dicentes legem Mahommeti nichil esse. Sed timore mortis non audent hoc confiteri publice quia statim decapitarentur.' Cf. Étienne de Bourbon, *Anecdotes historiques, légendes et apologues*, ed. A. Lecoy de la Marche (Paris, 1877), p. 275.

programme of action. The events of 1244 and 1291 were on the point of being reversed. On what conditions? The Lanercost Chronicle, a nearly contemporary document, records under the year 1336 terms reputedly offered by the sultan to the patriarch. Al-Nazir was willing to allow the return of the Latin clergy to Outremer; they might reopen all churches, worship freely and openly, run their own spiritual affairs without intervention, and take tithes as they had done in the past. Pilgrims and merchants would once again be welcomed in the country. However, the Christians would be permitted neither temporal power nor jurisdiction. In return for this great concession to the Latin church, the sultan demanded no monetary compensation; but he insisted that the pope revoke all sentences of excommunication against merchants who had traded with his people.[11]

These terms, although actually recorded in 1336 when a crusade was thought to be imminent, may well represent al-Nazir's normal negotiating position with the pope in the 1320s and 1330s. By ending the western blockade on Egypt he would greatly assist Mameluk commerce, in which he had a deep interest; the peace would enhance his already exalted personal prestige as a diplomat; and it would put an end to the irritation of crusading initiatives. Toleration of yet one more Christian sect in Palestine was a small price to pay for these advantages. On the other hand these conditions were almost certainly unacceptable to the pope and the king of France, both because they prohibited the restoration of the kingdom of Jerusalem, and because they treated the Latins on equal terms with the other Christian sects in Palestine. Nevertheless the sultan's evident interest in negotiation aroused expectation that more favourable terms might be wrung from him by a formal embassy to Cairo. Great optimism was in the air. Pierre's appointment as patriarch was the crucial step in a Franco-papal initiative to redraw the map of the Middle East.

By June 1329 the first steps were being taken towards fulfilling this ambitious programme: Pierre was preparing to leave for Cyprus. The immediate reason for his journey was a royal wedding.[12] In March 1328 King Hugh IV of Cyprus had sent proctors to France to negotiate a marriage between his son and heir Guy, prince of Galilee, and Marie, daughter of Louis de Clermont, duke of Bourbon. Hugh had chosen his son's bride

---

[11] *The Chronicle of Lanercost*, tr. Sir H. Maxwell (Glasgow, 1913), pp. 302–3.
[12] Meersseman, 'La chronologie', pp. 80, 82.

because he had confidence in Louis's attachment to a crusade, since the duke had in 1318 been named commander of an army intended to reconquer the Holy Land.[13] The projected union of the two houses would refurbish the Franco-Cypriot alliance, essential to any successful re-establishment of Christian power in Palestine. By 19 March 1329 the terms of the contract had been agreed, and Louis engaged with Sadoc Doria to equip four galleys for the transport of his daughter from Aigues-Mortes to Cyprus.[14] Then on 24 July the duke nominated Pierre de la Palud and two knights as his procurators for the lady on her journey.[15] Later Guillaume, bishop of Mende, Marie's confessor, was added to the group, doubtless to Pierre's pleasure because he was an old friend and sparring partner. And before it sailed the official party was joined by large numbers of pilgrims who hoped to journey on from Cyprus to visit the holy places in Jerusalem.[16]

From Pierre's point of view the one drawback to these splendid plans was financial. The revenues of Jerusalem, even when increased by those of Limassol (which had been granted to him *in commendam* for life on the day he was made patriarch[17]) still added up to a sum inadequate for the expenses he foresaw. Since his elevation he had acquired a household, soon to be swollen for the journey by the six Dominicans mentioned in the papal grant. All his entourage would have to be shipped to Cyprus and then to Cairo, since by August 1329 it had definitely been decided that he should negotiate face to face with al-Nazir.[18] The patriarch's aristocratic upbringing had doubtless taught him to despise cheese-paring, particularly on a diplomatic mission. How could the necessary costs be met? In response to his plea, Pope John gave him an unusual privilege: he might absolve forty merchants excommunicated for having traded with the Egyptians, and take half the profit thus accrued to cover his expenses on the voyage to Cairo. (This singular remission of papal rigour against offending merchants was presumably justified by the assumption that the end of the blockade was imminent.) John also conferred on Pierre

---

[13] *Titres de la maison ducale de Bourbon*, ed. M. Huillard-Bréholles, i (Paris, 1867), no. 1509.
[14] Ibid., no. 1888.
[15] Ibid., no. 1894.
[16] Continuation of *Chronique latine de Guillaume de Nangis*, ed. H. Géraud (Paris, 1843), ii. 110.
[17] *Lettres communes*, ed. Mollat, no. 44850.
[18] Ibid., no. 45363.

permission to raise a loan of 1,000 golden florins, along with the right to tax Limassol and the churches subject to the patriarchate, and exemption from such tithes as the Archbishop of Nicosia might wish to exact.[19] These concessions were, from the Cypriot point of view, ill-timed. Made at the expense of the Latin church on the island, they added to the burdens of the local clergy, who could ill tolerate further financial loss at a time when the pope's crusade taxation was affecting their revenues.[20] Some resentment against the patriarch was therefore inevitable.

In the autumn of 1329 the four galleys set sail for Cyprus. The journey was presumably as squalid, cramped, and miserable as crossings of the Mediterranean usually were in this period. But the fleet escaped danger and the party arrived in Nicosia in time for the wedding to take place in January 1330. Thus at least one of Pierre's commissions was fulfilled. While planning the second, the journey to Cairo, he may have stayed at the house in the citadel of Nicosia traditionally assigned to the patriarch of Jerusalem, where he would have had time to look round him. The sullenness of the local inhabitants usually exerted little charm over western visitors. In April 1330 the Venetian merchant Sanudo wrote:

The land of Cyprus which is inhabited by Greeks, and the island of Crete, and all the other lands and islands which belong to the principality of the Morea and the duchy of Athens are all inhabited by Greeks; and although they are obedient in words, they are none the less hardly obedient in their hearts, although temporal and spiritual authority is in Latin hands.[21]

Pierre had always regarded the Greeks as heretics; his prejudices were too strong to be overcome by a meeting—there is no reason to think he even tried to contact the Greek bishop of Limassol. And while the sophisticated court of Hugh IV appealed strongly to some Latins, Pierre was probably too austere

---

[19] *Lettres communes*, ed. Mollat, nos. 45366, 45955, 45470, 45471, 45472, 45473.

[20] G. Hill, *A History of Cyprus* (Cambridge, 1948), ii. 193–4 and n. 2 on future financial trouble over the concessions. On the taxation of the Cypriot church, Y. Renouard, *Les Relations des papes d'Avignon et des compagnies commercials et bancaires de 1316 à 1378* (Paris, 1941), pp. 164–5.

[21] Quoted by K. Setton, in J. M. Hussey, ed., *The Cambridge Medieval History*, iv. 1, 2nd edn. (Cambridge, 1966), p. 429. For trouble between the Greek and Latin hierarchies, see *Acta Ioannis XXII (1317–1334) e registris vaticanis aliisque fontibus collectis*, ed. A. L. Tautu (Vatican, 1952), pp. 68–75.

to be attracted by its southern culture. But he will surely have admired the great church of Hagia Sophia in Nicosia, the nave of which had only been completed in 1326;[22] and in the Dominican convent, its splendid church the mausoleum for the kings of Cyprus, he will have felt at home.

In the spring the patriarch and the bishop of Mende set off for Egypt. Their route led them first to Acre, where they waited for letters of safe conduct from the sultan; then they marched down the coast of Palestine by the Pilgrims' castle, Jaffa, Rama, and Gaza, crossed the desert to Alexandria, and finally came up the Nile to Cairo.[23] It is unfortunate that Pierre, normally given to exploiting his visual memory for striking similes, never later referred to his Egyptian journey in his sermons—his diplomatic failure perhaps caused him to banish the whole episode from his mind. There is therefore no direct evidence of the impression the city made on him. A Dominican friar, Humbert de Dijon, who was in his party, was impressed by the fortification of the sultan's palace; otherwise his description of the ruler's retinue as containing 10,000 armed guards, 10,000 trumpeters, actors, and entertainers, and 1,500 wives, surely owed more to Christian prejudice than to observation.[24] But an Italian traveller who visited Cairo in the same year was a more lively eye witness, talking in awe of the sultan's 14,000 troops, of his six elephants 'quos vidi et tetigi' (which I saw and touched), of his eight lions, and—most wonderful of all—his giraffe.[25] The patriarch had the advantage over the Italian merchant of penetrating into the Mameluk court, where the formalities of eastern protocol and the lavishness of dress must have all but taken his breath away.

But time for marvelling was strictly limited. The initial part of the negotiation was conducted with underlings; before settling down to the real business, the envoys had a small commission to fulfil for Philip VI. The king wanted to know the truth about Guillaume de Bonnesmenil's mission of 1327; had his failure really been due, as Guillaume asserted, to a Catalan rival's malice and acts of piracy? In Egypt Pierre easily

---

[22] T. S. Boase in H. W. Hazard, ed., *A History of the Crusades,* iv (gen. ed. K. Setton; Madison, Wisc., 1977), pp. 167 and 172.

[23] T. Kaeppeli and P. Benoit, 'Un Pélerinage dominicain inédit du XIVe siècle', *Revue biblique,* 62 (1955), 518–19. It is interesting that the party regarded the land route as far safer than a journey by sea from Jaffa.

[24] Ibid., p. 521.

[25] G. Golubovich, *Biblioteca bio-bibliografica delle Terra Santa e dell'Oriente francescano,* iii (Florence, 1919), p. 336.

acquired the evidence to vindicate Guillaume.[26] However, the incident should have alerted him to a continuing problem in Franco-Mameluk relations: al-Nazir's commercial interests in a treaty with the west could be satisfied in two mutually exclusive ways. He could either negotiate with the French and the papacy for a permanent lifting of the commercial blockade in return for a concession on Outremer; or he could keep the *status quo* in Outremer and follow his traditional alliance with the Aragonese. It was ominous for Pierre and Durand that in February 1330 the sultan had written to King Alfonso IV of Aragon, renewing the relationship he had enjoyed with the king's predecessor.[27] Therefore on Pierre's arrival in Cairo Aragonese influence may even have been at work covertly to combat the French initiative.

A Mameluk annal records a French mission received by the sultan on 15 April 1330, and given leave to depart nine days later;[28] but what happened during the neotiations can only be conjectured. According to the continuator of Guillaume de Nangis, Pierre's task was to discover if the Holy Land could be recovered for Christians by any means other than war.[29] If this is an accurate statement, then the embassy was instructed to demand some kind of political control within Palestine, and to back that demand with the threat of a crusade.[30] Pierre seems to have tried a legalistic form of persuasion—since the sultan reverenced the law, he should hand back the lands his ancestors had conquered by force.[31] Reasonably enough, al-Nazir's spokesman replied that the Christian armies had them-

---

[26] M. H. Lot, 'Essai d'intervention de Charles le Bel en faveur des chrétiens d'Orient, tenté avec le concours de Pape Jean XXII', *BEC* 36 (1875), 588–600; Golubovich, *Biblioteca bio-bibliografica*, p. 36.

[27] Atiya, *Egypt and Aragon*, p. 63.

[28] Ibid., p. 64.

[29] Continuation of *Chronique latine de Guillaume de Nangis*, ed. Géraud, ii. 130–1.

[30] Golubovich, *Biblioteca bio-bibliografica*, iii. 366–7, contains an undated account by Ibn Fadl Allāh al ʿUmarī taken from his *al Taʿrīf bi 'l-muṣṭalaḥ al-sharīf* of what he said was the only French mission to the sultan during the reign of al-Nazir. On this occasion the envoys proposed that in return for a hefty annual payment, the area from Caesarea to Ascalon should be returned to the Latins. The sultan, infuriated by their presumption, became belligerent, warning them that if they dared to attack Jerusalem he would crucify them. If this is indeed, as Golubovich conjectured, an account of Pierre's embassy, al-Nazir's unexpected ferocity towards the envoys—he was, after all, renowned for his diplomatic skills—was aroused by his anger at Coptic support for the French delegation.

[31] The argument was described in Pierre's sermon on Corpus Christi, Clermont Ferrand, Bibliothèque municipale, MS 46, fo. 140ᵛ.

selves conquered Palestine by force, therefore the Egyptian victory of 1291 had simply restored the *status quo ante*. There was no case for cession. And as soon as the ambassadors actually entered al-Nazir's presence it became crystal clear that the sultan had every intention of preserving intact Mameluk rule in Outremer, a land he valued not only as a buffer against any future Mongol aggression but also for its religious significance to all devout Muslims. On this there could be no negotiation. For his part Pierre apparently would not settle for less than some kind of Christian political hegemony over Jerusalem. (Joinville pride and an intensive diet of crusading literature may not have been the ideal preparation for a mission requiring flexibility of mind.) The consequent stalemate meant that the patriarch's plan of returning to Palestine, taking the Holy Sepulchre under his protection, and re-establishing Latin Christianity there proved to be a pipe-dream. And this time, unlike 1327, there was no one extraneous to blame; the only culprit was the Mameluk ruler himself. So totally had Pierre failed to move him that he did not even carry back a letter from al-Nazir to the pope.[32] Therefore the patriarch and Guillaume returned to Cyprus in deep disappointment, without even making a pilgrimage to Jerusalem. For although permission for this was granted, and many of their party actually went,[33] had Pierre accepted the offer he would have seemed to endorse Egyptian rule in the holy places.

Guillaume must by then have been a sick man; he died at Beaulieu in July 1330. Pierre sent the sad news of their failure in Cairo to the pope, and while awaiting John's orders fulfilled other commissions that had been imposed on him before he left: he arranged a dispensation for Balien of Ibelin, count of Jaffa, to marry within the prohibited degrees, and he began to inquire into the imprisonment of a papal nuncio in 1327. Since the alleged criminal in that affair was Pierre de Castre, the vicar general of the Dominican Province of the Holy Land, it was a highly embarrassing inquest for Pierre. It was therefore with relief that he received, on 11 September 1330, a summons from the curia for his immediate return 'pro quibusdam arduis negotiis' (to deal with certain serious problems).[34] He delegated

[32] See Kaeppeli and Benoit, 'Un Pèlerinage dominicain inédit', pp. 514–15.
[33] Humbert de Dijon went, in company with many 'noble and illustrious persons'; ibid., p. 516.
[34] *Lettres communes*, ed. Mollat, no. 46004; J. Richard, *Chypre sous les Lusignans: Documents chypriotes des Archives du Vatican XIV et XV siècles* (Paris, 1962), pp. 51–8, esp. p. 52 n. 1.

the rest of the trial to the bishop of Beyrouth and set sail at once.

When he arrived back in the west, the patriarch's bitterness at his rebuff in Cairo was evident to all contemporaries. The continuator of Guillaume de Nangis attributed to him in 1331 a tirade before the king and a large number of prelates and barons on the obstinacy of the sultan.[35] It is unfortunate that this was the only personal characteristic Pierre chose to record after his meeting with one of the most remarkable personalities of his age. To a less prejudiced mind, that the Mameluk ruler should refuse to hand over Outremer to the westerners in exchange for only a small political advantage— for what, apart from peace, could the papacy offer?—was not obstinacy but reason. In the absence of external enemies (al-Nazir had made peace with the Mongols in 1323), Egypt was invulnerable to western pressure.[36] Furthermore, the central plank of the Latin case for ownership was religious: the lands in which Christ lived and died ought to belong to His followers —a thesis regularly expounded by canon lawyers since Pope Innocent IV had first developed it.[37] Al-Nazir Muhammed could scarcely be expected to favour this plea, especially since the Christians had not been notably tolerant of Muslim claims on Jerusalem during their tenure of the city. The Egyptian court had access to historical sources quite as effective in its cause as those Pierre had accumulated to plead for Christian title; and in possessing the country, the sultan held the trump card. Pierre's outburst in Paris was the result of pent-up frustration. He had got nowhere and saw no hope.

One very small consolation for his deep disappointment: he brought back with him a recipe for pills which, it was claimed, would cure headaches, stomach aches, wind, nausea, poor vision, or any other sensory weakness. The mixture of pulverized aloes, myrrh, and saffron advocated was expensive, but unusually simple in composition for a medieval remedy. According to the prescription, in winter the resultant pills should be drunk in the best wine, in summer in rosewater; the appropriate

[35] Continuation of *Chronique latine de Guillaume de Nangis*, ed. Géraud, ii. 131. C. Tyerman, 'Philip VI and the Recovery of the Holy Land', *EHR* 100 (1985), 27 and n. 5.

[36] For a recent brief description of al-Nazir Muhammed's reign, see P. M. Holt, *The Age of the Crusades: The Near East from the Eleventh Century to 1517* (London, 1986), pp. 207–20.

[37] J. Muldoon, *Popes, Lawyers and Infidels: The Church and the Non-Christian World, 1250–1550* (Liverpool, 1979), p. 6.

number to take depended on the location of the malady. But no matter what the problem, they would comfort a man's five senses, making him feel young and happy again.[38] We should perhaps picture Pierre in the months after his Cyprus visit, fighting off the gloom and dampness of a Paris winter with a potion redolent of a more colourful and sunny world.

(b) *Plans for the Crusade and Other Business*

Pierre halted at Avignon to give Pope John his report containing the melancholy conclusion that war was the only remaining means of recovering the Holy Land. With the pope's approval he then set out for Paris, which he reached before the end of 1330, intent on persuading King Philip VI of the need to launch a crusade. The son of a man who had devoted much energy to the defence of the Latin East, Philip seemed a fair target; his own concern for Christendom had earlier been demonstrated in a plan to fight the Moors in Spain.[39] Furthermore, as the first king in a new line, with an insecure title and commanding only divided loyalties, he might be attracted to holy war by political expediency: a victory in Outremer would confirm his hold on his newly acquired crown, permitting comparisons with St Louis. Therefore there were grounds for hope.

The patriarch was fortunate. In response to his strenuous plea, Philip permitted him to address a meeting of twenty-six prelates and a large number of barons which had been convened to deal with the business of the realm. Before that august company Pierre set forth all the possible grounds for an immediate French crusade. After his speech, perhaps fortified by a prophecy he reported that Islamic law was due to perish in 1335, the prelates upheld his cause and the barons requested the king to lead them to war against the infidel.[40] Their display of interest was crucial because it permitted planning for the great venture to begin. Although it was to be two years before the king finally committed himself, he wrote immediately to

---

[38] Paris, Bibliothèque nationale, MS Latin 3528, fo. 114; see E. Wickersheimer, 'Les Pilules de frère Pierre de la Palud', *Bulletin de la Société française d'histoire de la médecine*, 16 (1922), 139–41.

[39] Housley, *Avignon Papacy*, pp. 23–4, 57; Tyerman, 'Philip VI and the Recovery of the Holy Land', *EHR* 100 (1985), 27. Continuation of *Chronique latine de Guillaume de Nangis*, ed. Géraud, ii. 131.

[40] Baluze-Mollat, *VPA*, ii. 288–9, taken from a sermon of Pierre Roger, Paris, Bibliothèque nationale, MS Latin 3293, fo. 164[r].

Pope John, asking him to license Pierre to preach the crusade in France.[41] From now until the beginning of 1336 the patriarch was to be closely involved in the life of the French court, both as adviser on the projected campaign and as trouble-shooter in affairs that threatened to block it. His conviction that holy war was the only way forward in the east had thus set him on the path to becoming an *éminence grise*.

Crusade preachers had to expect a rough ride from their audience,[42] and expressions of scepticism about their motives. The *Grandes Chroniques* records that in the 1330s men were slow to take the cross because they thought it futile, and cynically regarded crusading sermons as a means of extorting money from them.[43] The patriarch's Dominican minions who went out into the city parishes and the surrounding countryside were doubtless harassed on this score; but Pierre himself was sheltered from any veiled hostility by the king's protection. The quality of his crusading sermons can be assessed from the only one extant, that for the feast of the exaltation of the cross in Clermont Ferrand, Bibliothèque municipale, MS 46, fos. 215^r–220^v. References, especially those to the lilies of France, imply that it was preached before the king; the date was 14 September, the year probably 1332. Pierre began his concerto in four movements with a loud indictment of those true knights and champions of Antichrist who wasted their substance in processions, tournaments, games, and extravagant clothing. (The criticism was entirely appropriate if it was made during the lavish preparations for the knighting of King Philip's eldest son, which took place in October 1332.) In the patriarch's opinion such knights ought to turn away from the path of sin and fight against the heathen under the banner of the cross. His words were not propitiatory; but the violence of his tone may even have contributed something to the ultimate success of his cause. For the continuator of Guillaume de Nangis described how, only two and half weeks later (on 2 October 1332), the king, accompanied by the kings of Bohemia and Navarre and the dukes of Burgundy, Brittany, Lotharingia, Brabant, and Bourbon, repaired to the Sainte Chapelle, there to announce publicly his intention of going on crusade.[44]

---

[41] *Lettres communes*, ed. Mollat, no. 58207.

[42] *Lettres secrètes*, ed. Coulon, no. 5220, warning preachers of the difficulties they might meet.

[43] Ed. Viard, ix (Paris, 1937), p. 134.

[44] Continuation of *Chronique latine de Guillaume de Nangis*, ed. Géraud, ii. 133–4.

The rest of Pierre's sermon was less critical, more hortatory. The slower second section began with a meditation on the similarities between the cross and the fig-tree: as the fig-tree is prolific in fruit, so is the cross; Christians ought to defend the cross in the knowledge that, after battle, they will eat figs to satiety. As munching figs calms wild animals, so will they, once victorious, find peace. But now they should emulate angry bulls by goring open Syria and Egypt, destroying Islam, and totally extirpating Muhammad's wicked people. The knights of Charlemagne, Duke Godfrey de Bouillon, and the Count of St Gilles[45] were humble on their journeys; so must the king of France and his followers be. As the lilies of France stood tall yet bowed their heads, so should they combine uprightness with humility. If they could not be humble, they would find themselves consigned to the lower circles of hell, since much was expected of those to whom much was given. They must follow the example of Charlemagne and Godfrey who confessed, communicated, and heard sermons before they fought. Those who left penance until too late would be prevented by the demons in hell from obtaining mercy; but those who confessed first would acquire the indulgence that steeled them to face with total equanimity whatever befell them. If they were captured, their captivity would count towards their salvation; if they were wounded, they would display their wounds on the Day of Judgement; if they were killed, they would obtain from Christ in the world to come a glorious and immortal body.

In quieter vein Pierre recounted a legend then current about the history of the cross: that it was hewn from the tree in paradise on which grew the fatal apple Eve gave to Adam; an angel subsequently presented it to Seth, Adam's son; the Queen of Sheba later discovered it and brought it to Solomon. After it had been used for many long years in Jerusalem as an instrument of torture, during which time Christ was crucified, it was abandoned and left to rot until found by St Helena, mother of Constantine the Great, who then restored it to the proper veneration of Christians. The upright of the cross was said to have been made of cedar of Lebanon, the highest of trees, its cross-shaft of palm, the purest of trees. Christians should reflect on the symbolism.

The sermon ended with a story of a crusading fleet, intent on

---

[45] The appearance of Raymond of St Gilles among the crusading heroes (in contrast with the earlier emphasis on Godfrey alone) should be ascribed to Pierre's hard work on the *Liber bellorum Domini*.

reaching Outremer, which was blown by adverse winds to a place on the coast of Spain where the inhabitants owed the Moorish emir a hundred Christian heads each year as a form of tribute. The local population begged the new arrivals to assist them in battle against their cruel overlord; since it was winter and Outremer now impossible of access, the crusaders agreed. Seven Christian knights subsequently totally defeated a Saracen army of a hundred mounted men. After the victory one of the captives asked his new Christian overlord what had happened to the white-clad knights with crosses on their shoulders who had assisted them in the battle. The moral of this story was that Christ was the protector and defender of all crusaders; Christians should therefore fight for their Lord until death, as bees fight for their king (*sic*).

Pierre took trouble to vary his images and the pitch of his diatribe. Because his message was exactly the one that had reverberated across Europe at regular intervals since 1095, to give it new emotional impact he had to spice it up with fresh illustrations. If subtlety was unnecessary, a spanking pace and an element of suspense were vital to commanding attention. This achieved, he could both scare his listeners into taking the cross by threatening them with hell, and lure them to it by romantic allusions to the heroes of the past. He aimed to send them off convinced that the crusade, as an extension of the church's normal penitential practice, provided a sure access to heaven not lightly to be ignored; and conscious of their duty to fight for Christ, the most benevolent of lords. A man who could resist this double call was hardly a man at all.

What part this and similar sermons played in recruiting soldiers for the campaign is very difficult to estimate, since motives for the Jerusalem journey were as mixed in the early 1330s as they had always been before. King Philip had probably determined before Pierre's diatribe to use the assembly for his son's knighting as the occasion for public commitment to the crusade. Too much should not be attributed to the patriarch's oratorical skill alone. On the other hand Pierre's sermon may have had some effect in swaying aristocratic opinion. The blatant cynicism expressed across France in 1336 after the crusade's failure was less evident during its planning. Though the Aragonese ambassador in Avignon was convinced as early as 1333 of the futility of the project,[46] in Paris there was a measure of confidence in it, since once the king had demon-

---

[46] Housley, *Avignon Papacy*, pp. 18–19.

strated interest, many important lords had been drawn in; and the unswerving adherence of the chancellor Guillaume de St Maure was seen as a guarantee of the court's genuine enthusiasm. Therefore in September 1332 Pierre was preaching to ears not unwilling to hear, especially since at this stage he was only demanding goodwill, not firm promises.

The Sainte Chapelle announcement inaugurated the planning of a three-stage crusade, which was to culminate in a general passage in 1336. Then on 1 October 1333, the archbishop of Reims, Pierre Roger, preached before a huge assembly at Préaux-Clercs. After his rousing sermon the king, the patriarch of Jerusalem, many other masters, and a large crowd of nobles took the cross.[47] Thenceforth they were bound by their vows. In theory, nothing could now stand between the French and the Holy Land.[48] The impressive ceremony was stage-managed to highlight the bond between the king and the patriarch, thus underlining Pierre's position as the prelate almost certain to be nominated papal legate when the general passage was on the point of departure. Philip and Pierre in partnership symbolized the synthesis between martial courage and Christian wisdom. State and church were setting forth hand-in-hand to the reconquest of the Holy Land; together they could not fail. On a less elevated note, Philip was probably glad to have among his intimates for the journey one who had only recently returned from Cyprus and Egypt, who could give him advice on practical matters. Though the chief strategic decisions had by now been taken, there was much detailed planning still to be done; and over the next two years he often called on the patriarch for assistance. (One of three papers drawn up for a meeting of the king's council at this time contained a brief description of European princes' journeys to the Holy Land from the time of Charlemagne onwards, surely the product of Pierre's researches for the *Liber bellorum Domini*.)[49]

---

[47] Continuation of *Chronique latine de Guillaume de Nangis*, ed. Géraud, ii. 135.

[48] For the conditional vows taken by some French aristocrats, see Housley, *Avignon Papacy*, pp. 150-1.

[49] The three documents are to be found in Paris, Archives de l'Empire, Chambre des comptes, P. 2289, and were described by L. de Mas Latrie in *Histoire de l'Île de Chypre sous le règne des princes de la maison de Lusignan* (Paris, 1857), p. 726. Pierre was also involved in secret negotiation with the sultan, as the evidence of the Lanercost Chronicle implies. In this connection the imprisonment for spying of Fr. Alfonso Buenhombre in Cairo in 1336 reinforces the supposition that he was in Egypt on the patriarch's business. See Meersseman, 'La Chronologie des voyages', pp. 83-4.

But the single-minded commitment of 1 October 1333 was not typical of the years 1330–5. For most of this period, the crusade was woven into the backdrop of other political concerns. As always, before an offensive could be launched successfully against the infidel, peace had to be concluded among Christians, and Pierre played his part in forwarding this. In 1331 he was sent by the pope with the archbishop of Rouen to conciliate the Viscount of Carlat and the Count of Comminges as a preliminary to holy war.[50] More importantly, he was involved in the settlement of the knottiest political problem of Philip's early years, the Artois succession.[51] Since the death of Robert II of Artois at the battle of Courtrai in 1302, his daughter Mahaud, who had inherited his estates under local custom, had faced determined opposition from Robert II's grandson Robert III, count of Beaumont-Roger, who would have inherited from his grandfather under French law, and who was able on several occasions to exploit Mahaud's unpopularity in Artois. Despite Robert's appeals against it, the 1309 judgement of Parlement in Mahaud's favour was upheld in 1318 and 1322. But the accession of Philip VI in 1328 tilted the balance sharply towards Robert, both because he was the new king's brother-in-law and trusted friend, and because Philip, whose title to the French throne depended on the exclusion of claims derived through the female line, would find it awkward to favour Mahaud. When the countess died in late November 1329 there was a real chance that the decision of 1309 might be overturned.

Mahaud's heir Jeanne, widow of Philip V, became seriously ill only a few months after her mother. Before her death, in accordance with her will of 1319 (see Ch. 4a), she designated as her sole heir her elder daughter Jeanne, the wife of Eudes IV, duke of Burgundy. The opposition to Robert III's claims on Artois thereby acquired a formidable leader; Eudes too was a brother-in-law of the king—his sister was Philip's wife. And the duke was swiftly joined by Louis of Nevers, who stood to lose by Robert's accession in Artois. In September 1330, Louis linked the quarrel over Artois with that over the throne of France by allying with Edward III. And at the same time, the affair

---

[50] *Lettres communes*, ed. Mollat, no. 4737. This mission also suggests Pierre's competence as a linguist.

[51] The clearest and most easily accessible account of the origin of this thorny problem is Charles T. Wood, *The French Apanages and the Capetian Monarchy, 1224-1328* (Cambridge, Mass., 1966), pp. 59–63, 119–34; on the events of 1329–32, see R. Cazelles, *La Société politique et la crise de la royauté sous Philippe de Valois* (Paris, 1958), pp. 75–105.

became entangled with another dispute over the succession to Savoy. Thus at the end of 1329 and for most of 1330, two powerful parties were emerging among the French princes, the duke of Burgundy, the count of Flanders, and the count of Savoy on the one hand, opposed by Robert of Beaumont-Roger, the duke of Brittany, and the dauphin of Vienne on the other. Whichever side he supported, King Philip had something to lose. John XXII, clearly concerned at the danger to the French throne, warned the king against committing himself too far in favour of the duke of Brittany and the dauphin of Vienne;[52] he probably regarded them as having the weaker case. But as long as the Flemish-Burgundian party threatened to support the claims of Edward III, Philip was bound to feel happier with Robert III and his allies.

Had Robert been content just to wait, he might at last have obtained his heart's desire. But in a fit of impatience he determined to accelerate the process by producing 'proof' of the rightness of his claims. He had, he maintained, by good fortune found a marriage contract drawn up for his parents Philip and Blanche of Brittany, in which his grandfather Robert II ceded Artois immediately to his father. (Had this actually been the case, then Robert III, as Philip's heir, would have had plain title to the county.) He produced a copy of this document, along with a letter purportedly written by Thierry d'Hireçon on his deathbed, containing a confession that he had suppressed the contract in his anxiety to help Mahaud obtain Artois. Later, however, it emerged that these documents had both been forged by a certain Jeanne de Divion, a former servant of Thierry now in Robert's pay.

When Robert produced his letters, they evoked a wave of sympathy for his cause; but doubts soon arose. And these were fanned by the patriarch of Jerusalem on his return from his Cyprus mission. Pierre's interest in the affair went back to 1319 when he had acted as executor to Jeanne's will; his warm feelings for the Burgundian ducal family were well established. His investigation in 1329 of Thierry d'Hireçon's affairs, very soon after the prelate's death, may have convinced him that Robert's story was untrue; possibly he also spotted the wrong date on the newly found marriage contract; he may even, as Blanche's confessor, have seen the original.[53] For whatever

[52] Cazelles, *La Société politique*, p. 87.

[53] *Inventaire du Trésor des chartes du roy*, MS AN. JJ. 20, fos. 84^r-85^r; see Wood, *French Apanages*, p. 61 n. 60. On Pierre's earlier relationship with Blanche, see Ch. 5a.

reason, he at once took the lead in attacking the authenticity of Robert's new finds. As soon as he arrived in Paris in November 1330 he was sent by the king to the count to warn him not to rely on forgeries. According to Robert's advocate Guillaume de Breuil, the patriarch's admonition impressed the count's counsellors, who advised Robert against exploiting the documents if he knew anything at all to their discredit. Foolishly Robert swore to their authenticity, temporarily silencing his accusers —including, Guillaume thought, Pierre de la Palud. The contract and letter were therefore submitted in support of Robert's case.[54] But the confidence the count's oath initially generated was swiftly dissipated. At the Parlement in 1331 the original decision of 1309 was reaffirmed, the Duchess of Burgundy was granted Artois, and the letters were publicly condemned as forgeries. Then Jeanne de Divion and Robert's confessor, a Dominican called Jean Aubri, were imprisoned, and the count, recognizing the danger of his position, fled to Brabant. King Philip, relieved to have his dilemma solved, was spared the ill effects he had anticipated, since the duke of Burgundy cheerfully abandoned his projected English alliance and Edward III was willing to make peace. Therefore Philip felt strong enough to inaugurate proceedings against Robert.

In the public aspect of this affair Pierre had nothing to reproach himself with. Far from it; he had unmasked a plot that had threatened the security of the realm. But in a sideshow he appeared in a less attractive light. Presiding over a bench of Masters of Theology, most recruited from the mendicant orders, he put pressure on Jean Aubri to reveal what Robert had told him about the forgery. Jean regarded himself as bound by the seal of the confessional; but he undertook to bow to the superior moral authority of the doctors, should they instruct him to break it. Pierre then publicly assured him that sins alone were covered by the seal of the confessional; if he told them Robert's confidences he would not be committing an offence but rather helping the kingdom and thus serving justice, both meritorious acts. This advice was approved by the other masters.[55] However, it caused scandal among some other Paris clerks, who accused the Dominicans in particular of abandoning a deeply held conviction of the order, so as to curry favour with the king.[56] (Modern Roman Catholic theologians do not

[54] H. Moranvillé, 'Guillaume de Breuil et Robert d'Artois', *BEC* 48 (1887), 641–9. [55] *CUP* ii. 348, no. 917a.

[56] Continuation of *Chronique latine de Guillaume de Nangis*, ed. Géraud, ii. 127–9; *Grandes Chroniques*, ed. Viard, ix. 129.

agree with this judgement.[57]) Impressed by the masters' unanimity Jean Aubri agreed to speak; Pierre took him to the bishop's chapel where, to the delight of the king's servants, he told all. After that, despite the assurances he had been given, he was taken back to prison and never heard of again.[58]

On the precise issue of his words to Jean Aubri, Pierre's conscience was clean. Although he had himself insisted on the secrecy of confession in his commentary on the Book 4 of the *Sentences*, 21. 2, the particular circumstances of Robert's crime were held by all the Masters to justify his advice. But the perpetual imprisonment of the priest, like the subsequent execution of Jeanne de Divion, was a different matter. Besides, Pierre's statement that any action which assisted the kingdom of France served justice was at odds with the tenor of much of his earlier writing, *a fortiori* of his most potent sermons. Furthermore, the final outcome of his intervention was unjust to the count of Beaumont-Roger. Robert can scarcely have imagined, when he first stooped to forgery, that one sin would lead to his total disgrace, his exile, and the loss of all his possessions. But so, by May 1332, it turned out. And if the sentence was Parlement's, Pierre fully shared its intransigence.

The second affair to absorb Pierre's energy was the complicated propaganda war over the beatific vision. Here, too, he played a leading role; under his influence what might have been an isolated theological difference of opinion was allowed to merge into a power struggle between Avignon and Paris. The first scenes in the drama were Avignon-based. On 1 November 1331 Pope John XXII preached a sermon in the city, arguing that the souls of the blessed would not enjoy the beatific vision until the Day of Judgement. He followed this up, on 5 January 1332, with the corollary that the damned too remained unpunished until the Day of Judgement.[59] The pope made it clear that he was speaking as an individual, not in his capacity as bishop of Rome, and that the thesis he propounded was open to debate. Nevertheless, he must have been surprised by the violence of the reaction he unleashed. The reason was that his opponents

---

[57] On this see A. Duval, 'Pierre de la Palu', *Dictionnaire de spiritualité*, xii. 2 (Paris, 1986), col. 1632. Cf. Fournier, *HLF*, p. 50 n. 1.

[58] Continuation of *Chronique latine de Guillaume de Nangis*, ed. Géraud, ii. 129. See also the testimony of Richard Lescot, *Grandes Chroniques*, ed. Viard, ix. 129.

[59] See *CUP* ii. 414–15, no. 970. A. Maier, *Ausgehendes Mittelalter: Gesammelte Aufsätze zur Geistesgeschichte des 14 Jahrhunderts*, iii (Rome, 1977), pp. 319–72, 415.

were apprehensive about the effects of his position on the penitential teaching of the church; as John of Naples argued in 1332, the papal case called into question both purgatory and the value of prayers for the dead. In the Dominican master's opinion the traditional thesis that the beatific vision was enjoyed by the saints from the time of their deaths was far safer.[60] This also was the line taken by Pierre de la Palud when he was invited to Avignon to dispute the issue at the end of 1332;[61] there he produced eight Scriptural passages purporting to support his interpretation. But John XXII, who also produced Scriptural backing, remained unconvinced. When the friar Thomas de Waleys violently attacked the pope's sermons in January 1333, he was imprisoned—though ostensibly for other reasons.[62] John then invited Durand de St Pourçain, now bishop of Meaux, to examine the prisoner; but Durand upheld Thomas's views with passion, and therefore was forced to appear before a commission of inquiry. Next the pope consulted Jacques Fournier, the future Pope Benedict XII, but to no better purpose. Exasperated, he then circulated a tract entitled 'Whether the souls of the dead, purged of all sin, see the divine essence' ('Utrum anime sanctorum ab omnibus peccatis purgate videant divinam essenciam'), replete with Scriptural quotations. But it, too, failed to sway hostile theological opinion. Finally, at the end of 1333 he established a very large commission to investigate the issue, telling it before it began what he hoped its conclusion would be.[63] Once more, however, he had to face disappointment. During the course of 1334, as the views of the commissioners trickled in, his self-assurance was undermined. On 3 December 1334, he finally recanted—though he died before he had had time to seal the bull setting out his change of heart.

Had the dispute been contained within Avignon, its significance might have been small. But to the theologians grouped around Lewis of Bavaria, who were already committed to the belief that Pope John XXII was a heretic, the affair came as an unlooked-for corroboration of their judgement. Bonagratia of Bergamo and Michael of Cesena launched appeals against the

[60] P. T. Stella, 'Giovanni Regina di Napoli, O.P., e le tesi di Giovanni XXII circa la visione beatifica', *Salesianum*, 35 (1973), 65-6; Maier, *Ausgehendes Mittelalter*, iii. 501. On the doctrine cf. J. Le Goff, *The Birth of Purgatory*, tr. A. Goldhammer (Chicago, 1984), p. 309.

[61] Maier, iii. 427-8.

[62] *CUP* ii. 428, no. 975. See T. Kaeppeli, *Le Procès contre Thomas Waleys O.P.* (Rome, 1936).

[63] *CUP* ii. 434-7, no. 983.

pope's errors, Lewis kept a copy of the papal commission's inquiry,[64] and William of Ockham made political capital out of John's early sermons in the *Opus nonaginta dierum*.[65] Munich's intervention was, from the pope's point of view, unfortunate but almost inevitable. But the involvement of Paris was less expected. News of the pope's sermons percolated there very rapidly—John later blamed certain Avignon theologians for the leak, and complained bitterly that they had misrepresented what he had said.[66] The king opportunistically seized on the rumour, expressed deep shock, and refused to take any notice of John's many efforts at self-justification. In his anxiety to overcome the royal displeasure, John sent the Franciscan Master General Giraud d'Ot (Geraldus Odonis) to Paris in the summer of 1333, on his way to participate in peace negotiations between the kings of England and Scotland. According to instructions, Giraud there expounded in the schools the papal thesis on the beatific vision. His disputation, which has survived,[67] was more moderate than the French chronicler's account of it. But far from vindicating the pope, it played straight into the king's hands. On 18 December Philip consulted ten Masters of Theology, including four Franciscans; all disagreed with Giraud. By the weight of their authority, Giraud himself was induced to accept the majority view.

On this occasion the Paris opposition was levelled specifically against Giraud d'Ot. No mention was made of the pope. Nevertheless the incident clearly put pressure on John, and it can reasonably be assumed that this was intended. So the intervention of King Philip in a purely theological difference of opinion begins to look sinister. The letters between Avignon and Paris in the course of 1332 and 1333[68] reveal without ambiguity that it was the king, not his bishops, who made the running on the issue. Why should the orthodox Philip have copied the excommunicated Lewis of Bavaria in exploiting the controversy? The answer may have been money. In 1331–3 Philip badly needed papal assistance for the financing of the crusade; he knew he could not hope to cover the costs from French resources alone. Therefore his ambassadors at Avignon had been pressing since the end of 1331 for the grant

---

[64] Maier, *Ausgehendes Mittelalter*, iii. 420.
[65] *Guilelmi de Ockham: Opera Politica*, ed. R. F. Bennet and H. S. Offler, ii (Manchester, 1963), p. xvii.
[66] *CUP* ii. 428–9, no. 980.
[67] Ed. in Maier, *Ausgehendes Mittelalter*, iii. 335–68.
[68] *CUP* ii. 416–17, no. 972; 417–18, no. 973; 418, no. 974.

of a six-year tenth on clerical revenues throughout Christendom. In 1333 Pope John XXII finally and reluctantly agreed to this demand,[69] despite its contravention of his usual practice and his certainty of its impracticability.[70] He may have conceded so much in the hopes of moderating Philip's indignation about the sermons. But success, far from silencing the king, simply made him more demanding. In order to convert his paper victory into hard cash he needed constant papal support, since John alone could force the non-French churches to pay their share of the newly granted tax.[71]

It was therefore probably in the hope of acquiring ascendancy over him and making him serve French interests that Philip decided to embarrass John yet further. Royal agents set to work in Paris, whipping up feeling against Giraud d'Ot and what they represented as his heresy.[72] The public concern they generated justified Philip in taking the next step in his campaign. On 19 December 1333 he called all the French masters of the Paris Theology faculty, including Pierre Roger, archbishop of Reims, Nicolas de Lyre, and Durand d'Aurillac, to meet at Vincennes under the chairmanship of Pierre de la Palud, in order to give formal judgement on the disputed question of the beatific vision. The choice of Vincennes for the hearing scarcely disguised the king's interest in the matter; yet more pointed was the presence of large numbers of princes, prelates, and royal counsellors sitting around the chamber in which the masters were to debate.[73] According to the continuator of Guillaume de Nangis, Philip controlled the proceedings, telling the masters, in French, that he wanted answers to two questions: whether the souls of the saints saw the face of God after their deaths, and whether on the Day of Judgement that vision would cease, to be superseded by a new and different one. The outcome was predictable.[74]

On 2 January 1334 the masters introduced their verdict by pointing out that they were bound to reverence the king and obey his orders 'as our lord, our dearest founder, the guardian of the Paris *studium* and of our Theology faculty'. They stated

69 *Lettres communes*, ed. Mollat, nos. 61206–7, 61234.

70 Housley, *Avignon Papacy*, pp. 178–9.

71 Ibid., p. 178.

72 Continuation of *Chronique latine de Guillaume de Nangis*, ed. Géraud, ii. 137.

73 *CUP* ii. 430, no. 981.

74 Continuation of *Chronique latine de Guillaume de Nangis*, ed. Géraud, ii. 138–9.

that in seeking for a decision on the matter, the king was not intending in any way to injure the pope, whose devoted sons they all were, since John had only discussed and not upheld the contrary opinions. They then declared: 'Since the death of Christ ... the souls of the faithful, ... separated from their bodies, exempt or delivered from purgatory, enjoy a plain, clear, beatific, intuitive and immediate vision of the Divine Essence and of the most blessed Trinity.'[75] Afterwards, despite their request to be spared the ordeal, the king required them to seal their sentence as a precaution against subsequent recantation. Thus he converted it into a semi-legal document, to be stored in the royal archives. Philip, through Pierre's actions, had got what he wanted. The threat to John's standing was subtler than that launched by Philip IV against Boniface VIII in 1303; but it was quite dangerous enough to render him malleable.

The Vincennes declaration had a long-term significance in the evolution of the Gallican church: under Pierre's leadership the authority of the university of Paris had been pitted against that of the pope in a doctrinal matter. In the letter the patriarch wrote to Avignon accompanying a copy of the statement, he gently but firmly asked John to terminate discussion of the issue by confirming the theologians' judgement.[76] This was as good as an assertion that the Paris theologians were the guarantors of orthodoxy; the pope should bow to their rulings. Though Pierre's letter was courteous in tone, the continuator of Guillaume de Nangis ascribed to the king an accompanying epistle lacking in civility: Philip informed the pope that the Masters of Theology at Paris knew better than lawyers (among whom he counted John) what should be believed in matters of faith. It was now up to John to correct those who disagreed with the faculty.[77] If this is a fair summary of what he said, then Philip's letter approached the tone his predecessor had used in 1302–3. In any case, the claim of 1334 that overriding doctrinal authority might be vested in the Paris Theology faculty was more precise than any similar claim made during the more famous conflict between Boniface VIII and Philip the Fair. From the declaration of Vincennes onwards French kings could find in the university on their own doorstep a certainty on

---

[75] *CUP* ii. 430, no. 981.
[76] Ibid., no. 982.
[77] Continuation of *Chronique latine de Guillaume de Nangis*, ed. Géraud, ii. 138–9.

matters of faith that eluded them in Rome. The scene was set for the events of the Great Schism.

The Vincennes declaration provides yet another twist to the problem of determining Pierre's views on authority in matters of faith. He had consistently encouraged popes to discuss issues of faith with the masters of universities and *studia*, while stipulating that the authority to promulgate was exclusively papal. Necessary antecedent consultation was compatible with his belief in the inerrancy of the Roman and universal church. Equally Pierre had always accepted the possibility of individual popes falling into error; in his commentary on Book 4 of the *Sentences*, he had gone so far as to assert that if the pope did publicly preach an error then it was necessary to rise and contradict him publicly (19. 3). In the case of the beatific vision there had been no official pronouncement; therefore the orthodoxy of the Roman church had not been tested. In pointing out that the opinion attributed to John was wrong, the king and the Paris theologians were simply preventing the unthinkable, and saving John from himself. So Pierre doubtless reasoned.

But there were underlying tensions between the events of 1334 and Pierre's previously stated views. In the first place, the Vincennes declaration had not been elicited by a papal request for advice—rather, it was gratuitously forced on the pope's attention; and that at a time when John was engaged in extensive enquiries on the matter at Avignon. Secondly, the ground for believing in the Roman church's inerrancy—Christ's promise to Peter—seemed to imply more than that officially promulgated statements on faith could not be wrong. If Christ was indeed praying for Peter's successor, then the pope should not need to be chided into correct belief by others who had no similar Scripturally warranted claim to divine protection; far less could anyone simply dismiss him as an ignorant lawyer, as King Philip apparently wished to do. John's belief[78] that the guardianship and protection of Holy Scripture and the Catholic faith lay principally with the Universal Vicar of Christ seems closer to Pierre's own interpretation of Christ's promise in his Quodlibet and in *De potestate Papae*. Furthermore, in *De paupertate* Pierre had denied Michael of Cesena's right as an individual to criticize the pope; yet the Vincennes declaration assumed that right for a corporation of Masters of Theology (though they did cover themselves by denying that John really adhered to the condemned views). Also in *De paupertate* Pierre

---

[78] *CUP* ii. 435, no. 983.

had argued that unless what the pope said went clean contrary to Scripture, he should be obeyed. Though in the case of the beatific vision the patriarch had produced eight Scriptural references to controvert John's view, he was aware that John too had assembled his Scriptural support. Yet he would not give the pope the benefit of the doubt. If Pierre saw no contradiction between what he had said in the past and what he did in 1334, neither the supporters of Jean de Pouilly nor those of Michael of Cesena could have regarded him as consistent.

Vincennes was a public humiliation for John XXII, all the more painful because it had been inflicted through the connivance of a man he had regarded as an old friend, and whom he had promoted to a venerable and dignified position in the church. Pierre, along with many contemporaries, regarded the beatific vision as a nodal point of penitential theology. He was convinced that Pope John was wrong and that through his error the church might be diverted from the truth. It would have been impossible for him to keep silent. But not content simply to dispute the issue he allowed King Philip to make political capital out of it; by presiding over the Vincennes assembly he led the university theologians in their open challenge to John. No churchman in the age of Lewis of Bavaria could be unaware of the dangers in such a stand. Thus Pierre's enthusiasm for the crusade had seduced him into an action at odds with many of the principles he had enunciated earlier in his career. As in 1318, he had faced the painful choice between impotence and compromise that confronts most intellectuals in politics; and though he acted on this occasion with neither hesitation nor concession to the other side, the pope's death in 1334 must have filled him with relief.

7. The Last Years

While the theologians wrangled, plans for the crusade went on apace. And in the summer of 1334 the Latins scored a victory which seemed an excellent omen for the future: a fleet drawn from several western countries and with Byzantine aid inflicted a defeat on the Turkish pirates of Asia Minor in the gulf of Adramyttium. Encouraged by this, the French prepared first for an attack on Anatolia, to be led in 1335 by Louis de Clermont, duke of Bourbon, and then for the main crusade to be launched in 1336.[1] To this end the patriarch and the king worked hand-in-glove. Pierre demonstrated his influence over Philip early in 1335 by acquiring for his nephew, Aimon's son, his first post at court.[2] This crucial step on the ladder was to lead Pierre de la Palud the Younger to a distinguished career in royal service, as Master of Requests, governor of the bailliage of Amiens, seneschal of Carcassonne and Béziers, and finally seneschal of Toulouse and Albi, with the title 'king's captain in Languedoc'. His uncle's faith in his abilities was to be amply justified.

Meanwhile, after the death of John XXII in December 1334, the cardinals swiftly elected in his place Jacques Fournier, the one-time Cistercian abbot famous for his inquisition into Catharism in Montaillou and the surrounding area.[3] Fournier, who chose the name Benedict XII, had had much recent experience in curial affairs, so slipped easily into the driving-seat. Initially he displayed enthusiasm for the crusade by confirming all Pope John's bulls and privileges for Philip; and in July he regranted Pierre de la Palud the bishopric of Limassol *in commendam*, an indication that he still hoped the patriarch would re-establish himself in Jerusalem,[4] albeit now by force. But during the course of 1335 Philip's concentration on Palestine began to be threatened by King Edward III's challenge to his throne. Long-standing disagreements about Gascony rapidly

---

[1] N. Housley, *The Avignon Papacy and the Crusades, 1307-1378* (Oxford, 1986), pp. 25-6.

[2] R. Cazelles, *La société politique et la crise de la royauté sous Philippe de Valois* (Paris, 1958), p. 337.

[3] *Le Registre de l'Inquisition de Jacques Fournier (évêque de Pamiers) 1318-1325*, ed. J. Duvernoy (2 vols.; Paris, 1978).

[4] *Lettres communes*, ed. Vidal, no. 21.

fed Anglo-French enmity to the point where Philip felt obliged to call off Louis de Clermont's Anatolian expedition because of fear of war. At once Benedict became seriously concerned that money raised for the crusade would actually be used to fight the English. Therefore on 13 March 1336 he postponed the general passage and absolved the king from his crusading oath. In just over a year he had completely changed course.

Philip VI had no reason to welcome Benedict's doubtless well-founded suspicions about his intentions. But a worse blow was soon to befall him from the same quarter: at the end of 1336 the pope converted postponement of the crusade into cancellation, and revoked the 1333 grant of a six-year tenth on clerical property, insisting that funds already collected should be returned.[5] As a consequence, in addition to financial loss—Philip had, after all, incurred expenses for the campaign which he was now expected to absorb without assistance—the king was exposed to much bitter comment from his disillusioned subjects, who retrospectively interpreted the whole crusading episode as nothing but a plot to extract money from them. He became very unpopular. The contrast between his arrogant treatment of Pope John and his temporary vulnerability to Benedict's darts is striking;[6] and the explanation lies at least partly in the realm of theological debate. For Philip no longer had a stick with which to beat the pope.

Immediately on his election Benedict had shown his determination to extricate the papacy from the awkwardness of the beatific vision controversy. Within two months of his consecration he summoned seventeen Masters of Theology, including Pierre de la Palud, to Sorgues, to assist him in defining orthodoxy on the matter. (Pierre was paid 100 gold florins to cover his expenses, an astonishing sum for a Dominican to request, and far more than the other masters received.[7]) At Sorgues the patriarch took a leading part in the debate, and the final verdict, entitled 'An Abridged Concordance of the Replies Given by the Venerable Fathers, Masters and Experts in

---

[5] Housley, *Avignon Papacy*, pp. 28, 178–81; C. Tyerman, 'Philip VI and the Recovery of the Holy Land', *EHR* 100 (1985), 45–7; *Benoît XII: Lettres closes et patentes intéressant les pays autres que la France*, ed. J. M. Vidal and G. Mollat (Paris, 1950), no. 786; *Benoît XII: Lettres closes, patentes et curiales se rapportant à la France*, ed. G. Daumet (Paris, 1920), nos. 251 and 252.

[6] Edward III's alliance with Lewis of Bavaria altered the balance again in Philip's favour by 1338; Housley, *Avignon Papacy*, pp. 182–3.

[7] J. M. Vidal, 'Notice sur les oeuvres de Pape Benoît XII', *Revue d'histoire écclesiastique*, 6 (1905), 789 n. 4.

Theology, Pierre de la Palud and Others', was partially incorporated into the bull *Benedictus Deus* of 29 January 1336.[8] By citing the masters' opinion in his bull, Benedict deferred to Philip's argument that only trained theologians were competent to decide questions theological. But he spiked the king's guns by calling theologians from a range of places in southern Europe as well as from France, and by consulting them on his own terms in a town close to Avignon. He could hardly have made plainer his conviction that the Paris Theology faculty had no monopoly of sound judgement.

Benedictus Deus put an end to the dispute by stating that the souls of the departed were rewarded or punished before the Day of Judgement. Pierre will have welcomed the decision heartily since it restored his peace of mind—he was far from sharing King Philip's sense of loss at the end of the controversy. Besides, he was naturally drawn to Jacques Fournier's austere, reforming temperament, in some respects like his own, and Benedict's commitment to extirpating abuses in the religious orders, particularly among the troubled Franciscans,[9] was an aspiration after his own heart. So the first year of the new pontificate was a time of calm co-operation between pope and patriarch. On 8 July 1335 Benedict wrote to Philip, asking him to excuse Pierre's absence from the next Parlement because he was needed at Avignon; by the following month Pierre was administering the bishopric of Rodez during a vacancy.[10] As the prospects for the crusade receded in the course of the year, the patriarch again put off his return to Paris, perhaps because he was being consulted over the projected reforms of the Cistercians, the Benedictines, and the Austin canons.

But the March 1336 postponement of the general passage necessarily altered Pierre's position. Since he could no longer expect to resume control over the Latin church in the east, his patriarchate would be titular until another crusade was launched; consequently the financial arrangements from which

[8] A. Maier, *Ausgehendes Mittelalter: Gesammelte Aufsätze zur Geistesgeschichte des 14 Jahrhunderts,* iii (Rome, 1977), p. 427.

[9] P. C. Schmitt, *Un Pape réformateur et un défenseur de l'unité de l'Église: Benoît XII et l'ordre des Frères Mineurs, 1334-1342* (Florence, 1959).

[10] *Benoît XII: Lettres closes, patentes et curiales,* ed. G. Daumet, no. 77; *Lettres communes,* ed. Vidal, no. 2484. Pierre's presence at Parlements did not make him a member of them; important figures were invited just to witness. But his familiarity with Parlement's proceedings was evident in one of his sermons, in which he explained 'In my father's house there are many mansions' in terms of the different tiers of seats at that assembly (Clermont Ferrand, Bibliothèque municipale, MS 46, fo. 69ᵛ).

he had benefited were no longer justified. Therefore in response to Benedict's request he surrendered the bishopric of Limassol. When his gesture became known, the chapter of Cambrai was inspired to elect him to its rich and powerful bishopric;[11] but Benedict quashed the election and provided another man. Shortly afterwards, he conferred on Pierre the tiny and very poor see of Couserans on the Spanish border by Comminges, which was regularly at the Avignon popes' disposal, and which had been held by a Dominican before him (ironically St Dominic had refused to accept it). At the same time he requested the repayment of a loan of 1,000 gold florins[12]—presumably the one granted in 1329.

The loss of Limassol and Cambrai, along with Pierre's appointment to the diminutive Couserans, led Paul Fournier[13] to speculate that the patriarch had already fallen foul of Benedict XII on the issue of the Dominican constitution. But that clash did not come before December 1338; and I doubt if this explanation does justice to either man. Pierre had often preached against those who led the life of poverty in their youth at the schools but who, once appointed to bishoprics, abandoned those values totally to concentrate on self-enrichment at the expense of the poor (Clermont Ferrand, Bibliothèque municipale, MS 46, fo. 214^r). To accept Cambrai, had he been offered the opportunity, would have gone against his own expressed principles as well as against Dominican tradition; and Benedict was not the man to encourage others to backslide. As to Limassol, a titular patriarch could claim no special privilege, and although John XXII had granted him the bishopric *in commendam* for life, Benedict had subsequently quashed all such grants except those held by cardinals.[14] Pierre was therefore obliged to concur in his own deprivation. Even so, the grant of Couserans alone was sufficiently ungenerous as to suggest a breach of some kind between the two men. A likely cause of such coolness would be an attempt by Benedict to persuade Pierre to take up residence in Cyprus, the patriarch of Jerusalem's

---

[11] *Lettres communes*, ed. Vidal, nos. 2528 and 4078; and Fournier, *HLF*, p. 51 n. 2. See also *Chronique de Giles le Muisit*, ed. J. J. Smet in *Recueil des Chroniques de Flandre*, ii (Brussels, 1841), p. 217: 'Dominus autem papa, hoc cognito, considerans non esse congruum neque decens, quod tam excellens persona et in tam altiori statu, demisso statu patriarchatus, efficeretur episcopus, cassavit electionem.'

[12] *Lettres communes*, ed. Vidal, no. 2530, and ii. 328.

[13] *HLF*, pp. 51-2.

[14] By *Supra gregem dominicam* of 18 May 1335.

traditional home since 1291.[15] We may imagine Pierre, aware of increasing pressure on the Eastern Mediterranean, resisting this demand, pleading old age or ill health as grounds for remaining in France; and Benedict reluctantly agreeing, on condition that he live inconspicuously and austerely.

Where Pierre made his home for the last five years of his life is unclear. The patriarch of Jerusalem's church and houses in Avignon were probably no longer congenial to him. He may have spent much time in Couserans; he certainly confirmed the statutes of its church in 1337, which suggests at least a temporary stay. He is recorded, though not reliably, as having attended in 1341 the consecration of the chapel of the college of Autun in Paris. The chronicle of Fr. Stephen of Lusignan asserted that he was in Cyprus when he died on 31 January 1342.[16] This, however, was almost certainly mistaken, since he was buried at St Jacques in Paris. But whatever the detail, the main picture is clear: after his participation at the Sorgues conference, he retreated from the public stage. Neither king nor pope demanded his services.

Nevertheless, as the events of 1338 were to show, there was still life in him. In that year Benedict XII, having dealt with all the other religious orders, turned his attention to the reform of the Dominicans. Struck by the inconsistency between the order's constitutions and its practice in relation to property,[17] he asked Hugues de Vaucemain, the master general, and the chapter to put the order at his mercy. This request they promptly refused. But his initiative created a sense of vulnerability in the order; at a general chapter held between 1336 and 1339, certain convents were accused of owning houses and revenues in violation of their vows of poverty. Concerned lest the matter provide the pope with ammunition, Hugues consulted various important friars, among them Pierre de la Palud, on whether owning property went against the Dominican vow of poverty, and what should be done about certain specific revenues possessed by some houses.

---

[15] That Benedict thought the patriarch ought to reside in Cyprus may reasonably be inferred from the appointment of the archbishop of Nicosia to the post in 1342, G. Golubovich, *Biblioteca bio-bibliografica delle Terra Santa e dell'Oriente francescano*, iii (Florence, 1919), p. 403.

[16] L. de Mas Latrie, 'Les Patriarches latins de Jérusalem', *Revue de l'Orient latin*, 1 (1893), 16; Fournier, *HLF*, p. 52 and S. Guichenon, *Histoire de Bresse et de Bugey* (Lyons, 1650), 2. 2. 287–8.

[17] See W. A. Hinnebusch, *History of the Dominican Order*, i. *Origins and Growth to 1500* (New York, 1966), p. 269.

Pierre's reply[18] demonstrates that even in his old age he remained capable of fine distinctions.[19] In his opinion owning property in common could not contravene the oath of poverty, for if it did, then all monks would be in trouble. Neither was it incompatible with the Rule of St Augustine, since all Austin canons had property. It did, however, contravene the Dominican constitutions. But Dominicans had not vowed to preserve their constitutions, only to obey in accordance with them.[20] A general chapter could revoke any constitution it thought fit, provided its decision was ratified by the next two general chapters. However Pierre did not recommend the revocation of the prohibition on property. Rather, since the violations complained of had been committed only by a few convents, he advocated the lawyer's remedy of dispensation from the rule where a reasonable case could be made out. The Paris convent, needing peace and quiet for study, had acquired the neighbouring houses; the Metz convent had done likewise to protect its access. These were legitimate grounds for breaching the constitution. Similarly, houses might be bought for friars to stay in while they preached and heard confessions at some distance from their home bases; it would, after all, be a more serious violation of the Dominican way of life to leave souls unsaved than to possess houses. As to the various forms of monetary income about which Hugues had asked, most of them did not need a dispensation because they fell within the limits permitted under receipt of alms—though Dominicans should not pursue in the lawcourts those who failed to keep their promises on alms-giving. The acceptance of annual rents, however, went beyond the permitted limits and should always be covered by dispensation. Having sorted out these specific problems without demanding any real change in the *status quo*, Pierre went on to voice his opinion that the underlying cause for all these irregularities was a clause in *Super cathedram* of 1300, reinforced by the Council of Vienne. This, by ordering friars to pay a quarter of their earnings from funerals and gifts *in articulo mortis* to the parish priest, had unreasonably impoverished the order and

---

[18] Printed in Mortier, iii. 131–6.

[19] In addition to the letter addressed to Hugues de Vaucemain, Pierre wrote a tract apparently making the same points but in scholastic form. Of this only a fragment remains, quoted by Henry of Bittenfelt. See V. J. Koudelka, 'Heinrich von Bittenfeld († 1465), Professor an der Universität Prag', *AFP* 23 (1953), 25–7.

[20] Here Pierre was entirely correct. Dominican tradition had always stressed that the constitutions were only human law. On this see S. Tugwell, ed., *Early Dominicans: Selected Writings* (New York, Romsey, and Toronto, 1982), p. 22.

forced it into petty expedients. Rather than interfere with the Dominicans, the pope should modify that hated stipulation.

If Benedict XII knew of Pierre's opinion, he did not grant his request. But neither, on the other hand, did he succeed in changing the Dominican practice on property. In 1339 he called twenty-two members of the order to Avignon; together they produced a series of relatively minor emendations of the kind general chapters usually provided. In 1340 he summoned seventeen Dominicans with a specific brief to reform the constitutions; on this occasion also Hugues de Vaucemain and his henchmen succeeded in fighting off the threat. In the relative safety of Italy Gualvagno de la Flamma dared to assert that the pope had no right whatever to alter the Dominican constitutions.[21] Had his words penetrated to the court of Lewis of Bavaria they would have evoked high glee. Hugues and the official negotiators were presumably more circumspect; but they were every bit as determined, and in the end their dogged resistance won the day. Alone of all the religious orders, the Dominicans remained unreformed by Benedict XII—a fact later generations of friars came to regret.[22]

Pierre's last letter, with its criticism of *Super cathedram*, highlights a thread that ran through much of his adult life: that of adapting to the changed situation after the Council of Vienne. Deeply though he detested *Multorum* (which extended bishops' rights in the inquisition) and the reimposition of *Super cathedram*, though he denied to general councils any authority beyond that delegated to them by popes, Pierre had had to bow to the conciliar canons. A lawyer to his fingertips, on almost all occasions he practised the obedience he demanded from others. And in one respect Vienne had provided an inspiration for his later career: there the whole of the Catholic church had been mobilized to provide money for a crusade. The failure of Clement's grand design had obliged Philip VI and Pierre to take up the challenge; the recovery of the Holy Land remained for the patriarch an enduring aspiration. Because so much effort had gone into planning the general passage, the disappointment of 1336 was proportionately deep. But had he lived long enough to see it, he would have been consoled by the eastern exploits of Pierre, his namesake and nephew. In 1344 an expedition of which the young Pierre was among the leading laymen captured

---

[21] Mortier, iii. 97—a marked contrast with Gualvagno's usual enthusiasm for papal power.
[22] See ibid., p. 522 n. 2.

Smyrna, the only territorial conquest of western armies in the fourteenth century; though Pierre himself was killed during the siege that followed, he had made La Palud a name of distinction in crusading annals.

On 31 January 1342 the patriarch died. He was buried at St Jacques, at the entrance to the church, in a coffin bearing the patriarchal double cross and the La Palud arms[23]—to the end he remained an aristocrat. Although he had been given permission to make a will, his movable goods (or a large proportion of them) found their way into the papal coffers at Avignon, as usually happened in the case of holders of Languedoc sees.[24] However, the dispersion of his property was not the end of his story. Within his own order, his reputation as a great teacher and preacher survived for at least two centuries. St Antoninus of Florence and Capreolus plagiarized from him; Cardinal Julian of Torquemada exploited his political writings in the conciliar epoch; and his commentaries on Books 3 and 4 of the *Sentences* were highly regarded by the moralists of the early sixteenth century.[25] Even the less scholarly had reason to hear of him. In the fifteenth century Louis of Valladolid produced a short tract about the great Dominican writers connected with St Jacques,[26] containing a list of Pierre's works, most of which were still to be found then in the St Jacques library. His name was included in 'trees' (based on the tree of Jesse) from which novices learned about the great Dominicans of the past.[27] And in the early sixteenth century he was one of the subjects of a humanistic poem 'Naumachia ecclesiastica' by Gaudanus.[28]

But Pierre was too much a man of his time, too taken up with the aims and complexities of early fourteenth-century life, to

---

[23] Guichenon, *Histoire*, 2. 2. 288. The coffin was found and identified by workmen in St Jacques in 1631; J. D. Levesque, *Les Frères Prêcheurs de Lyon: Notre Dame de Confort, 1218-1789* (Lyons, 1979), p. 103.

[24] D. Williman, *Records of the Papal Right of Spoil, 1316-1412* (Paris, 1974), p. 174, no. 905. I assume that the 1345 collection in Apulia related to the Patriarch's goods in Cyprus.

[25] J. Miethke, 'Eine unbekannte Handschrift von Petrus de Paludes Traktat *De Potestate Papae* aus dem Besitz Juan de Torquemadas in der Vatikanischen Bibliotheke', *QFIAB* 59 (1979), 474-5; L. Vereeke, 'Les Éditions des œuvres morales de Pierre de la Palu († 1342) à Paris au début du xvie siècle', *Studia Moralia*, 17 (1979), 267-82.

[26] Ed. H. C. Scheeben, 'Die Tabulae Ludwigs von Valladolid im Chor der Predigbrüder von St. Jakob in Paris', *AFP* 1 (1930), 254.

[27] A. Walz, 'Von Dominikanerstammbaümen', *AFP* 34 (1964), 231-75.

[28] G. M. Löhr, 'Die kölner Dominikanerhumanist Jacobus Magdalius Gaudanus und seine Naumachia ecclesiastica', *AFP* 18 (1948), 295-6.

be valued in the days of the reformation and counter-reforma-
tion. Unlike the great theologians and lawyers in whose steps
he trod, he had left little of permanent intellectual value on
which the sharper minds of that troubled era could brood. He
therefore passed into oblivion. For the next three centuries
only the more historically minded of his own order even mentioned his name. Then, with the papally inspired revival of
Thomism in the last two decades of the nineteenth century, his
relatively small part in the preservation of Thomist teachings
first attracted attention among Catholic theologians. At the
same time, galvanized by Ranke's commitment to recovering
historical facts, secular French historians began to sift through
the medieval royal records; their patient labours revealed
Pierre as a minor figure in a number of disconnected episodes.
It was not until 1938, when Paul Fournier wrote his seminal
article in *Histoire littéraire de la France*, xxxvii, that the pieces
of the patriarch's life were put back into place, and his significance in ecclesiastical politics could be appreciated.

Yet the very diversity of Pierre's enterprises, which hid him
so long from historians' gaze, might constitute an argument for
his insignificance. A man who failed in the three political tasks
imposed on him—peace-making in Flanders, negotiating with
the sultan, and launching a crusade—and who dabbled in
many kinds of intellectual activity but only rarely achieved
excellence, might seem undeserving of our attention. In the
Introduction I justified writing a whole book about Pierre on
grounds of his value as an example, his participation in important controversies, and the usefulness of his writings in
re-creating for us some of the tensions in his world. I would
now like to make one more claim for his historical importance.

Pierre's fleeting public appearances on the fourteenth-century
stage were not the sum of his contribution to the drama. Behind
the scenes he advised pope and king on appropriate goals of
action; he defined the limits of their competence, but he also
attempted to encourage co-operation. There was, of course,
nothing unique about this; indeed, he was one of a sizeable
band. Nevertheless, his high reputation among his contemporaries is some measure of his influence. When the question
arises, as it inevitably must, of how the church was able to ride
out storms in the pontificate of John XXII quite as dangerous as
those that later tore it apart, the most straightforward answer
is that disruption of the *status quo* was not then a popular
cause among influential laymen. Though there was some sympathy for Lewis of Bavaria, there was little for the schismatics

he sheltered. In France after 1324 this was clearly the case. (Philip VI's skilful manipulation of the beatific vision affair was blackmail, not schism.) Therefore the way in which a public opinion favourable to the church was maintained becomes historically interesting. Pierre de la Palud and the others like him who strove to serve two masters, to uphold the rights of each and create harmony between them, constituted an important force in French society. Equally important was their determination to convince both sides and their supporters that this harmony was both possible and desirable. From the pulpit and in the confessional they preached the message of co-operation to a people disposed to listen, since it had no desire to return to the uncertainties of Philip IV's conflict with Boniface VIII. That the flock in fact entered the sheepfold undivided should largely be ascribed to the dogs' energetic rounding up of would-be wanderers, and to their firm if noisy direction of all their master's lambs towards the gate.

Bibliography

1. MANUSCRIPT SOURCES

Clermont Ferrand, Bibliothèque municipale, 46.
Inventaire du Trésor des chartes du roy, Reg. JJ. 55, vol. ii; AN. JJ. 20; and Testaments J. 403.
Naples, Biblioteca Nazionale, I. A. 4; VII. F. 29.
Oxford, Bodleian Library, Holkham Miscellaneous 10.
Paris, Bibliothèque mazarine, 199; 233.
—— Bibliothèque nationale, Latin 3293; 3528; 4046; 14799; nouvelle acquisition 1759.
—— Bibliothèque Ste Geneviève, 865.
—— Bibliothèque de l'Université, 168.
Princeton University Library, Garrett 84.
Toulouse, Bibliothèque municipale, 744.
Vatican, Latin 1073; Regina Christiana 547.
Vienna, Österreichische Nationalbibliothek, 2168.
Worcester Cathedral, Q. 100.

2. PRINTED SOURCES

Acta capitulorum generalium Ordinis Praedicatorum, ab anno 1220 usque ad annum 1844, ed. B. M. Reichert (Monumenta Ordinis Fratrum Praedicatorum Historica, 3 and 4), i (Rome, 1898) and ii (Rome, 1899).
Acta Ioannis XXII (1317-1334) e registris vaticanis aliisque fontibus collectis, ed. A. L. Tautu (Vatican, 1952).
Acta sanctorum, Bollandists (Antwerp, 1643-).
AUBRET, L., *Mémoires pour servir à l'histoire de Dombes* (4 vols.; Trévoux, 1864-8).
BALUZE, S., *Miscellanea novo ordine digesta*, ed. J. Mansi (Lucca, 1756-62).
—— *Vitae Paparum Avinionensium*, ed. G. Mollat (4 vols.; Paris, 1914-28).
BARBICHE, B., ed., *Les Actes pontificaux originaux des Archives nationales de Paris*, iii. *1305-1415* (Vatican, 1982).
Benoît XII: Lettres communes, ed. J. M. Vidal (3 vols.; Paris, 1903-11).
Benoît XII: Lettres closes et patentes intéressant les pays autres que la France, ed. J. M. Vidal and G. Mollat (Paris, 1950).
Benoît XII: Lettres closes, patentes et curiales se rapportant à la France, ed. G. Daumet (Paris, 1920).
Cartulaire de l'église de Notre Dame de Paris, ed. B. Guérard (4 vols.; Paris, 1850).

CASSIODORUS, *Historia tripartita*, ed. W. Jacob and R. Hanslik (Vienna, 1952).

Chartularium Universitatis Parisiensis, ed. H. Denifle and E. Chatelain, ii (Paris, 1891).

The Chronicle of Lanercost, tr. H. Maxwell (Glasgow, 1913).

Chronique latine de Guillaume de Nangis de 1113 à 1300, avec les continuations de cette chronique de 1300 à 1368, ed. H. Géraud (2 vols.; Paris, 1843).

Corpus iuris canonici, ed. E. Friedberg (2 vols.; Graz, 1955).

DUPUY, P., *Histoire du différend d'entre le Pape Boniface VIII et Philippes le Bel, roy de France* (Paris, 1655).

Durand de St Pourçain, *In sententias theologicas Petri Lombardi Commentariorum Libri Quatuor* (Lyons, 1587).

ÉTIENNE DE BOURBON, *Anecdotes historiques, légendes et apologues*, ed. A. Lecoy de la Marche (Paris, 1877).

Gesta Dei per Francos, ed. J. Bongars (Hanover, 1611).

GILES OF ROME, *De ecclesiastica potestate*, ed. R. Scholz (Weimar, 1929).

Les Grandes Chroniques, ed. J. Viard, viii and ix (Paris, 1934 and 1937).

GUALVAGNO DE LA FLAMMA, *Cronica Ordinis Praedicatorum ab anno 1170 usque ad 1333*, ed. B. M. Reichert (Rome and Stuttgart, 1897).

GUI, BERNARD, *Le Manuel de l'Inquisiteur*, ed. and tr. G. Mollat (Paris, 1964).

HUILLARD-BRÉHOLLES, M., ed., *Titres de la maison ducale de Bourbon* (Paris, 1867–74).

Jean XXII: Lettres secrètes et curales relatives à la France, ed. A. Coulon and S. Clemencet (3 vols.; Paris, 1906–72).

Jean XXII: Lettres communes, ed. G. Mollat (16 vols.; Paris, 1904–47).

JOHN OF NAPLES, *Quaestiones variae parisiis disputatae Fr. Johannis Napoli*, ed. D. Gravina (Naples, 1618).

Les Journaux du Trésor des chartes de Charles IV le Bel, ed. J. Viard (Paris, 1917).

JULLIEN DE POMMEROL, M.-H., ed., *Sources de l'histoire de l'Université d'Orléans, i. Le Chartrier au debut du XVIe siècle* (Paris, 1974).

LECLERQ, J., ed., *Jean de Paris et l'ecclésiologie du XIIIe siècle* (Paris, 1942).

Lettres de pape Jean XXII (1316–1334), ed. A. Fayen (Rome, Paris, and Brussels, 1908–12).

LIZERAND, G., ed., *Le Dossier de l'affaire des Templiers* (Paris, 1923).

MARSILIUS OF PADUA, *Defensor pacis*, ed. C. W. Previté-Orton (Cambridge, 1928).

MATTHEW PARIS, *Chronica majora*, ed. H. R. Luard (London, 1872–83).

Obituarium Lugdunensis Ecclesiae, ed. M.-C. Guigue (Lyons, 1867).

Obituaires de la Province de Lyon, i, ed. G. Guige and J. Laurent (Paris, 1951).

Ordonnances des roys de France de la troisième race, ed. E.-J. de Laurière et al. (Paris, 1723–1857).

PALUDE, PETRUS DE, *Articulum circa materiam confessionum*, ed. Barbier (Paris, 1506).

PALUDE, PETRUS DE, *Quartus Sententiarum liber*, ed. Vincent Haerlem (Vincent of Haarlem) (Paris, 1514).
—— *Scriptum super tertium Sententiarum*, ed. Peter of Nimeguen (Paris, 1517).
—— *Tractatus de potestate Papae*, ed. P. T. Stella (Zurich, 1966).
PERCIN, J. J., ed., *Monumenta Conventus Tolosani Ordinis FF Praedicatorum* (Toulouse, 1693).
RAYNALDUS, O., *Annales ecclesiastici ab anno 1198*, ed. J. D. Mansi (Lucca, 1747–56).
Registre de l'inquisition de Jacques Fournier (évêque de Pamiers), *1318-1325*, ed. J. Duvernoy (3 vols.; Paris, 1978).
Les Registres de Boniface VIII, ed. G. Digard, M. Faucon, A. Thomas, and R. Fawtier (4 vols.; Paris, 1884–1939).
Registres du Trésor des chartes, ii. 1. Règnes de Louis X et de Philippe V le Long, ed. J. Guérout (Paris, 1966).
RICHARD, J., ed., *Chypre sous les Lusignans: Documents chypriotes des Archives du Vatican* (Paris, 1962).
TUGWELL, S., ed., *Early Dominicans: Selected Writings* (New York, Romsey, and Toronto, 1982).
VALENTIN-SMITH, M. M. and GUIGUE, M.-C., eds., *Biblioteca Dumbensis* (Trévoux, 1854–85).
WILLIMAN, D., *Records of the Papal Right of Spoil, 1316–1412* (Paris, 1974).

3. SECONDARY WORKS

ATIYA, A. S., *Egypt and Aragon: Embassies and Diplomatic Correspondence between 1300 and 1330* (Leipzig, 1938).
BARBER, M., *The Trial of the Templars* (Cambridge, 1978).
BAZAN, B., WIPPEL, J., FRANSEN, G., and JACQUART, D., *Les Questions disputées et les questions quodlibétiques dans les facultés de théologie, de droit et de médecine* (Brepols, 1985).
BENTON, J. F., 'Theocratic History in Fourteenth-Century France: The Liber bellorum Domini by Pierre de la Palu', *University of Pennsylvania Library Chronicles*, 40 (1974), 38–54.
BEYSSAC, J., *Les Chanoines de l'église de Lyon* (Lyons, 1914).
—— *Les Lecteurs et théologaux: Notes pour servir à l'histoire de l'église de Lyon* (Lyons, 1926).
—— *Les Prévots de Fourvière* (Lyons, 1908).
BRETT, E. T., *Humbert of Romans: His Life and Views of Thirteenth-Century Society* (Toronto, 1984).
BRUNDAGE, J. A., *Law, Sex and Christian Society in Medieval Europe* (Chicago and London, 1987).
BURNS, J., ed., *The Cambridge History of Medieval Political Thought* (Cambridge, 1988).
BURR, D., *The Persecution of Peter Olivi* (Transactions of the American Philosophical Society, n.s. 66. 5; Philadelphia, 1976).

CATTO, J., ed., *The History of the University of Oxford, i. The Early Schools* (Oxford, 1984).

CAZELLES, R., *La Société politique et la crise de la royauté sous Philippe de Valois* (Paris, 1958).

CENCI, C., *Manoscritti Francescani della Biblioteca Nazionale di Napoli* (Florence, 1971).

CHABANNE, R., 'Pierre de la Palu', *Dictionnaire de droit canonique*, vi (Paris, 1957), cols. 1481–4.

COBBAN, A. B., *The Medieval Universities: Their Development and Organization* (London, 1975).

CONGAR, Y., 'Aspects ecclésiologiques de la querelle entre mendiants et séculiers dans la seconde moitié du XIIIe siècle et le début du XIVe', *AHDLMA* 28 (1961), 35–151.

COURTENAY, W. J., *Schools and Scholars in Fourteenth-Century England* (Princeton, NJ, 1987).

—— 'The Dialectic of Omnipotence in the High and Late Middle Ages', in T. Rudavsky, ed., *Divine Omniscience and Omnipotence in Medieval Philosophy* (Dordrecht, Boston, and Lancaster, 1985), pp. 243–69.

COX, E. L., *The Eagles of Savoy: The House of Savoy in Thirteenth-Century Europe* (Princeton, NJ, 1974).

—— 'Political and Social Institutions in Bresse (1250–1320)', Ph.D. thesis (Johns Hopkins University, Baltimore, 1958).

CREYTENS, R., 'Santi Schiattesi O.P., disciple de S. Antonin de Florence', *AFP* 27 (1957), 200–318.

D'ALVERNY, M. T., 'Un adversaire de St Thomas: Petrus Johannis Olivi', *St Thomas Aquinas, 1274–1974: Commemorative Studies* (Toronto, 1974), ii. 179–218.

D'AVRAY, D., *The Preaching of the Friars: Sermons Diffused from Paris before 1300* (Oxford, 1985).

—— 'The Gospel of the Marriage Feast of Cana and Marriage Preaching in France', in K. Walsh and D. Wood, eds., *The Bible in the Medieval World* (Oxford, 1985), pp. 207–24.

DELABORDE, H. M., 'Un arrière petit-fils de St. Louis: Alfonse d'Espagne', *Mélanges Julien Havet* (Paris, 1895), pp. 411–27.

DONDAINE, A., 'Documents pour servir à l'histoire de la province de France: L'Appel au concile (1303)', *AFP* 22 (1952), 381–439.

—— 'Guillaume Peyraut: Vie et oeuvres', *AFP* 18 (1948), 162–236.

DUNBABIN, J., 'Careers and Vocations', in J. Catto, ed., *The History of the University of Oxford, i* (Oxford, 1984), pp. 565–605.

—— 'From Clerk to Knight: Changing Orders', in C. Harper-Bill and R. Harvey, eds., *The Ideals and Practice of Medieval Knighthood*, Papers for the 3rd Strawberry Hill Conference (Bury St Edmunds, 1988), pp. 26–39.

—— 'Government', in J. Burns, ed., *The Cambridge History of Medieval Political Thought* (Cambridge, 1988), pp. 477–519.

—— 'The Lyon Dominicans: A Double Act', in J. Loades, ed., *Monastic Studies: The Continuity of Tradition* (Penarth, forthcoming).

DUVAL, A., 'Pierre de la Palu', Dictionnaire de spiritualité, xii. 2 (Paris, 1986), cols. 1631–4.

FAVIER, J., Philippe le Bel (Paris, 1978).

—— Un Conseiller de Philippe le Bel: Enguerran de Marigny (Paris, 1963).

FÉDOU, R., Les Hommes de loi lyonnais à la fin du moyen âge: Étude sur les origines de la classe de robe (Paris, 1964).

FINKE, H., ed., Aus den Tagen Bonifaz VIII: Funde und Forschungen (Münster, 1902).

—— Papsttum und Untergang des Templarordens (2 vols.; Münster, 1907).

FOURNIER, P., 'Durand de S. Porcien', HLF 37 (Paris, 1938), 1–38.

—— 'Notes tirées des sermons inédits du frère prêcheur Pierre de la Palu', Mélanges A. Dufourcq (Paris, 1932), pp. 102–23.

—— 'Pierre de la Palu, théologien et canoniste', HLF 37 (Paris, 1938), 39–84.

Les Genres littéraires dans les sources théologiques et philosophiques médiévales: Définition, critique et exploitation, Proceedings of the international conference at Louvain-le-Neuve, 25–7 May 1981 (Louvain, 1982).

GILLINGHAM, J., and HOLT, J. C., eds., War and Government in the Middle Ages (Cambridge, 1984).

GILSON, E., A History of Christian Philosophy in the Middle Ages (London, 1955).

GLORIEUX, P., La Littérature quodlibétique (2 vols.; Paris, 1925 and 1936).

—— 'Jean de Saint-Germain, maître de Paris et copiste de Worcester', Mélanges A. Pelzer (Louvain, 1947), pp. 513–29.

GOLUBOVICH, G., Biblioteca bio-bibliografica della Terra Santa e dell' Oriente francescano, iii (Florence, 1919).

GROPPO, G., 'La teologia e il suo "subiectum" secondo il prologo del commento alle Sentenze di Pietro da Palude, O.P. († 1342)', Salesianum, 23 (1961), 219–316.

GUICHENON, S., Histoire de Bresse et de Bugey (Lyons, 1650).

GUILLEMAIN, B., La Cour pontificale d'Avignon (1309–1376): Étude d'une société (BEFAR; Paris, 1962).

—— La Politique bénéficiale du Pape Benoît XII, 1334–42 (Paris, 1952).

GUIMARAES, A. de, 'Hervé Noël († 1323): Étude biographique', AFP 8 (1938), 5–81.

HARPER-BILL, C. and HARVEY, R., eds., The Ideals and Practice of Medieval Knighthood, Papers for the 3rd Strawberry Hill Conference (Bury St Edmunds, 1988).

HAURÉAU, B., 'Guillaume de Macôn, canoniste', HLF, 25 (1869), 380–403.

HEDDE, R. and AMMAN, E., 'Pierre de la Palu', Dictionnaire de théologie catholique, xii. 2 (Paris, 1935), cols. 2033–6.

HEFT, J., John XXII and Papal Teaching Authority (Lewiston and Queenston, 1986).

HÉLIN, E., 'Opinions de quelques casuistes de la Contre-Réforme sur l'avortement, la contraception et la continence dans le mariage', *La Prévention des naissances dans la famille: ses origines dans les pays modernes* (Institut national des études demographiques, handbook 35; Paris, 1960), pp. 235-51.

HENNEMANN, J. B., *Royal Taxation in Fourteenth-Century France: The Development of War Financing, 1322-1356* (Princeton, NJ, 1971).

HEYNCK, V., 'Zur Datierung des Sentenzenkommentars des Petrus de Palude', *Franziskanische Studien*, 53 (1971), 317-27.

HILL, G., *A History of Cyprus*, ii (Cambridge, 1948).

HINNEBUSCH, W. A., *The History of the Dominican Order*, i. *Origins and Growth to 1500* (New York, 1966), and ii. *Intellectual and Cultural Life to 1500* (New York, 1973).

HOLT, P. M., *The Age of the Crusades: The Near East from the Eleventh Century to 1517* (London, 1986).

HOUSLEY, N., *The Avignon Papacy and the Crusades, 1307-1378* (Oxford, 1986).

—— *The Italian Crusades: The Papal-Angevin Alliance and the Crusades against Christian Lay Powers, 1254-1343* (Oxford, 1982).

HUNECKE, V., 'Die kirchenpolitischen Exkurse in den Chroniken des Galvaneus Flamma O.P. (1283-ca.1344): Einleitung und Edition', *DA* 25 (1969), 111-312.

KAEPPELI, T., *Scriptores Ordinis Praedicatorum Medii Aevi* (3 vols.; Rome, 1970-80).

—— and Benoit, B., 'Un Pélerinage dominicain inédit du XIVe siècle', *Revue Biblique*, 62 (1955), 513-40.

KEDAR, B. Z., *Crusade and Mission: European Approaches toward the Muslims* (Princeton, NJ, 1984).

KOCH, J., 'Durandus de S. Porciano O.P.: Forschungen zum Streit um Thomas von Aquin zu Beginn des 14 Jahrhunderts', *Beiträge zur Geschichte der Philosophie des Mittelalters*, 26. 1 (1927), 1-436.

—— 'Der Prozess gegen den Magister Johannes de Polliaco und seine Vorgeschichte (1312-1321)', *RTAM* 5 (1933), 391-422.

—— 'Der Prozess gegen die Postille Olivis zur Apokalypse', *RTAM* 5 (1933), 302-13.

—— 'Die Jahre 1312-1317 im Leben des Durandus de S. Porciano', *Studi e Testi*, 37 (1924), 265-306.

—— 'Zu codex 35 des Archivo del Cabildo Catedral de Barcelona', *AFP* 13 (1943), 101-7.

KOUDELKA, V. J., 'Heinrich von Bittenfeld († 1465), Professor an der Universität Prag', *AFP* 23 (1953), 5-65.

LABORDE, H.-F., *Jean de Joinville et les seigneurs de Joinville* (Paris, 1884).

LAMBERT, M. D., *Franciscan Poverty: The Doctrine of the Absolute Poverty of Christ and the Apostles in the Franciscan Order, 1210-1323* (London, 1961).

—— 'The Franciscan Crisis under John XXII', *Franciscan Studies*, 32 (1972), 123-43.

LE BRAS, G., *Histoire du droit et des institutions de l'Église en Occident*, vii. *L'Âge classique, 1140-1378* (Paris, 1965).

LEE, H., REEVES, M., and SILANO, G., *Western Mediterranean Prophecy: The School of Joachim of Fiore and the Fourteenth-Century 'Breviloquium'* (Toronto, 1989).

LEFF, G., *Heresy in the Later Middle Ages: The Relation of Heterodoxy to Dissent, c.1250-1450* (2 vols.; Manchester and New York, 1967).

—— *Paris and Oxford Universities in the Thirteenth and Fourteenth Centuries* (New York, 1968).

—— 'The Franciscan Concept of Man', in A. Williams, ed., *Prophecy and Millenarianism* (Harlow, 1980), pp. 217-38.

LE GOFF, J., *The Birth of Purgatory*, tr. A. Goldhammer (Chicago, 1984).

LEHUGEUR, P., *Histoire de Philippe le Long, roi de France 1316-1322* (reissue Geneva, 1975).

LEJEUNE, R., and STIENNON, J., *La Légende de Roland dans l'art du moyen âge* (2 vols.; Brussels, 1967).

LERNER, R. E., 'Poverty, Preaching and Eschatology in the Revelation Commentaries of "Hugh of St. Cher"', in K. Walsh and D. Wood, eds., *The Bible in the Medieval World* (Oxford, 1985), pp. 157-90.

LEVESQUE, J. D., *Les Frères Prêcheurs de Lyon: Notre Dame de Confort, 1218-1789* (Lyons, 1979).

LEWIS, A. W., *Royal Succession in Capetian France: Studies on Familial Order and the State* (Cambridge, Mass. and London, 1981).

LOT, M. H., 'Essai d'intervention de Charles le Bel en faveur des chrétiens d'Orient, tenté avec le concours de Pape Jean XXII', *BEC* 36 (1875), 588-600.

LOTTIN, O., *Psychologie et Morale au XIIe et XIIIe siècles* (6 vols.; Gembloux, 1942-60).

LUCAS, H., 'The Great European Famine of 1315, 1316, 1317', *Speculum*, 5 (1930), 343-77.

LUSCOMBE, D. E., 'Thomas Aquinas and Conceptions of Hierarchy in the Thirteenth Century', *Miscellanea Mediaevalia*, 19 (1986), 261-77.

MCCREADY, W. D., *The Theory of Papal Monarchy in the Fourteenth Century: Guillaume de Pierre Godin, 'Tractatus de causa immediata ecclesiastice potestatis'* (Toronto, 1982).

—— 'Papalists and Anti-papalists: Aspects of the Church–State controversy in the Later Middle Ages', *Viator*, 6 (1975), 241-74.

MAIER, A., *Ausgehendes Mittelalter: Gesammelte Aufsätze zur Geistesgeschichte des 14 Jahrhunderts* (3 vols.; Rome, 1964-77).

MARCUZZI, C., 'L'Usura, un caso di giurisdizione controversa in un responsum inedito di Pietro de la Palu (1280-1342)', *Salesianum*, 40 (1978), 245-92.

MARTIN, C. M., 'The Enforcement of the Rights of the Kings of France in the Duchy and County of Burgundy, 1285-1363', B.Litt. thesis (Oxford, 1965).

MAS LATRIE, L. DE, *Histoire de l'Île de Chypre sous le règne des princes de la maison de Lusignan* (Paris, 1957).

—— 'Les Patriarches latins de Jérusalem', *Revue de l'Orient latin*, 1 (1893), 16–41.

MEERSSEMAN, G., 'L'Architecture dominicaine au XIIIᵉ siècle', *AFP* 16 (1946), 136–90.

—— 'La Chronologie des voyages et des œuvres de frère Alphonse Buenhombre O.P.', *AFP* 10 (1940), 77–108.

MEIJERS, E. M., *Études d'histoire de droit*, iii. *Le Droit roman au moyen âge* (Leiden, 1959).

MESNIL, E. R. DU, *Armorial historique de Bresse, Bugey, Dombes, Pays de Gex, Volromey et Franc-Lyonnais* (Lyons, 1873).

MICHEL, A., 'Pénitence', *Dictionnaire de théologie catholique*, xii. 1 (Paris, 1933), cols. 1001–4.

MICHELET, J., *Le Procès des Templiers* (Paris, 1841 and 1851).

MIETHKE, J., 'Die Traktat *De potestate papae*: Ein Typus politik-theoretischer Literatur', *Les Genres littéraires dans les sources théologiques et philosophiques médiévales*, (Louvain, 1982), pp. 193–211.

—— 'Einer unbekannte Handschrift von Petrus de Paludes Traktat *De Potestate Papae* aus dem Besitz Juan de Torquemadas in der Vatikanischen Bibliotheke', *QFIAB* 59 (1979), 4368–75.

MISKIMIN, H. A., *Money, Prices and Foreign Exchange in Fourteenth-Century France* (New York, 1970).

MOLLAT, G., 'Jean XXII (1316–1334) fut-il un avare?', *Revue d'histoire écclesiastique*, 5 (1904), 522–34; 6 (1905), 33–46.

MORANVILLÉ, H., 'Guillaume de Breuil et Robert d'Artois', *BEC* 48 (1887), 641–9.

MORTIER, D. A., *Histoire des maîtres généraux de l'ordre des Frères Prêcheurs* (8 vols.; Paris, 1903–20).

MULDOON, J., *Popes, Lawyers and Infidels: The Church and the Non-Christian World, 1250–1550* (Liverpool, 1979).

ORME, N., *From Childhood to Chivalry: The Education of the English Kings and Aristocracy, 1066–1530* (London and New York, 1984).

OWST, G. R., *Literature and Pulpit in Medieval England* (Cambridge, 1933).

PENNINGTON, K., *Pope and Bishops: The Papal Monarchy in the Twelfth and Thirteenth Centuries* (Pennsylvania, 1984).

PIANA, C., 'Scritti polemici fra Conventuali ed Osservanti a metà del '400, con la participazione dei giuristi secolari', *AFH* 71 (1978), 339–405.

POU Y MARTI, J. M., *Visionarios, beguinos y fraticelos catalanes (siglos xiii–xv)* (Vich, 1930).

La Prévention des naissances dans la famille: Ses origines dans les pays modernes (Institut national des études demographiques, handbook 35; Paris, 1960).

RASHDALL, H., *The Universities of Europe in the Middle Ages*, ed. F. M. Powicke and A. B. Emden, 3rd edn. (3 vols.; Oxford, 1936).

REEVES, M., *The Influence of Prophecy in the Later Middle Ages: A Study of Joachimism* (Oxford, 1969).

RIANT, COUNT, 'Déposition de Charles d'Anjou pour la canonisation de Saint Louis', *Notes et documents publiés pour la Société de l'histoire de France*, 335 (1884), 155–76.

—— and GIORGI, I., 'Description du *Liber bellorum Domini*', *Archives de l'Orient latin*, 1 (1881), 289–322.

RICHARD, J., *La Papauté et les missions d'Orient au moyen âge* (Rome, 1977).

RICHÉ, P. and LOBRICHON, R., eds., *Le Moyen Âge et la Bible* (Paris, 1984).

ROUSE, R. H. and M. A., *Preachers, Florilegia and Sermons: Studies on the 'Manipulus Florum' of Thomas of Ireland* (Toronto, 1979).

—— 'The Verbal Concordance to the Scriptures', *AFP* 44 (1974), 5–30.

SCHEEBEN, H. C., 'Prediger und Generalprediger im Dominikaner Orden des 13. Jahrhunderts', *AFP* 31 (1961), 112–41.

SCHMITT, P. C., *Un Pape réformateur et un défenseur de l'unité de l'Église: Benoît XII et l'ordre des Frères Mineurs, 1334–1342* (Florence, 1959).

SETTON, K. M., *The Papacy and the Levant, 1204–1571*, i (Philadelphia, 1976).

SHEEHAN, M. W., 'The Religious Orders, 1220–1370', in J. Catto, ed., *The History of the University of Oxford*, i (Oxford, 1984), pp. 193–221.

SIKES, J. G., 'John de Pouilli and Peter de la Palu', *EHR* 49 (1943), 219–40.

SMALLEY, B., *The Study of the Bible in the Middle Ages*, 3rd edn. (Oxford, 1983).

—— 'Use of the "Spiritual" Senses of Scripture in Persuasion and Argument by Scholars of the Middle Ages', *RTAM* 52 (1985), 44–63.

SOUTHERN, R. W., 'The Changing Role of Universities in Medieval Europe', *BIHR* 60 (1987), 133–46.

STEGMÜLLER, F., *Repertorium Biblicum Medii Aevi* (7 vols.; Madrid, 1950–61).

STELLA, P. T., 'A proposito della attribuzione a Pietro di la Palu del *Tractatus de causa immediata ecclesiasticae potestatis*', *Salesianum*, 27 (1965), 382–409.

—— 'Giovanni Regina di Napoli, O.P., e le tesi di Giovanni XXII circa la visione beatifica', *Salesianum*, 35 (1973), 55–99.

—— 'Intentio Aristotelis, secundum superficiem suae litterae: La "replicatio contra Magistrum Herveum praedicatorem" di Giovanni di Pouilly', *Salesianum*, 23 (1961), 481–528.

STRAYER, J., *The Reign of Philip the Fair* (Princeton, NJ, 1980).

TABACCO, G., *La casa di Francia nell'azione politica di papa Giovanni XXII* (Istituto storico Italiano per il medio evo; Rome, 1953).

St Thomas Aquinas 1274–1974: Commemorative Studies (Toronto, 1974).

TIERNEY, B., *The Origins of Papal Infallibility, 1150–1350* (Leiden, 1972).

TUGWELL, S., *The Way of the Preacher* (London, 1979).

TURLEY, T., 'Infallibilists at the curia of Pope John XXII', *Journal of Medieval History*, 1 (1975), 71–101.

TYERMAN, C., 'Philip V of France, the Assemblies of 1319–20 and the Crusade', *BIHR* 57 (1984), 15–34.

—— 'Philip VI and the recovery of the Holy Land', *EHR* 100 (1985), 25–52.

—— '*Sed nichil fecit?* The Last Capetians and the Recovery of the Holy Land', in J. Gillingham and J. C. Holt, eds., *War and Government in the Middle Ages* (Cambridge, 1984), pp. 170–81.

VAN DEN AUWEILE, D., 'À propos de la tradition manuscrite du *De causa immediata ecclesiasticae potestatis* de Guillaume de Pierre Godin († 1336)', *RTAM* 21 (1984), 183–205.

VEREECKE, L., 'Les Éditions des oeuvres morales de Pierre de la Palu († 1342) à Paris au début du XVIᵉ siècle', *Studia Moralia*, 17 (1979), 267–82.

VERGER, J., 'L'Exégèse de l'Université', in P. Riché and R. Lobrichon, eds., *Le Moyen Âge et la Bible* (Paris, 1984), pp. 199–232.

VICAIRE, M.-H., 'Les "Jacobins" dans la vie de Toulouse', *AFP* 57 (1987), 1–24.

VIDAL, J. M., 'Notice sur les oeuvres de Pape Benoît XII', *Revue d'histoire écclesiastique*, 6 (1905), 557–65; 785–810.

VOLLERT, I. O., 'The Doctrine of Hervaeus Natalis on Primitive Justice and Original Sin', *Analecta Gregoriana*, 42 (1947).

WALSH, K. and WOOD, D., eds. *The Bible in the Medieval World: Essays in Memory of Beryl Smalley* (Oxford, 1985).

WATT, J. A., 'Spiritual and Temporal Powers', in J. Burns, ed., *The Cambridge History of Medieval Political Thought* (Cambridge, 1988), pp. 367–423.

WEISHEIPL, J. A., 'Peter of la Palud (Paludanus)', *New Catholic Encyclopaedia*, 11 (Washington DC, 1967), pp. 220–1.

WICKERSHEIMER, E., 'Les Pillules de frère Pierre de la Palud', *Bulletin de la Société française d'histoire de la médecine*, 16 (1927), 139–41.

WILLIAMS, A., ed., *Prophecy and Millenarianism: Essays in Honour of Marjorie Reeves* (Harlow, 1980).

WIPPEL, J. F., 'The Quodlibetal Question as a Distinctive Literary Genre', in *Les Genres littéraires dans les sources théologiques et philosophiques médiévales* (Louvain, 1982), pp. 67–84.

WOOD, C. T., *The French Apanages and the Capetian Monarchy, 1224–1328* (Cambridge, Mass., 1966).

ZUCKERMAN, C. A., 'Dominican Theories of the Papal Primacy, 1250–1320', Ph.D. thesis (Cornell University, 1971).

Index